Desert, Garden, Margin, Range

Literature on the American Frontier

Desert, Garden, Margin, Range

Literature on the American Frontier

Edited by Eric Heyne

TWAYNE PUBLISHERS · *New York*
MAXWELL MACMILLAN CANADA · *Toronto*
MAXWELL MACMILLAN INTERNATIONAL · *New York   Oxford   Singapore   Sydney*

Twayne Publishers   Maxwell Macmillan Canada, Inc.
Macmillan Publishing Company   1200 Eglinton Avenue East
866 Third Avenue   Suite 200
New York, New York 10022   Don Mills, Ontario M3C 3N1

Macmillan Publishing Company is part of the Maxwell Communication Group
of Companies.

Library of Congress Cataloging-in-Publication Data

Desert, garden, margin, range: literature on the American frontier/
   edited by Eric Heyne.
      p.   cm.
   Includes bibliographical references and index.
   ISBN 0-8057-9027-6 (hc). — ISBN 0-8057-9031-4 (pb)
   1. American literature—History and criticism.   2. Frontier and
pioneer life in literature.   I. Heyne, Eric.
PS169.F7D47   1992
810.9'3278—dc20   91-46365
                                                                       CIP

The paper used in this publication meets the minimum requirements
of American National Standard for Information Sciences—Permanence
of Paper for Printed Library Materials. ANSI Z3948-1984.∞™

10 9 8 7 6 5 4 3 2 1 (hc)
10 9 8 7 6 5 4 3 2 1 (pb)

Printed in the United States of America

Contents

Introduction

The Lasting Frontier: Reinventing America

Eric Heyne

Columbus ended earth's romance:
No New World to mankind remains!
—Herman Melville, *Clarel*

. . . the front of the sperm whale's head is a dead, blind wall . . .
Melville, *Moby-Dick*

History is increasingly being understood as a matter of texts and descriptions, rather than events and physical realities. The weaker version of this theory of historical understanding states merely that we are strongly constrained in our understanding of the past by surviving texts. The stronger version, however, argues that history has always been constituted by texts to a profound degree. According to this model, the history of a physical place, such as the American frontier, must be understood largely as the history of writing about that place. When Frederick Jackson Turner said that "the United States lies like a huge page in the history of society,"[1] he was speaking figuratively. But contemporary understanding of the frontier takes that statement much more literally. In a very important sense, the frontier always existed primarily as a text written and read by Americans and would-be Americans. The West had to be not inhabited but invented. The frontier was less a demographic threshold or the line of trees at the edge of town than an advertisement for free land out West and a sermon about what lay beyond the trees.

Moreover, the textual frontier was shaped almost entirely by "Easterners." Writing about the frontier was seldom done *on* the frontier.[2] As

3

Annette Kolodny observes of one particular genre of frontier writing, "Though the bulk of its story line is usually played out on some prairie frontier, the domestic novel of western relocation was nonetheless a response to eastern—and not western—concerns."[3] Edwin Fussell points out, in his defense of what might be called the "frontier thesis" of American literature, that American authors have created their West in unlikely places, such as Concord, Salem, and the mid-Pacific. Not surprisingly, those with enough leisure and education to write lived mostly in more settled areas (or in a settled future, looking back to an earlier frontier period).

American literary studies have generally treated the frontier as a brute historical fact, a given, adopted as an element of setting. But some critics (including most in this anthology) are supplementing that static understanding of the frontier with one that recognizes its fundamentally creative and figurative use in American literature. Just as, in the words of Henry Louis Gates, Jr., "Race [often] pretends to be an objective term of classification, when in fact it is a dangerous trope,"[4] so the frontier, once treated as an objective term of geographical classification (or as an archetype that was then often reified), is increasingly being understood as a trope.

The first part of the title of this anthology—*Desert, Garden, Margin, Range*—emphasizes the competition among different versions of the frontier, the contrasting and self-contradictory images by which Americans have characterized their most American places. The title's four terms represent the four poles of two figurative axes: *desert* and *garden* on the axis of utility, and *margin* and *range* on the axis of spatial representation.

Land that had not yet been populated by whites was usually characterized by terms representing extremes, as *desert* or *garden*, depending entirely on whether the land in question could yield immediate profit. If Europeans did not yet have a use for a given piece of land, it was not merely wild but a desert, a place of danger and deprivation. If the technology was available to exploit the land (via farming, mining, ranching), the wilderness was a garden, a pastoral refuge needing only a civilizing hand to make it bloom. The land itself never changed, of course. But, to take the most well-known instance, the invention of a stronger plow turned what had been the great American desert into the American breadbasket, as two centuries earlier cotton and tobacco profits built on the comparative advantage of slave labor metamorphosed a dangerous, unprofitable interior jungle into rich estates. John Seabrook illustrates the same kind of economic reality today in the gold-mining "deserts" of Nevada: "The marketplace can turn a mass of waste rock into an ore body virtually overnight. The definition of gold ore . . . is

4

rock that can be mined profitably. . . . If the price of gold rose high enough, the Empire State Building would turn into a skyscraper of gold ore."[5]

Of course, writers are interested in a different kind of profit, but in its pursuit they too characterized the frontier according to what they could retrieve from it. As Louise K. Barnett argues in her essay in this volume, Cooper saw the wilderness as a privileged site for speaking the truth, a kind of prelapsarian verbal garden. Susan Scheckel demonstrates the ways in which Mary Jemison's portrayal of the wilderness (including Native Americans) as domestic and healthy, as a garden rather than the wild desert of earlier captivity narratives, was particularly threatening to early-nineteenth-century readers. Similarly, in tracing out the different versions of the character of Daniel Boone, Mary Lawlor notes the various descriptions of Kentucky as dangerous or bountiful, depending on the different biographers' rhetorical purposes.

Moreover, American terms for the frontier not only clash with one another but also contain contradictions within themselves. Two of the best studies of the process by which Americans have named their frontier, Henry Nash Smith's *Virgin Land* and Annette Kolodny's *The Lay of the Land*, compare the tangled metaphors for the wilderness with the equally ambivalent metaphoric webs in which men have placed women. As the virgin is both desirable and useless in the male gaze, so the frontier is both a sacred site and a waste of untapped resources, and the desert is both a place to shun and a space to fill. Nor has the "closing" of the frontier changed the dominant thinking: "We may indeed have long ago ceased to self-consciously or attentively *think about* the feminine in the landscape, but that does not mean we have ceased to *experience* it or to act in such a way that our behavior apparently manifests such experience at its deepest level of motivation."[6] Many Americans continue to live as though they had a frontier available, to remake them as they need it, and to have their way with when they want it. They can do that because the frontier has always been a rich textual field—generating advertising and all sorts of other texts for the readers of our demanding culture—rather than a place on a map.

Metaphors such as "virgin land" reveal that just as women—and often nonwhite men as well—have been the body and voice of the Other for the white male author, so the frontier has been the place of the Other. Perhaps because of very common instincts regarding territoriality, most human cultures have felt a need to locate in space, in a distant place that yet borders on the familiar, the voice of the unconscious that seems to speak from both far away and intimately near. In an essay on "Aggressivity," Jacques Lacan focuses on the human need to displace aggression to a particular place:

Let us say that animal psychology has shown us that the individual's relation to a particular spatial field is, in certain species, mapped socially, in a way that raises it to the category of subjective membership. I would say that it is the subjective possibility of the mirror projection of such a field into the field of the other that gives human space its originally "geometrical" structure, a structure that I would be happy to call *kaleidoscopic*.

    . . . Yet does it offer us a place of rest? Already in the ever-contracting "living space" in which human competition is becoming ever keener, a stellar observer of our species would conclude that we possessed needs to escape that had very strange results.[7]

As territorial animals, Americans have fought over the kaleidoscope of their frontier, but no one, not even the winner, is able to rest. Americans are especially marked by their restlessness, their "needs to escape," and when physical struggle and escape are impossible, they turn in imagination to the realm of myth. Thus the frontier becomes the place where Americans locate the violence and hand-to-hand combat they cannot allow at home, and the West remains a ritualized, mythical place that lives on in novels and advertisements. This flight to the American West of the late nineteenth century is not exclusive to Americans, as the popularity of Westerns abroad indicates, but it is indeed "very strange." As Reginald Dyck explains below, the twin frontier myths of the peaceful garden and a legitimate, licensed frontier violence have not provided Americans with a "place of rest," only an uneasy truce.

    Laid across this spectrum of utilitarian names for the frontier is another set of terms, which may be defined by the opposition of *margin* and *range*. As Edwin Fussell noted, the frontier has meant both the border one crossed to reach new places and the places themselves, "sometimes a line and sometimes a space."[8] Metonymic terms—those describing the line—focus on movement and transition, in directions (west, southwest, northwest) and across distinct lines (trans-Mississippi, transmontane, across the border, into the woods). Metaphoric terms—those describing the space—are usually proper nouns themselves expanded metonymically from particular features (the West Coast, Oregon, the Dakotas, the Plains, the Territories). Sometimes the metonymic and metaphoric operate simultaneously and there is confusion about what is meant, as when Huck Finn explores the wild stretches of the Mississippi, and then contemplates "lighting out for the Territories," across a line into a still wilder place.

    As a margin the frontier was continually on the move, in the narrative progression that Turner traced across the continent. Ray Allen Billington characterized this aspect of the frontier as *process*, which he contrasted with frontier as *place*.[9] But this process has nevertheless always been described by means of a spatial figure, often an indistinct or shifting line. Crossing the frontier is a quintessentially American act, our national (male) rite of passage (as when Deerslayer follows Hurry Harry into "the deep shadows of the forest," Melville's Ishmael sails out of sight of land, or Faulkner's Isaac leaves behind his compass and rifle). Interestingly, this passage is generally either open-ended or circular, leading not into adulthood but into mystery or back to childhood. As John Cawelti says of Westerns in general and the Lone Ranger in particular, movement "in and out of society might be interpreted as another symbolic expression of the conflict between a fascination with the adult world and a real hesitation to become committed to it."[10] Insofar as the frontier is understood *only* as a boundary, what lies beyond it is fundamentally an aporia, an emptiness—uncivilized, unmapped, unsurveyed, without clear title. The frontier-as-margin is a negation and a challenge. In order for that challenge to be answered, we require the complement: the frontier-as-range.

The "home on the range" is always a relatively empty place (except for its original inhabitants, of course, who must be eliminated). These are the wide open spaces, "Big Sky" country, the open range, the wild. Crossing into this place is just the beginning. Once there, one needs to know one's way around in order to survive. It is the place Americans go to test social conventions against the old standard of nature, to take the measure of their civilization. Ironically, Americans have reduced what is left of the real wilderness to a charity case that exists in national parks and preserves—rather like keeping a once-independent parent confined in a rest home. "[T]his vast, savage, howling mother of ours, Nature," as Thoreau called "her" in "Walking,"[11] now howls only if we suffer "her" wolves to be reintroduced.

Nevertheless, the psychic wilderness lives on in imaginative writing. The peculiarly frontier genres, such as the Western novel, are set on the frontier-as-range. The border does not appear in such texts, except as a distant line across which Easterners travel in order to be tested. When the frontier-as-border does appear, it is usually a signal that the conventions of the Western are going to be challenged or parodied, as in Edward Abbey's *The Brave Cowboy*, with its contrasts between Albuquerque and the surrounding desert and mountains. Margin-as-range is a charmed place, Americans' own sacred lands, the white (and hence symbolic) equivalent of particular sacred Native American (and therefore real) places like the Black Hills.

The continuing power of all four of these views of the frontier may be illustrated by contemporary examples from Alaska. Near the end of her history of the Yukon, Melody Webb talks about the "romanticization" of "throwback" occupations like fur trapping and their tendency to "perpetuate the myth and mystique of 'the last frontier' ": "In the

1970's the cliché ["the last frontier"] became the official state motto. Those who most often take up the refrain reside in cities and resort to rural excursions as vacations or hobbies rather than as committed life-styles."[12] If the frontier has always been created rather than discovered, and if most of that creation took place long after the physical work of settlement was finished, there is no contradiction (though much painful humor) in the prospect of self-styled "settlers" in modern Alaska re-peating precisely all the mistakes of their pioneer forebears. Most Alaskans today want to see the "desert" of "empty" tundra and taiga developed for their own profit, as it has been in the case of the Prudhoe Bay oil field, the royalties on which this year will pay the entire state budget and yield every Alaskan a check for more than eight hundred dollars. Alaska's senators and representatives vigorously pursue open-ing the Arctic National Wildlife Refuge to oil exploration, battling inter-ference from Californians, New Yorkers, and other distant federal taxpayers.

But these same prodevelopment Alaskans want to preserve their "garden" for hunting, trapping, fishing, boating, snowmobiling, and other rugged outdoor pastimes. They also want more jobs, but only for themselves—"local hire" is a major political issue. Tourists are officially welcomed though unofficially despised, just as government is and for the same reason: money. The Alaska Independence Party claims it acts in the spirit of the American Revolution, by the right of self-determina-tion. But it seems to some observers that what its members chiefly desire is the right to go wherever they want and do whatever they wish to the land. Independence Party gubernatorial candidate Joe Vogler has sued local government to let him enforce on his tenants the mandate that they must cut down aspens; and he has abandoned in midwilderness, in protest against federal regulators, the bulldozer with which he was cut-ting a road to his mining claim across hundreds of empty miles of govern-ment land.

The land Alaskans quarrel over is a huge expanse, a range both immense and fragile, beautiful and inaccessible, full of unnamed moun-tains and almost entirely without trails by which to reach those moun-tains. Alaska is also marginal in many ways: stranded far west in its own time zone and far north in its own climate, with few roads (and none to its capital); strung together by dogsled and airplane; hemmed in by cold in the winter and by mosquitoes and bears in the summer; hostilely divided between urban and rural cultures, interior and southeastern political agendas, Anchorage and the rest of the state, Native Americans and whites, tree huggers and oil suckers. The oil companies dominate Alaska in much the same way that the railroads dominated the old West (ranching and cowboy mythology notwithstanding). Winter remains the best time to travel, except during a severe cold snap, when it can be

8

deadly. Teachers draw the highest salaries in the country, but more parents teach their children at home than in any other state. Government seems to be fiercely resented, although it is by far the largest employer. There is no hint that such contradictions will be quickly resolved; terms such as *frontier, wilderness, pioneer*, and *freedom* will remain in circulation among people who use them to mean entirely opposite things.

In its more ambitious literature, as in the popular literature of letters to the editor and campaign speeches, Alaskan texts embody the contradictions of the frontier tradition. Alaskan writing is overwhelmingly a "tourist literature," written by short-term visitors like John Muir, John McPhee, Jack London, James Michener, Barry Lopez, Robert Service, and Joe McGinnis. The reason is partly numbers: odds are slim that such a small population as Alaska's will produce a bumper crop of excellent writers. However, there is another reason for this tourist literature, related to the paradox of the wilderness that Kolodny notes in her discussion of Cooper. How can writers "alone enjoy the darkened forest recesses without threatening to become either destructive or intrusive" (Kolodny 1975, 89)? The frontier-as-range exists only so long as it is uninhabited; Americans cannot have their frontier and live in it too. Their solution is to write and run, to touch lightly and so believe that it can all be left the way they found it. Thus, ironically, Alaska is left in the hands of outsiders who can leave the frontier and therefore feel free to romanticize it.

It is the radically evasive quality of the frontier—disappearing precisely as Americans attempt to inhabit it—that makes it so hard to write about, but also so endlessly compelling. The frontier is, to use Melville's term, America's "Loose-fish." Anything is possible out there—including, as so many utopian colonizers have gambled, human perfectibility. Frontier-as-margin represents all boundaries between pairs of human conditions; frontier-as-range contains whatever possibilities lie outside each person's condition. Since walls may be solid or porous, and since the next valley may be lush or sterile, the frontier may be used to provoke either hope or despair. This gives it a powerful emotional charge, a risky energy that Harold Simonson discusses in *The Closed Frontier*: "Desire is the fatal flaw, and tragedy the freedom to act upon it. . . . The tension we know as humans is precisely between our necessity to live in this old world and our desire to break through and beyond. . . ."[13] The frontier symbolizes both limitation and a land beyond limitation, and both concepts have always seemed peculiarly concrete and accessible to Americans. The gunfight justice of the Old West myth is built on this paradox of free choice and self-willed confinement. Oppositions are clear and extreme, but everything interesting happens on the bloody ground between. This is the same paradox John Cawelti identifies when he talks about the "rules" for playing the Western "game": "The dialectical structure of the Western—its opposition of townspeople and savages with the hero in the middle—encourages the expression of value oppositions" (Cawelti, 73). The hero who negotiates the middle ground must, of course, ride off into the sunset at the end, for he cannot be accommodated by the stable community, as Leatherstocking cannot live in the settlements. Thus the Western is always "dialogic," to use Mikhail Bakhtin's term, and a variety of voices speak behind the rattle of six-guns, ironically similar to the dialogism James Ruppert examines in his essay on Native American contact narratives in this collection. Both the cowboys and the Indians seek to define themselves in their contacts with the Other.

The best literature about the frontier uses this "dialectical structure" to explore new modes of self-knowledge. For instance, the "Indiana" section of Hart Crane's *The Bridge* is such a moving and profound treatment of the frontier in American life largely because it exposes some of the gaps left by traditional Western narratives. A mother saying goodbye to her grown son recalls their family's earlier journey on the wave of American expansion. Crane's pioneers, however, did not settle out West: "But we,—too late, too early, howsoever— / Won nothing out of fifty-nine." Turning to the east, against the tide, they join the backwash of settlers who have been forgotten in the myth of steady westward progression. On that return trail the mother meets "a homeless squaw— / Perhaps a halfbreed," with whom she shares a wordless moment of communion.

In the brief dramatic monologue of "Indiana" many other familiar stereotypes are undermined. Women, not men, meet on the frontier; white and red come together rather than do battle; the settlers and would-be miners miss their chance and are forced to travel back from Colorado to Indiana; the son is raised by his mother (and stepfather) in the absence of his father, rather than being raised by his father or another male relative in the familiar pattern of the absent mother; and the son goes to sea rather than taking up the family farm. This work is not realism exactly; it's more like a remixing of romantic imagery, a new perspective on panoramic American movements. The same westering energy that drove European-Americans to cover the body of the continent persists in driving them outward across the world. White Americans may be so sentimental about home precisely because they feel so driven to abandon it.

The Bridge is always a bridge up and out, rather than across. Even in the foggy morning of "The Harbor Dawn," in archurban Manhattan, "a forest shudders in your hair," and when the fog rolls away it exposes nothing less than that old "city up on a hill" and our Manifest Destiny, now circled back upon themselves: "Under the mistletoe of dreams, a star— / As though to join us at some distant hill— / Turns in the waking west and goes to sleep." With its echoes of Whitman's elegy for Lincoln and the irrepressible American urge to travel in mind and body, this passage suggests that Americans are caught in mourning, obsessed with their frontier and the fear that it may be slipping away from them.

Crane wrote *The Bridge* a generation after Turner had mourned the passing of the frontier, but Crane knew that it was still open, still out there, "an empire wilderness of freight and rails," ranged by anachronistic "hobo-trekkers" like modern-day ghosts of the mountain men. Nor has the frontier faded any further since Crane. It lives in American commercial rhetoric with a special fierceness, in the number of advertisements that use cowboy imagery to persuade men who have never seen a cow up close to buy a particular brand of beer because it is passed around a fictional bunkhouse. A more interesting and complex manifestation of the continuing power of the frontier in American consciousness is the phenomenon of American science fiction. No other genre has produced such a dedicated and talented community of writers and readers. The opening line of "Star Trek"—"Space: the final frontier"—captures the essentially romantic inspiration of science fiction.

In science fiction as in much other American literature (but emphatically not in commercials), such escape often ends tragically. Frederick Pohl's bitter novel *Jem* reenacts the white settlement of the New World and extermination of Native Americans through the vehicle of alien species on a distant planet that is being conquered by humans. The future's more powerful technology enables a quicker conquest and a more durable slavery. The planet Jem, its name a public-relations ploy to solicit funding for its development, was to be a new chance for humans, who have drained just about all of Earth's resources. But the totalitarianism that develops on Jem, after Earth's nuclear war over dwindling resources, is exactly the opposite of the freedom promised by the myth of the frontier. In Pohl's bloody and competitive universe, "there are no survivors. There are only replacements."[14] The potential of the frontier for remaking humanity remains illusory; space to grow is no guarantee of real growth.

Most science fiction remains firmly within the American romantic tradition, which has always sought to remake humanity on the site of the frontier and has frequently conflated the notions of frontier and nature. In Emerson's words, no one can "be happy and strong until he too lives with nature in the present, above time."[15] Along with this enobling, encircling quality, however, is the contradictory but equally powerful notion that "nature is thoroughly mediate. It is made to serve."[16] As James Barszcz argues in this volume, for Emerson the frontier is primarily the place where consciousness meets external reality, and so any human possibility for good or bad may be found at the edge of the woods. There is therefore no ultimate or final meaning to the frontier. As Melville says of that wilderness-ranger Moby Dick, "the front . . . is a dead, blind wall."[17] Like the "face" of the whale, or of a coin, the frontier means only what we make it mean. Thus it is true both that "Columbus ended earth's romance" and that five hundred years later frontier romances have never been more popular. The challenge for critics is to recognize, analyze, reconcile, deconstruct, and otherwise read into the enormous variety of frontier experiences.

Investigations of the role of the frontier in American literature generally proceed along one of two tracks: through the canon or around it. The former attempts to isolate and explain the frontier function, as it were, in canonical American literature. The essays in part 1 of this anthology take this approach. Each deals with traditionally valued literature that is patently "about" the frontier, but all attempt to revise the accepted views of exactly what that means. Louise K. Barnett's "Speech in the Wilderness: The Ideal Discourse of *The Deerslayer*" argues that in Cooper's "novel of speech," Deerslayer's epistemological "purity" is only possible in the "harmony of the woods," not in the "contradictions of the settlements." The place of the Other, ironically, is the only place where Americans can be purely themselves, in the immediacy and presence of speech. Just as Cooper sought to make the wilderness an epistemological paradise, so, argues Mary Lawlor, the various biographers and novelists who used the Daniel Boone figure constantly remade the wilderness by remaking the character of Boone. In "The Fictions of Daniel Boone," Lawlor explains that the essence of Boone's character is precisely its lack of essence; his stature as totemic figure derives mainly from his mutability, from the ease with which he can be turned to the various purposes of different Western mythmakers.

In "Hawthorne, Emerson, and the Forms of the Frontier," James Barszcz argues against the common notion that the frontier was seen by classic American writers as a boundary between culture and nature. Hawthorne and Emerson both saw a "radical continuity" between town and forest; the latter was always immediately politicized in the presence of humans (according to Hawthorne) and was grist for the mill of human consciousness (according to Emerson). For both Hawthorne and Emerson, the real frontier lies on the edge of human consciousness and is merely displaced temporarily, for particular rhetorical purposes, to the edge of the woods or beyond. Like Barnett and Lawlor, Barszcz illustrates the particular ways in which American writers have actively created frontiers on an originally undifferentiated American "mythotopography."

In "Frontier Violence in the Garden of America," Reginald Dyck explores the contradictions between two powerful myths, those of the peaceful garden and the violent frontier. In order to portray both the natural beauty and the energizing savagery of American settlement, such authors as Willa Cather and Wright Morris have developed narrative strategies to accommodate both myths within one story. The human costs are tremendous, and, rather than experiencing "regeneration through violence," as Richard Slotkin argues,[18] Cather's and Morris's characters suffer tremendously in trying to reconcile the contradictory self-images of "innocent and noble farmers" and "powerful individualists." Linda S. Pickle also addresses violence in the writings of Great Plains authors. Her essay, "Foreign-Born Immigrants on the Great Plains Frontier in Fiction and Nonfiction," explores the variety of narrative methods by which Cather, Ole Rölvaag, Marie Sandoz, and John Ise dramatize the conflicts of Plains frontier life. The physical and emotional struggles of foreign-born immigrants are handled differently by these four writers. For Pickle the most interesting differences arise from the choice to write fiction or nonfiction, especially the degree to which fiction writers "endow their subject matter with a sense of universality and of epic and even mythic significance."

Part 2 of *Desert, Garden, Margin, Range* includes essays that primarily take the other route of frontier studies: interpretation and evaluation of previously neglected texts. The canon of American literature is currently growing at a rate that threatens to overwhelm the institutional framework for teaching it, as anthologies are swollen by works previously considered subliterary. Among these are many texts by women and minorities, others previously dismissed as "popular," and still others on the fringes of traditional belletristic genres. The essays by Susan Scheckel and Carol J. Singley argue for both the radical thematic implications and the genuine aesthetic value of neglected American texts by women. In "Mary Jemison and the Domestication of the American Indian," Scheckel argues that Jemison inhabited the frontier in a fundamentally different way than Boone and other male avatars of the settler. This "domestic" rapprochement with wilderness and with the figure of the Native American was intensely threatening to American exploitational ideology, and so Jemison's story was itself partly "domesticated" by its "author," James E. Seaver. However, enough of the original story and language remain for us to understand Jemison's unique contribution to American letters. In "Catharine Maria Sedgwick's *Hope Leslie*: Radical Frontier Romance," Singley argues that Sedgwick successfully employed the conventions of historical romance, including acceptably feminine heroines, well enough to be extremely popular in her day. But at the same time she undercut those conventions, creating powerful female protagonists and questioning the morality of Puritan settlement. Thus Sedgwick would seem a likely candidate for inclusion in the American literary canon, though she has been excluded thus far. Singley wonders, for instance, whether "the ending of *Hope Leslie* is too discomfitting for literary historians and readers who prefer retreat into a fantasy world where one can ignore the injustices to nature by escaping further into the wilderness."

In "Southwest of What?: Southwestern Literature as a Form of Frontier Literature," Reed Way Dasenbrock explores the long struggle over who will define the American Southwest and in what terms. Is regional literature a celebration of regional essence or an exploitation of exotic regional differences? In his survey of nineteenth-and twentieth-century novels, Dasenbrock concludes that exoticism, rather than realism, has been the norm with Anglo writers, even among supposedly realistic novelists, and he concludes that "if major writing about the Southwest is to emerge from Anglo writers as well as Chicanos and Native Americans, then the first task is a more critical examination of the received notions about the Southwest than any of these [Anglo] writers have engaged in so far."

Aron Senkpiel's observations about the North are similar to Dasenbrock's about the Southwest. Senkpiel's thesis is that the frontier has moved "from the Wild West to the Far North," and that much contemporary literature set completely or partially in the North repeats the mythopoetic gestures of frontier literature. This has been especially true of Canadian texts. However, as more genuinely indigenous writers are published, a new view of the northern frontier is taking shape: one that sees the vast taiga and tundra not as a boundary or a testing margin but as a "homeland."

At the end one comes around once again to the beginning. Columbus may have ended the European "romance" of exploration, but by the same act he initiated the Native American tragedy of near-annihilation. The final essay in this collection, James Ruppert's " 'Difficult Meat': Dialogism and Identity in Three Native American Narratives of Contact," could also have been the first essay, as it explores the Native American perspective on European invasion. Ruppert uses a Bakhtinian framework, because "oral tradition creates an environment that is similar to [Bakhtin's notion of] heteroglossia." In the course of his analysis we learn a great deal both about Native American perspectives on the white myth of the frontier and about how oral texts are fundamentally structurally different from Western "authored" narratives.

One hundred years after the 1890 census, which was the occasion for Turner's elegiac essay on the closing of the frontier, that frontier remains very much open in American consciousness, which is where it has always actually resided. Historians have argued over Turner's thesis for the last century—demonstrating, for instance, that "pioneers moved westward when times were good and did not when times were bad" (Billington, 29), undercutting the "safety valve" component of Turner's theory. But those professional debates have never mattered much to the general reception of Turner's frontier thesis, because the boundary whose passing he lamented has always been more psychic than physical. By 1893 writers had already lamented the wiping out of the buffalo, the passing of the mountain man and the gunfighter, and the end of free land. After 1893 others mourned the passing of particular kinds of life in New Mexico and California, on the Great Plains, and in the small-town South. Americans have always been nostalgic, despite priding themselves on looking ahead and moving forward. The frontier is, among its other manifestations, the place many Americans go to mourn their lost youth.

In 1988 two of America's most popular Western writers, Edward Abbey and Louis L'Amour, died. Between them they explored many of the contradictions Americans assume when they talk about "Western," "frontier," and "wilderness." Between the gunfighters, mountain men, and meticulously researched settings of L'Amour, and the boatmen, rangers, and threatened riverine settings of Abbey, there are tremendous thematic and methodological gaps. But which is more real to American consciousness? L'Amour and Abbey had a lot in common; they shared a deep respect for the wild places of the West and a similar fascination with its most common mythical inhabitant, the strong, lonely, courageous man. Of course, they developed those shared interests in very different directions. L'Amour wrote within (and set some of the standards for) the genre of frontier romance; Abbey deliberately challenged the conventions of that genre.[19] Millions of readers of L'Amour likely do not have much use for Abbey, and many of Abbey's following doubtless do not read L'Amour. But both writers built their stories on the same mythic groundwork, and together their books illustrate some of the huge range of possibilities available to writers who choose to fuel their writing with the cultural energy of the frontier.

Investigating the frontier in American literature is one way for Americans to try to understand, even as they unavoidably participate in, their continuing national obsession with exploration. The essays in this book inquire into the repeated American motif of pushing against limits, always "growing"—that is, changing in some way. Growth without displacement is of course impossible. One virtue of self-reflective writing like the essays in this volume is that it interrogates the terms of Western desire. Such cultural introspection may be the best hope for survival on those future frontiers where Americans will undoubtedly re-create the West, without, I hope, reenacting their mistakes.

Part 1

Revisiting the Canon of Frontier Literature

Speech in the Wilderness: The Ideal Discourse of *The Deerslayer*

Louise K. Barnett

In one of the early romantic masterworks of the American novel, *The Deerslayer*, language is envisioned as adequate to the needs of speakers. The ever-present dialectic between speech and silence is represented only in terms of intentionality: that is, when characters speak they are able to express themselves eloquently, but they may *choose* silence as the preferable course. Problems of verbalization are social in *The Deerslayer*, never linguistic. Its fictive world demonstrates full confidence in the ability of language to articulate accurately a world outside itself and to achieve congruity between intention and utterance and between speaking and understanding—in short, a faith in the ability of characters to speak and be understood.

Given this confidence in spoken language to communicate meaning, it is hardly surprising that *The Deerslayer* is significantly shaped by issues of speech. It is in fact a speech-act drama in which speaking or withholding speech has profound consequences for the entire fiction. The text is dominated by Deerslayer's massive discourse, a series of assertions that physical reality and the behavior of other characters constantly validate.[1] Moreover, a particular speech act is climactically crucial—Deerslayer's promise to the Hurons to return to captivity and probable death. The commitment to speech, more than action, is a public commitment to the values of the word and an ultimate test of character in which a man's word literally becomes his bond.

Successive literary revolutions have made Cooper's ideas of novelistic praxis increasingly remote, but *The Leatherstocking Tales* continue to invoke a central conflict of the American experience—the tension be-

19

tween wilderness and individual freedom. The pastoral is the ideal genre for Cooper's acute sense of these polarities, and no text of his is more successful as a model of American pastoral than *The Deerslayer*, the last and "most fascinating" of *The Leatherstocking Tales*.[2] Cooper's wilderness is not the howling desert of the Puritan imagination, which, in their traditional imagery, must be "cultivated" and "made to bloom," but a nurturing presence whose pristine existence is superior to any other environment.

However, nature is the perfect place for men and women only insofar as they live there according to those principles of right conduct that have been learned within a social group; consequently, the mythic protagonist must be acculturated enough to have imbibed correct values without similarly acquiring the corrupt practices of existence in society.[3] That Deerslayer is "at heart, a Moravian," as Hurry Harry accuses, might reasonably be inferred from his frequent citing of the Moravian missionaries and his adherence to their teachings, yet his rejection of society is equally emphatic. Moreover, as Donald Darnell shows, "its rich romantic, mythic, and pastoral elements notwithstanding, [*The Deerslayer*] is, in a very substantial way, about social hierarchy and class. . . ."[4] Cooper is as inflexible as Zola in predicating Judith Hutter's fate upon her mother's failure to find her proper social level, first aiming too high and bearing children out of wedlock, then marrying beneath her. Deerslayer's commentary on such violations of hierarchy asserts the superiority of rigidly maintained class distinctions. Without prior knowledge of her mother's history Judith has already repeated the first phase of it, and she makes vigorous efforts to complete the pattern by marrying Deerslayer, a man who is—whatever his virtues—socially beneath her and as removed from class affiliation as Thomas Hutter.

Judith's story is simply the most dramatic encapsulation of the principle that governs *The Deerslayer*'s perfect economy: nothing is suitable that is out of character. This is the "matrix-sentence" of Deerslayer's truth, to borrow a Barthesian term, and it applies equally to the twin spheres of nature and gifts, what is inborn and what is acculturated.[5] Nature is the unalterable life stuff that each society shapes into a distinctive culture by developing the appropriate gifts. For every nature, there is natural behavior, the basic core of being that experience cannot modify. Environment determines the acquisition of "gifts," which are built upon the foundation of nature, and certain gifts are more suited to certain natures.[6] As Deerslayer tells Judith and Hetty, "Stick to your gifts and your gifts will stick to you." Such deterministic reasoning reveals a world organized into fixed hierarchies that unite nature and society according to the divine plan, a system in which everything is not only explicable but classifiable in language.

1

In spite of its token gesturing toward the plot action of frontier romance, the hackneyed staple of Indian captivity, *The Deerslayer* is a novel of speech much more than action, almost static when compared to *The Last of the Mohicans*. While the text as moral tract presents a schematization akin to a morality play, in which the familiar virtues and vices can be readily assigned to the characters,[7] the text as romance explores the familiar issue of identity. Who the characters are is finally the novel's greatest preoccupation, and it is constantly revealed first through speech and only later through some other form of behavior. Even the torture scene is a ritualized tableau in which speechifying outweighs the Indians' physical assault and Deerslayer's reaction.

Although language shares the divided nature of society, capable of ordering and corrupting, no writer has more confidence than Cooper in its power to achieve an ideal discourse. In the categorizing of Deerslayer and of the authorial voice, there is no indication that language may be anything other than a transparent medium to present an organization that inheres in the world itself. When words are used to express this order (i.e., nature), they can always be understood. "Such language," Deerslayer affirms, "is as plain in one tongue as in another; it comes from the heart, and goes to the heart, too" (*Deerslayer*, 448). Cooper's fictive world contains no ambiguities, no complexities, no realities that stubbornly withhold their nature from language. The world is fallen, so it often swerves from the divinely appointed order, yet even these departures from universal decorum can be adequately labeled as aberrations and be made to serve the system they flout. A perfect correspondence between signifier and signified governs *The Deerslayer*'s universe of discourse.

This perfect correspondence is possible only in the specifically enabling site of the wilderness, the pastoral margin. In the macrocosm of town and settlement, language is deformed by hypocrisy, affectation, and deceit. But even in the wilderness language is threatened by deception and self-interest, for ultimately it is only as good as its speakers. As Deerslayer tells Hetty, "Men are deceived in other men's characters, and frequently give 'em names they by no means deserve. You can see the truth of this in the Mingo names, which, in their own tongue, signify the same thing as the Delaware names . . . and no one can say they are as honest or as upright a nation. I put no great dependence, therefore, on names" (*Deerslayer*, 56). Such assertions suggest that Deerslayer values nature as presence over any representations of it.

Deerslayer's own credibility as a speaker joins the novel as moral tract to the novel as romantic fiction, allowing him to function both as sage, the passive hero who enlightens others through speech about the nature of the world, and as potential martyr, the active hero who risks death to preserve his integrity. Thus the keyword of the novel's discourse is nature, and the keyword of its metadiscourse is truth. That nature can accurately be revealed in language is the enabling principle of Deerslayer's discourse, but his own character as a truthful and moral speaker equally empowers his speech. Even the enemy acknowledges his veracity by allowing him to leave captivity on "furlough." Rivenoak tells his prisoner, "You are honest; when you say a thing it is so" (*Deerslayer*, 490).

Deerslayer monopolizes the novel's speech because his is the only truthful discourse in the twofold sense of conforming to nature and being spoken disinterestedly. Because the behavior of other characters and physical reality constantly validate his speech, agreement with Deerslayer is a touchstone for judging other characters. His reverse image, Hurry Harry, instructs misguidedly, expounding a system of classification that assimilates Indians to wolves and hence justifies killing and scalping them. Hetty's discourse articulates an unchanging moral imperative, but it frequently reminds us of the institutional nature of such supposed absolutes and the concomitant importance of verbal context.[8] When Hetty enjoins Deerslayer to return good for evil, he replies: "Ah Hetty, that may do among the missionaries, but 'twould make an oncertain life in the woods. . . ." (*Deerslayer*, 507). Because other speakers are all marked by some barrier to truthful speech—Judith's need to conceal her past, Hurry's prejudice, Hutter's rapacity, Hetty's feeblemindedness—they lack this power to assess experience precisely and verbalize it without distortion. Deerslayer is also able to weigh the speech of others accurately because "the ears of a man can tell truth from ontruth" (*Deerslayer*, 226). Thus, understanding as well as speaking depends upon character: Deerslayer condemns Hurry's innuendoes about Judith as unmanly behavior, yet at the end of the novel he confesses (for once speechlessly) that they have influenced him—presumably because they are true in spite of their dubious source.

In his role of "Straight Tongue," one of his earlier Indian names, Deerslayer constantly enlightens his error-prone associates. A "full-fledged fictional Adam,"[9] he exercises the Adamic function of naming—correcting Hurry's notions of race, reproving Judith's love of finery, admonishing the two trappers for wanting to scalp Indians, informing both whites and Indians of the differences between red and white gifts. Most of the failings Deerslayer exposes are errors of classification; like Hurry's categorizing of Indians they impose convenient but inaccurate labels to justify self-serving behavior. All of these instances conform to the novel's master paradigm of linguistic behavior, the ordering and classifying of experience.

The majority of Deerslayer's illocutionary acts belong in Searle's category of assertions, "those utterances which commit the speaker to something's being the case, to the truth of the expressed proposition" (Searle, 10). Such speeches tend to be long because each subject participates in complex patterns of discourse representing relationships in the physical world. Since reason and nature are in harmony, Cooper treats these statements as self-evident truths that will be instantly recognized as such by rational listeners. Accordingly, when Judith hints that she might becomingly wear some fine clothing discovered in her father's chest, Deerslayer's explanation of the decorum of clothes and social hierarchy immediately changes her frivolous attitude: " 'I'll take off the rubbish this instant, Deerslayer,' cried the girl, springing up to leave the room; 'and never do I wish to see it on any human being again' " (*Deerslayer*, 215). Although Judith is beginning to care for Deerslayer, and his exegesis is framed by skillful, if sincere, compliment, Cooper always shows her attachment to be rational: if she responds to his personal authority here, it is only because this authority is based upon his recognized character and expertise. Certainly this talk exchange is a model of ideal persuasive discourse, but it is a great deal more; it is also a model of discourse based upon proper personal credentials and a rational argument.

"Truth is truth," Deerslayer is fond of proclaiming, an assertion that recalls Falstaff's query to Prince Hal, "Is not the truth the truth?" But a world of verbal sophistication separates Shakespeare's protagonist from Cooper's; Deerslayer is both naive and forthright, an innocent truth teller who can only flourish in the wilderness context. Falstaff calls attention to the cleverness of his utterance and invites the larger audience to ponder the complexities of "truth." Indeed, if Falstaff's transparently outrageous story is truth, then such a concept is worthless as a means of conveying reality. His assertions are one ploy among others to be used to individual advantage. Deerslayer's truth is embodied in speech corresponding to realities and understood as such by a receptor who requires nothing further.

That difficulties of communication do occur in *The Deerslayer* fails to undermine either the accepted certainty of the assertion Deerslayer makes or its content. The dialogue bristles with self-reflexive references to its own procedures in which plain speaking is demanded and understanding is viewed as a process achieved through speech. At first no one comprehends Deerslayer's plan of returning to Huron captivity, but through his usual method of precise categorizing and defining he explains his position until everyone, even Hetty, understands: " 'You can understand what it is to give a promise, I dare to say, good little Hetty?' 'Certainly. A promise is to say you will do a thing, and that binds you to be as good as your word' " (*Deerslayer*, 477–78). The questions of

The Deerslayer's world always have answers, and it only remains for Deerslayer to link "furlough" with "promise" to satisfy Hetty's puzzlement about the invisible captivity: the binding power of language upon honorable men and women.

Failures of understanding, like those of speech itself, are governed by character, not by language. When Hurry interrupts Judith's account of why she refuses to marry him by insisting that he understands her, his statement expresses his own assessment of Judith's history. The Hurons are similarly unable to understand Hetty's reading of the Bible, not because the Word is defective, but because their gifts are for another sort of belief.

2

Talk exchange in *The Deerslayer*, as Mark Twain observed in his own parody of Cooper's long-windedness, is unrealistically prolix.[10] The novel's speech is so implausibly ponderous because Cooper's failure to differentiate the spheres of narrative and dialogue burdens direct discourse with a number of authorial jobs that are patently inappropriate to the speech situation. Talk habitually turns into protracted speech making in which intrusions of authorial purpose mix uneasily with a character's reason for speaking. When Judith exhorts Deerslayer, "Pull, Deerslayer . . . pull for life and death—the lake is full of savages wading after us!" (*Deerslayer*, 146), her relatively brief and simple communication is suited to the urgency of the speech situation. But she continues: "Pull, Deerslayer, for Heaven's sake! . . . These wretches rush into the water like hounds following their prey! Ah!—The Scow moves! And now the water deepens to the armpits of the foremost; still they rush forward, and will seize the ark!" In Judith's second speech the inclusion of description embellished with literary simile, material appropriate to the narrative but in language at odds with the speech occasion, diminishes the drama of the escape.

What is equally striking in the speech of *The Deerslayer* is not the irrelevance Twain complained of, but the absence of the irrelevance that at least occasionally characterizes any real conversation. Nothing is spoken that is truly irrelevant to the novel's single-minded display of Deerslayer's exemplary character and capabilities within the overall design of narrative cum moral tract, and it is in fact this weighty double purpose that transforms talk exchange into verbal essays of didactic generalizing. When Judith offers up her own finery to ransom Hutter from the Indians, it is germane to the action for Deerslayer to pose the question that he does: "But are you sartain, gal, you could find it in your heart to part with your own finery for such a purpose?" (*Deerslayer*, 202).

The lengthy speech that follows, an example of what Twain meant by irrelevance, is gratuitous to narrative progression but in keeping with Deerslayer's role as disseminator of wisdom.

Most of Deerslayer's assertive utterances follow some recognizable version of an expository pattern: definition, comparison, contrast, exemplification. They are sermons or lectures that might easily be arranged according to topic. Cooper realizes that the awkward mesh of narrative with set pieces of exposition needs to be acknowledged, and his reference to the "unpolished sincerity, that so often made this simple-minded hunter bare his thoughts" offers a rationale for Deerslayer's sententiousness. Free from social properties that would restrain or deflect speech in more socialized speakers, Deerslayer simply utters a whole and unvarnished truth regardless of consequence or context. This openness of speech, a reflection of wilderness simplicity, characterizes the other white speakers as well, although in their cases disingenuous rudeness reveals character traits less admirable than Deerslayer's love of truth.[11] The insensitive and boastful Hurry Harry tells Deerslayer three times in the same conversation that he isn't good-looking. Later, he remarks: "I don't expect you'll prove much of a warrior . . ." (*Deerslayer*, 92). Hutter's suspicions about Deerslayer, which he voices in his presence, express his own criminal asociality.[12]

While the authorial voice all too frequently intrudes in substance, speech is stylistically differentiated according to character. Hurry's rash and impulsive nature and his braggadocio, Hetty's naïveté, Hutter's taciturn and suspicious nature and Judith's settlement-influenced sophistication and natural vivacity are all embodied in their speech, in addition to the broader effects of education and social class.[13] The Indians speak a more formal and figurative language than the whites without sounding alike: speech reveals Chingachgook's stolid dignity, Rivenoak's slyness, and Hist's strong feelings.

These distinctive voices are all subordinated to that of Deerslayer, which is at times plausibly humble, at times implausibly poetic or philosophical. Shifts in level are often abrupt, as in the passage Twain singled out for particular ridicule, where Deerslayer justifies to Judith his participation in the recovery of Hist: "It consarns me, as all things that touches a fri'nd consarns a fri'nd" (*Deerslayer*, 132). As Twain reasonably objected, we would expect a man who speaks like this to have some difficulty in organizing the world verbally, yet in the next breath, Deerslayer responds to Judith's question about his sweetheart with a poetic speech containing no grammatical errors or deviant pronunciation. The two utterances might be used to illustrate Coleridge's description of rustic and cultivated speech: "The rustic, from the more imperfect development of his faculties, and from the lower state of their cultivation, aims almost solely to convey insulated facts, either those of his scanty experience or his traditional belief; while the educated man chiefly seeks to discover and express those connections of things, or those relative bearings of fact to fact, from which some more or less general law is deductible."[14]

Deerslayer speaks in both styles, sometimes even mixing them in the same speech, but while such obvious inconsistency is contrary to realistic expectation, Cooper's intention, as he wrote in the preface to the *Leatherstocking Tales*, is to encompass an ideal of character: "A leading character in a work of fiction has a fair right to the aid which can be obtained from a poetical view of the subject. It is in this view, rather than in one more strictly circumstantial, that Leatherstocking has been drawn" (*Deerslayer*, vi). Because Deerslayer's first response to Judith is so circumscribed, it is easily expressed within the limited resources of his frontiersman's mode of speaking. Nature, however, inspires his deepest feelings, and the elevation of his speech is Cooper's way of rendering in language what would, in a realistically conceived woodsman, remain inchoate and nonverbal. What is appropriate to Deerslayer is the feeling, which can be most effectively expressed in a language that is unsuited to this illiterate character.

In his discussion of voice in *As I Lay Dying*, Stephen M. Ross observes that objections to such inconsistencies and implausibilities in a character's speech reflect "the assumption that voice must be an index of personal identity. . . . It is assumed not only that a voice belongs to some person but also that it is in crucial ways 'appropriate' to that person—to his or her socio-economic class, level of education, and so on."[15] While Deerslayer's speech does not maintain a consistent level of class and education, there is a predictability of content and attitude that makes his voice recognizable throughout the novel and creates "personal identity," although this identity is not primarily determined by the form of his speech.

3

A series of speech acts, followed by corroborative actions, tests each character's identity in the novel's climactic crisis. Deprived of a selfish motive by Judith's rejection, Hurry announces that he will not remain to defend the Hutter daughters, while Chingachgook, Hist, and Judith all profess loyalty to Deerslayer. Hurry departs; the others act upon their words by attempting to free Deerslayer from the Hurons. The greatest proof of the significance of speech is of course reserved for Deerslayer himself, a coalescing of his roles as moral preceptor and active hero. Through repeated discussion, since everyone but Chingachgook and

Hist requires a separate explanation, the pledge given to the Hurons comes to represent the conditions of all speech, its capacity for character revelation and for an absolute of commitment that transcends "the wants of the body" and "the cravings of the spirit." When Hurry objects that Deerslayer need not keep his word to the Indians because they "have neither souls nor names," Deerslayer replies with his most comprehensive argument: "If they've got neither souls nor names, you and I have both . . ." (*Deerslayer*, 418). The social linguistic contract merely replicates the divine, according to which the integrity of the speaker ensures the invisible bond of meaning and intention. Speaking is always a moral act, and thus it is an index of the speaker's morality.

While it seems to be a matter of course for Deerslayer to keep his word to God and man, his final conversation with Judith imposes a more difficult test of his commitment to truthful speech. If, as Judith says, the "arts and deceptions of the settlements" do not enter into their discourse, social decorum is nevertheless a powerful influence on both speakers. To avoid the insult of telling Judith outright that he does not love her, Deerslayer substitutes a curious evasion of the honest speech of his credo: "If Father and Mother was livin', which, however, neither is—but if both was livin', I do not feel toward any woman as if I wish'd to quit 'em in order to cleave unto *her*" (*Deerslayer* 568). In the presence of an explicitly sexual overture, albeit one couched in the institutional form of marriage, the protagonist retrogresses to a juvenile dependency made doubly absurd by the contrary-to-fact condition. It is Judith who puts the rejection into direct language, preempting Deerslayer's role of instructor and truth teller and enjoining him to confirm her speech by his own silence. Cooper reinforces the image of Deerslayer's retreat from adulthood by describing him as obediently mute, "playing with the water, like a corrected schoolboy." Continuing their role reversal, Judith poses another probing question, to which Deerslayer fails to respond in words: "Truth was the Deerslayer's polar star. He ever kept it in view; and it was nearly impossible for him to avoid uttering it, even when prudence demanded silence. Judith read his answer in his countenance" (*Deerslayer*, 570). Ordinarily able to master the world through speech, and even impelled by personal intergrity to utter the truth, Deerslayer now says nothing, a reversal that requires explanation.

Since Cooper tells us that Deerslayer's heart was never touched by Judith, his failure to speak is evidently motivated by a conflict between the social injunction that forbids giving offense to a woman and his personal injunction against lying. This uncharacteristic silence, upon which Cooper ends the novel, emphasizes that, like other American Adams, Deerslayer eschews adult sexuality, and this trait, as much as his distaste for other aspects of life in society, accounts for his inability to live there permanently. In order to be understood in that world Deer-slayer's tongue would have to express the "contradictions of the settle-ments" rather than the "harmony of the woods." Only the latter site makes possible the ideal of speech that Deerslayer has always espoused and exemplified.

The Fictions of Daniel Boone

Mary Lawlor

The history of Daniel Boone is the history of a cultural figure and a literary character whose claim to authenticity is one of its most dominant components. In the many narratives that have conducted the Boone motif into contemporary culture, a similar claim is often made for the text's direct access to Boone's authenticity. Such worrying over the sources and processes of composition oddly puts any attempt to stabilize Boone's figure into doubt; and the close analysis of his ideal authenticity dissolves into a demonstration of the rhetoric in which certain classical American notions of subjectivity exist.

However they may contradict each other, Boone's most universal assets—his simplicity, innocence, spontaneous knowledge, and physical prowess—are commonly evoked to serve this notion that he is in some sense authentic. But authentically what? Authentically himself, the individual, the coherent self, different from anything before, after, or beside him. This essay examines such distinctions, not to dismantle the figure but to demonstrate how the anxious historicism that projects it is condensed in Boone's own adaptability and, with all of its concerns for representation and the drive to honor the real, inflates Boone with a dimensionality we might call character.

The terms *figure* and *character* are not intended to be used interchangeably in this essay, since I am reserving a certain complex of difficulties for *character* that *figure* in its status as simple notation avoids. *Figure* is most often meant to suggest a shape as well as a technical function active in the narrative process. The complexities that I refer to as *character* provoke snags in the more conventional operations of figure, in that they sustain a critical awareness that accompanies actions and statements—not an awareness of what acts and sayings might result

29

in, but an awareness of their sheer phenomenality. Thus I understand character as a kind of dialogue in which act and reflection are locked in mutual response, each performing for each.[1]

I have chosen Boone from among a number of figures in American culture whose behavior and whose stories might be cited as paradigms of Western manners and narrative style. The highly conservative structural procedures and thematic concerns of the genre are evident to anyone remotely familiar with American culture, and thus any of these figures might appropriately be chosen to stand for the others. I choose Boone because, rather than repeating the wish to be new that he proposes in his various avatars, I would like to keep my criticism within the traditional scope of Western literary and cultural analysis that situates Boone as the earliest well-documented and circulated figure of the wilderness hunter in the United States. During the revolutionary era, Boone's name appeared in promotional literature for the territory of Kentucky; and for various reasons that have been addressed by Richard Slotkin, his figure began to subsume a range of characteristics that, recognized as prototypically American, composed an icon for the new ideology to use in reproducing itself. In *Regeneration through Violence* Slotkin writes: "[I]t was the figure of Daniel Boone, the solitary, Indian-like hunter of the deep woods, that became the most significant, most emotionally compelling myth-hero of the early republic."[2]

From the history of Boone literature that Slotkin and Henry Nash Smith before him have provided, I will address the works of John Filson, James Hall, Timothy Flint, and James Fenimore Cooper, which seem to have had the widest circulation in the United States during the late eighteenth and early nineteenth centuries. I am not interested here in capturing some real sense of Boone in a transcendent analysis that has escaped these writers; my concern is to address the mechanics of representation, intended or otherwise, that have projected Boone as an exemplum of the rhetoric of subjectivity. His figure in many ways duplicates the ideal, unmarked tabula rasa of the wilderness that he inscribes.

1

The first biography of Daniel Boone appeared in John Filson's *The Discovery, Settlement and Present State of Kentucke*, published in Delaware in 1784. Filson was a schoolteacher from Pennsylvania whose fascination with Boone seems to have been mixed with an interest in land speculation. He most likely read of him in the promotional literature for lands Boone had surveyed; and *Kentucke* itself had something of this advertising mission in its narrative pressures.

In about 1782, Filson went to Kentucky where he met Boone and heard the story of Kentucky's history, which was largely Boone's history. In his preface, Filson writes that Boone "was earlier acquainted with the subject of this performance [the settlement of Kentucky] than any other now living, as appears by the account of his adventures, which I esteemed curious and interesting, and therefore have published from his own mouth."[3]

In this account of the composition, Filson casts himself as a recorder of Boone's first-person narration who has no literary designs of his own. But since Boone's language is rough and simple, Filson has to edit it so that diction and tone will suit the conventions of publication. Filson does not exactly claim that Boone was himself illiterate; but by calling attention to the rustic quality of his speech, he stresses a naturalness in the figure of Boone, a quality as little designed as the history that emerges from and with him. Filson expects his language, then, to express simultaneously a simple and natural speaking subject, a writer who yields authority to his source and does not intrude in the composition, and a natural world to which the language is intended to refer. The presences that issue in the reader's imagination from either "side" of the work—that of the speaker and writer, or that of the referent—do not seem to get in the way of each other's operations, and in fact do not appear as "other." Boone's simplicity means faithful representation; and his literature, recited or written, does not translate the world of objects but records them faithfully: to write a botanical description, for example, is a literary act, and the literature thus produced constitutes science.[4]

Filson's description of Kentucky is succinct in style: his narrative of the earliest white expeditions beyond the Cumberland Mountains is brief, and he organizes the data of the territory in categories such as "Situation and Boundaries," "Rivers," "Nature of the Soil," and so on. To a certain degree, his close analysis of detail and compartmentalizing of the territory's physical data seem to resist narrative fluency. One of the effects of such discretion is to place each object in relief and to compose, in a sense, a series of portraits where visual realism dominates at the expense of conceptual representation that narrative might impose. Periodically, and fortunately for the fate of the book's reception, he releases himself from the rhetorical measures of scientific notation and indulges in more lyrical descriptions: "The beautiful river . . . Ohio receives a number of large and small rivers, which pay tribute to its glory"; and Licking River "collect[s] its silver streams from many branches" (Filson, 311). Conflating for the moment the voice of transparent recorder with that of desirous observer, he writes, "The reader, by casting his eye upon the map . . . may view . . . the most extraordinary country upon which the sun ever shone" (Filson, 316).

What we periodically recognize as elaborate stylizations in Filson's landscape descriptions bring to mind Wordsworth and Coleridge in the attention drawn to an observing and desiring subject whose sensibility is momentarily composed in an exchange with the voluptuous designs of nature. While this elasticity allows for much pleasure in Filson's writing, it also strains against the pressure of scientific and material economics that constitute a good part of his text's interest. But all of these categories and oppositions swirl into each other on the issue of reproduction, or representation—the impulse by which the landscape is converted into knowledge, the myth of the West is perpetuated in terms of wealth, and the observing subject attempts to compose itself from the divisions that shape and reshape it.

Even the biography proper, with its necessary concern for fluent narrative logic, retains the chorography's indulgence in description, a mode that Filson clearly favors. The restraints of his botanical lists are repeated somewhat in the episodic arrangement of material and its focus on the separate moments of Boone's experience, one after the other, rather than on an overtly posed, general meaning or ideological value woven through the text. Not until the end do we read totalizing comments such as the following: "My footsteps have often been marked with blood . . . Many dark and sleepless nights have I been a companion for owls, separated from the cheerful society of men, scorched by the summer's sun, and pinched by the winter's cold, an instrument ordained to settle the wilderness. But now the scene is changed: peace crowns the sylvan shade" (Filson, 359).

In his elaborate closing, Filson releases a flood of romantic narration that the preceding text thus retrospectively appears to anticipate. Such contrast in style and tone induces a tension in Filson's "voice" that has much to do with the design of Boone as a character. We might well presume that Filson knew his reader would recognize that the story was not precisely "taken from [Boone's] mouth" verbatim, for the style of Filson's preface is exactly that of Boone's first-person narrative. If this lack of difference were presumed to be taken literally, it would effectively diminish the distinctions between Boone and Filson as persons as well as writers; Boone's character and the place of the recorder/writer would be blurred. In any case, Filson's "I have taken" suggests plainly enough that the text is his own interpretation. Thus Filson's ventriloquy is oddly the device that separates him from Boone; more precisely, it is what makes Boone the absent, somewhat mystified creature that elicits Filson's desire by eluding it. In this relation, traits that will become more openly addressed in later Boone narratives are nascent: his protean evasiveness, his illusory, retrospective presence, and his treacherous innocence.

The literary articulation of Kentucky in which Filson participated made it into a thing that could circulate as information, exchangeable in a market economy that typically equated land with the human life that would occupy and develop it. The map and chorography that Filson provides are thus literally and figuratively bound up with the biography of Boone. Generating the wilderness that generates him, Boone becomes the quintessential figure of the West, imaging the whole field of its possibilities in his presence or in the simple sound of his name. Together the two accounts appropriate the place and its "history" for the new ideology and for its circuit of scientific and commercial exchanges.[5] The lists of landscape details are simultaneously restrained in style, in order to appear mimetic, and expeditious, in order that the information be clear enough to sell the land. Boone thus provides a representative image for the already-functioning modality of the hybrid American self: land, money, and biography inextricably entwined in each other's meaning. Boone's figure becomes formalized and an established convention. After this point, there is every reason to suppose that his public movements reaffirm Filson's account at the same time that they are informed by it.[6]

While many accounts of Boone after 1784 drew heavily on Filson's narrative, we begin to see among them more of a divided sensibility between notions of scientific realism and literary extension in the representation of the western territory and of the figure of Daniel Boone. A concern in these later texts for fidelity to conditions that were presumed to exist before composition, and represented as quickly disappearing, is evidenced not only thematically but in attention drawn to the writing itself, since the very fact of representation contributes to the receding of time presumably recalled. Such fear of being too late, of course, imagines its own starting point, the true Boone story, as an object of the writer's desire crouched on a distant horizon. While all Boone tales, including Filson's, seem to be fueled to some degree by such an anxious interest, it is in the early nineteenth-century narratives that articulations of Boone become interesting for their varying ways of distributing rhetorical stress and tension in the incessant wish to settle the question of the real.

2

In James Hall's *Letters from the West*, begun in 1819 and published together in 1828, Daniel Boone is presented as a solitary individual, an exemplary instance of the "backwoodsman"; and this type is itself understood to subsume and magnify several traits of what Hall attempts to articulate as the "national character." Broadening his delineations from the particular to the general and bringing them back to the specific again, Hall repeatedly qualifies, contradicts, and practically erases the characteristics he attributes to each phase of Boone's metonymity, so that, rather than types, he suggests tendencies and countertendencies of a highly protean, elusive, and barely discernible figure. Although Hall's work is largely a eulogy, the slipperiness that his stylistic hedgings and rhetorical hesitancies lend the figure is repeated in the dissimulations, deceptions, and illusions that are so important to Boone's preservation of himself—ironically an occupation that, in this account, to a great degree makes him. Hall's attempts to anchor Boone's reference in a specific regionalism and at the same time to let it subsume American character types continue the sense of natural innocence so important in Filson's designs. In his particularity Boone is ignorant of any larger cultural implications that his figure might evoke; and by subsuming all types, he cancels differences crucial to the mechanisms of civil exchange. But Hall takes a major turn in continuously altering his Boone, so that he reverberates between representation of the particular and the general. Rather than conducting one continuous history that lends position and voice to this one presence, here Boone "hopskotches" among several stories that supposedly participate simultaneously in a larger, highly abstract history.

Hall's letter 4 assumes "national character" as the ultimate reality of personality in the United States, shared by all but expressed differently from region to region. Local manners are thus signifiers of a sure core of character. But Hall's emphasis on the general reality to which regional idiosyncrasies point alternates with writerly indulgence in the value of the local for its own sake; and the more general, national characteristics both restrain and affirm parochial manners: "In the great matters of religion and law, all of us in the United States are the same—as the children of one family, when they separate in the world, still preserve the impress of those principles which they imbibed from a common source; but, in all matters of taste and fancy, customs and exterior deportment, we find a variance."[7]

Among the equipment that each citizen possesses, according to Hall, are a "hardy frame and versatile spirit [which] easily accommodate themselves to new employments." This chameleonlike ability to adapt to unfamiliar conditions is accompanied by a certain duplicity, however, which sustains the traveler's own regional outlook as his primary orientation: "Though he still has the same heart, the same feelings, and the same principles, he is quite another person in his manners and mode of living" (Hall, 246). The versatility that marks American character permits it to slide from local to national identity; and it also serves a kind of savvy that introduces violence in the form of disguise, misleading behavior, and dissimulation.

A model for the regional type of the backwoodsman and an exemplary instance of national character's versatile craftiness, Boone is as movable as the Kentucky border. He, like all Kentuckians, is essentially a Virginian, but in his status as representative American man, he shares with the New Englander a remarkable shrewdness. He has what Hall terms "the ability to deceive" that is managed by a "moral principle to control the evil propensities of human nature . . . [the] sufficient weight of character to enlist pride as an auxiliary" (Hall, 242). By raising the moral issue in this context, Hall barely disguises his attempt to identify deception as some kind of admirable aptitude.

A stable national character is evidently an object of Hall's desire, something that continuously elicits and eludes his writing, in the manner that Boone dodges definition as he floats among national, regional, and individual representation; and his model versatility lends him the protean slip by which he eventually comes to be known. As a writer, Hall explains, "my object is only to gather the raw materials which may be woven by more skillful hand; you must judge *ex pede Herculeum*, of the whole from a part" (Hall, 247). In a similar mood, Hall writes in his preface to *Letters from the West* that he offers "a mere collection of sketches, with but little choice of subjects, and still less attention to the order in which they are arranged" (Hall, iv). These comments of course work rhetorically to diminish the author's presence in and responsibility for the material he composes. Stephen Fender's observation that "in Hall . . . the West brought out a deep unease about the validity of metaphors,"[8] points to this preoccupation with the propriety of writing and with its way of snatching the real from the source that it imagines and in which it finds its sanction. Boone, functioning in Hall's work as a trope more than as a presence in his own right, thus becomes implicitly suspect by absorbing the reality of what he represents, at the same time that he is *supposed* to be authenticity itself.

In letter 16, "The Backwoodsman," Boone is dramatized in a history of settlement that rather gothically plays on the troubles of his typical solitude. While the rest of the country directs its commercial energies outward toward the Atlantic and Europe during a period of postrevolutionary prosperity, the backwoodsman faces the interior, dark spaces of the continent. His purposes are peculiar: not interested in commercial or financial gain, and too solitary to seek power for himself in the hinterland, this "emigrant" "appeared to have been allured by the very difficulties which discouraged others" (Hall, 251). The settlers are remarkable for the suffering and sacrifices they endure, and their reward—the exchange value—of such pain and denial is not immediately evident, except in the facts of risk and loss themselves.

The deprivation that Hall so heavily emphasizes in the experiences of Boone and his companions is partly attributed to their self-imposed exclusion from the lively commercial activities of the larger population, and in this sense the notion of sacrifice is quite literal. Boone explores the western territory for the sake of those whose life is secure and easy and who will follow him eventually, when his primary labor is done.

But this negative meaning of his suffering is supplemented by the dark danger that surrounds him. Highly conscious of the risks involved, Boone's company "plunged into *the boundless contiguity of shade*" (emphasis Hall's). Here, in the region called the "Bloody Ground," presumably the original meaning of the word *Kentucky*, "they pursue yet deeper danger, having "boldly cut the tie which bound them to society" (Hall, 252).

For other citizens, Hall writes, the wilderness had been unattractive because of "the unsettled state of the country, its reputed unhealthiness, and the vicinity of the Indian tribes" (Hall, 250). For European travelers contemporary to Boone, it was "too remote, too insulated, too barbarous" (Hall, 251). This hell into which they "plunge" and the suffering they submit to is reserved for them; and it is its own reward. Much in the manner of classical narratives where the hero descends into the world of the dead, Boone's story is related in terms of the moment-by-moment dangers he encounters. As in Filson's history, this episodic technique to some degree resists narrative linkage and thus sets each segment as if in relief. But the landscape in which these events occur is frightening, ugly, depressing. Compared to the "vast interminable waste" of ocean on which the mariner gazes, this wilderness is worse, since Boone's dangers are entirely unrehearsed.

The place of death that Hall's representation of the landscape strongly suggests is an unarticulated realm, lacking difference or representation. The more this idea is perpetuated the more it secures the rhetorical illusion, as in other Boone stories, that a condition of disinterest—and of innocence—is what is being represented. The danger of the Cumberland Mountains is a dark, mute danger, all the more treacherous for its resistance to signification, to marks of itself that would diminish the traveler's risk in their readability. Such treacherous innocence derives its attraction from its apparent newness, in a manner similar to the way in which detail or anecdote, what Joel Fineman has called the "historeme,"[9] often seems to resist larger narrative or conceptual generalization in Western narrative. Hall's turn on the innocence of Filson's Boone is quite dramatic and oxymoronic, but the effect of its violence is always to elide, always to disrupt, and to be continuously somewhere— if not somebody—else.

But these notions are rhetorical ideals for Hall as for other Boone writers. The very notion of a realm of unarticulated indifference beyond culture, written in the metaphor of death or of a primitive paradise, is a constitutive motif in culture itself. Much of Hall's work, like that of Filson and others, is to make the wilderness appear undifferentiated in order for it to elicit the acts of reproduction that the protagonist will initiate. The interests of commerce, literature, and science are bound together in the image of the wilderness; what is presented as "adventure" and risk is the highly literary narrative means by which the former, very worldly exchanges come to take place. Thus the metaphor system of interiority, darkness, danger, and death by which the forest is represented in Hall functions as part of an economic activity of the same order as that conducted by the prosperous citizens whose eastern trade serves the quicker returns that Boone is apparently denied.

3

The contradiction that arises between the emphasis in Boone stories, as in Western narrative generally, on the integrity of the detail and on Boone's own representative status is an issue that Timothy Flint's 1833 *Biographical Memoire of Daniel Boone* seems to absorb as a narrative tension. Flint, an educated admirer of Boone from Massachusetts, had read Cooper's novels, as he had read and written about Filson's account of the adventures of Daniel Boone.[10] Henry Nash Smith writes that Flint's biography was "perhaps the most widely read book about a Western character during the first half of the nineteenth century";[11] and it is entirely plausible to think that those of Cooper's *Leatherstocking Tales* written after 1833 respond to the newer figure of Boone depicted in Flint's narrative.

As James K. Folsom argues in the introduction to his edition of the *Memoire*, Flint's interest seems to be in demonstrating Boone's service to civilization. Unlike Hall's Boone, for whom the notion of service means sacrifice and suffering, Flint's Boone is an upright, healthy figure who walks into a paradisiacal wilderness that welcomes him as its nurturing, naming Adam. Rather than being a victim of the forest's hellish powers and insidious traps, he is, like Cooper's Leatherstocking, the avant-garde of a civilization that will make the unknown land submit to its progress.

Folsom is correct to insist on the privilege given to culture and on the concern for history somewhat at the expense of character in Flint's account of Boone, for the longer narrative of American civilization is quite clearly the object of Boone's service. But that narrative, like the Boone and Leatherstocking stories that precede it, is justified by reference to nature. The space of the wilderness is already staked out for a new social order before Boone comes to it, and his acts are circumscribed by that predetermined order, that "sphere which Providence called him to fulfill." Rather than initiating plans or acting on any sort of individualistic impulses, he responds to this providential call, which he reads in the text of the wilderness: Flint writes that Boone "received his commission for his achievement and his peculiar walk from the sign manual of nature" (Flint, 23).

Construed here as a commissioner of Boone's project, nature is an official that designates the mission with political authority. Flint's narrating voice speaks as the mind of culture and of the law—the symbolic order that takes nature for its own expression. But just as the *Memoire* is preoccupied alternatively with history, or the narrative of American civilization, and the moments of Boone's experience, the Boone figure operates alternately as a functionary of culture and as a loner whose private adventure in the wilderness is itself of interest.[12] Nonetheless, the latter character's distinction from ideology—his innocence—serves rhetorically all the better to model a national interest.

Much of Boone's course is determined, as in Filson, Hall, and Cooper, by his reading of Indian passages. But the emphasis on knowledge in Filson and Cooper is turned around in a sense in Flint's account, since Boone's negotiation of woodland trails involves as much if not more attention to erasing and placing his own marks as it does to deciphering those of others. Thus Boone appears conscious of being read, or at least of others reading indications of his presence, and attempts to make himself as elusive as we find him in Hall, except that in Flint the attempt is overt and the elusive traces literal. On their initial journey into western Kentucky, Boone and his brother leave a series of marks as they go, with the intention of staking out a route along which they might later bring their families. Flint calls this process "blazing": "The brothers left such traces—or blazes as they are technically called—of their course, as they thought would enable them to find it again" (Flint, 69).

At one point in the narrative, Boone attempts to elude a group of Shawnee by periodically shifting his direction and receding into the hills. He cannot erase his path, however, and the group continues to follow; finally he seizes a large vine, swings over several yards of ground, and effectively conceals his trail (Flint, 65).

In pursuit of the apparently retreating enemy after an attack on Bryant's Station, Boone advises his fellow officers that the marks of the Shawnee trail indicate a willingness to meet, since they are not at all concealed. Trees have been actually cut along the way, "the most palpable of all directions as to their course." Such an open invitation to follow, Boone notes, is at the same time a misrepresentation, since each member of the large party has taken care to step only in the footprint of the preceding person, and "twenty warriors might be numbered from the foot marks only as one." Eventually the group comes into the settlers' view, sauntering casually up the side of a hill. Now Boone understands the treachery: a larger party is waiting nearby, and this vulnerable platoon is only a decoy, posed to draw the attack (Flint, 152).

In these and similar incidents, the paths of Boone and his people become crucial rhetorical matters for survival in the wilderness. Deception and recollection are the major functions for which they are "blazed"; interpretation, or the ability to read, is necessary on the part of the one who comes later, if the trails are to be recognized and thus exist as such. Perhaps one of the most noticeable effects of this process of articulating and reading the wilderness in Flint's *Memoire* is the way in which meaning resides in the traces rather than the presence of human life. Once bodies are perceived, the data of their mood, condition, and intention are already known. Thus presence is a distinctly belated phenomenon, actually serving as another image or representation in a series of traces rather than as the source or end of the marking processes by which Boone operates. The elusiveness of Hall's Boone suggests an equal lack of substance, in sliding from meaning to meaning, from representation of individualism to regionalism to nationalism, and in the diminishment of his presence through suffering. For Flint it is the reading and writing of Boone as a component of the textual wilderness that makes him so difficult to grab. Oddly, Hall's and Flint's apparent emphasis on the wild and the civil in Boone are reversed in these processes where the very missed shape that is supposed to coin him for civilization makes him after all quite wild; and the wildness is simply a result of the problems inherent in civilization's key constituent, representation.

4

As Lucy Lockwood Hazard, Henry Nash Smith, Richard Slotkin, Stephen Raillton, and many others have noted,[13] James Fenimore Cooper's Leatherstocking is in many ways emblematic of the white hunter that Filson, Hall, and Flint elaborated in Boone's name; appearing first in *The Pioneers* of 1823, he retains the clothing, speech, and manners of and relations with the settlers. Through the Leatherstocking series the hero negotiates the gap between settled and wild territories, just as Boone had done, repeating the dialectic of expansion and settlement with each phase of his own life and the life of the white culture.

The contradictions of innocence and treachery that we find in and between Filson's and Hall's versions of Boone are dramatized simultaneously in *The Pioneers*, where the first portrait of Leatherstocking appears. As Jane Tompkins has argued, Natty Bumppo is not a character in the sense of a representation of individual will that changes. To a great extent, all of Cooper's figures are, as Tompkins characterizes them, "elements of thought, things to think with; and the convolutions of the plots, the captures, rescues and pursuits of the narrative, are stages in a thought process, phases in a meditation on the bases of social life that is just as rigorous and complicated in its way as the meditations of

[Lambert] Strether by the river."[14] I would add that these "things to think with," whether they succeed or not as representations of wills that change, are articulated through modes of characterization that depend on allegories of rhetoric whereby the character recognizes or overhears himself, since what he is consists to a great degree in his mode of representing himself.

The distinctions between the sophistry of the narrating voice in *The Pioneers* and Natty's comic, rough tones have rhetorical effects similar to those that appear in the relation between the recorder and his hero in Filson's history. When Cooper's backwoodsman speaks, however, his style and his notions are trapped in the ambivalence of the simultaneously sentimental and condescending tones that characterize the narrator's relation to him. In later novels Leatherstocking's performances will more obviously serve the interests recognizable in the narrator's gentle voice, but his disposition in *The Pioneers* is distinctly antithetical to the processes of culture.[15]

The Leatherstocking novels that precede Flint's biography of Boone are preoccupied in general with an opposition between written law and proprietorship on the one hand and oral tradition and unarticulated land claims associated with Indian culture on the other, an opposition that they cannot successfully maintain. The post-Flint stories, however, shift the opposition to one between written and visual ways of knowing. It is as if the later novels relinquish the exhausting attempt in both the earlier Leatherstocking novels and Timothy Flint's *Memoire* to represent a Boone character who functions beyond culture. Instead they emphasize seeing as a power different not only from that of books and the mediated kind of knowledge with which they are associated, but from verbal epistemologies in general. Vision in this sense takes on the properties of revelation and of truth as unmediated presence in a highly romantic articulation of the wilderness.

Invoking nature as a power that precedes man and as a physical unity much larger than the specific location of his story, Cooper introduces his last Leatherstocking novel, *The Deerslayer*, in humble and self-effacing tones. The painterly descriptions of landscape attempt to recuperate a wilderness whose integrity exists in being untouched and in having a looming, unquestionable consciousness. Unlike the indifferent nature of later nineteenth-century writing, Cooper's woodland scenes absorb the desires of his characters—as in the exemplary mirroring of Glimmerglass—and effect a readable transference, understood as intelligence for military, commercial, or survival purposes, or more grandly as "the book of nature."

Such regard for nature as either the province of an absolute, masculine deity, or as the privileged signifier of the most transcendent signifier Himself, is countered by a second tropical system that operates perhaps closer to the ground and cathects the wilderness with a feminine, sexual design. Natty's orientation is with the less specific, more disseminated manifestations of nature's power as father; Judith Hutter, a virtual frontier Venus, most demonstratively stands for the variations of bodily, reproductive nature that women represent in the novel. In this opposition, the representation of gender in *The Last of the Mohicans* is turned around; Hawkeye, whose physical and sensory energies are so crucial for knowledge, acquires as the Deerslayer a nearly spiritual integration with nature wherein his differentiation exists largely in his eye. Serving like a window, Natty's eye presupposes a subject-object relation between him and the environment, but like the opaque quality of Glimmerglass, reflection between him and nature is mutual. Like Filson's Boone, one determines the other; but here the figure of the hunter is almost mystically dissolved in the texture of the landscape. Glimmerglass attracts Leatherstocking not because it is picturesque but because it possesses an "air of deep repose—the solitudes that spoke of scenes and forests untouched by the hands of man."[16] The repeated admiration of Glimmerglass and of Judith's face, and the use of the "glass" to focus on long distances, sustain attention to the act of looking in the text—not, as in the earlier representations, the act of looking for trails, but a more overtly romantic process of narcissistic contemplation that partakes of the Emersonian pun "eye/I," as elaborated in his essay "Nature," published in 1836.

Judith, in subsuming the other women of the novel as well as feminine sexuality in general, is represented as picturesqueness itself, her good looks always arresting those who look at her. Attached to this power is Judith's notorious vanity that leaves her open to sexual exploitation by the British officers and really marks the difference between her kind of knowledge and Deerslayer's. The adventure's general ethic is to denounce the kind of physicality that Judith represents, weaving its tedium of biblical lessons through the utterances of Hetty and Leatherstocking, and through the narrator's continuous moralizing of the story. Deerslayer rejects Judith's affections and proposal of marriage for the sake of his continued existence as an individual par excellence, but his Moravian sensitivities inflect this decision with a priestly mission: to serve the masculine god of nature by refusing to submit his body to the terms of Judith's desire and by sustaining his celibate character. But nature becomes distinctly androgynous in his response to Judith's insinuating question, "Where, then, is your sweetheart, Deerslayer?" He replies: "She's in the forest, Judith—hanging from the boughs of the trees, in a soft rain—in the dew on the open grass—the clouds that float out in the blue heavens—the birds that sing in the woods—the wet springs where I slake my thirst—and in all the other glorious gifts that come from God's providence!" (Cooper, 616–17).

This long-winded answer that Twain ridiculed with such delight is indication of Natty's priestly service to a list of traces that he considers his bride. Unlike the version of nature understood as an abstract consciousness, this version seems to exist in the aesthetics of the visible prospect. His repeatedly mentioned devotion to truth telling is necessary because in both understandings nature is everywhere, and anything he might say is registered by its implicit witness. As a lover, nature looks on Leatherstocking from a different perspective than his own. Metaphorically, such an account is the record of his behavior that will be tallied at his death; and it might be argued that the metaphor has value as a note of self-consciousness in the storytelling process, a note that recalls Cooper's earlier anxieties in the elaboration of Natty's character, and of Hall's and Flint's in the representation of Boone, as something beyond culture. But the pressure of truth telling is also indicative of Deerslayer's great self-consciousness in the form of a narcissism that assumes his every utterance has meaning and effect; and in this sense nature is a presence simultaneous with his own, that extends beyond him but in his own line of vision. Contrary to Deerslayer's denials of vanity in relation to his physical appearance, this close attention to his own utterances amounts to an equivalent fetish of himself as voice rather than body. In both cases, consciousness is simultaneous with self-representation; listening to and looking at oneself are recording acts that imply a departure from the immediacy of being and cancel Leatherstocking's as well as Judith's innocence.

In a curious reversal of reproductive powers, *The Deerslayer* ends with Natty's return to Glimmerglass fifteen years after the incidents that precede it, only to find that Judith's name is no longer remembered and no account of her whereabouts can be secured beyond a vague rumor that she is living on the estate of a British officer who has not married her. The sexuality that exists for its own sake in her portrait is posed against that of Hist, who marries Chingachgook and gives birth to Uncas, the Apollonian hero of *The Last of the Mohicans*. Hist has died by the time of Natty and Chingachgook's return to Glimmerglass. None of the other women in the novel are presented as younger versions of characters introduced in the other parts of the series. The impression *The Deerslayer* leaves is that this kind of nature—specific, bodily, sexual, and feminine—does not reproduce but dies in the expenditure of its narcissistic and biological desires. On the other hand, the Leatherstocking, like Uncas and Chingachgook, continues into time, reproducing himself in new names and adventures through a kind of disembodied vision, never allowing domesticity to touch or to limit him and never representing himself through the inheritance of a family lineage. Thus his figure, as aware of itself as Narcissus, represents and reproduces ideology in sterility, while Judith, who bears all the marks of a fertile sexuality, is frustrated in her desire to marry Natty and reproduce in the form of children. The family lineage that she wishes to initiate is of course one of the most dominant means by which the European order is able to secure its articulations of the wilderness and to ejaculate its ideals of property and representation onto the tabula rasa of the forest. But families must always be alien to Natty Bumppo's wilderness, even though the narrative of generation derives from the same phallic episteme as Bumppo's celibate progressions.

5

The Boone figure's reading of the landscape and interpretation of physical data as if they functioned like a code seems to cast the territory itself in many ways as a text for him to negotiate, a tendency that becomes emphatic in nineteenth-century accounts. His innocence is progressively compromised as he penetrates the forest and absorbs its wily ways, a fearsome initiate of its unholy mysteries. Thus his ego is constituted by virtue of this wilderness, as a claimed innocent working against it. His violence and highly sophisticated machinations, however, demonstrate the very civilized, codified wilderness that he is. Finding his interests in the landscape and absorbing what he perceives to be its own desire—the language of the natives, the tempers of nature—he inscribes the forest with paths that lead progressively to the rivers that run westward for the subsequent traveler to follow quite naturally.

The issues of character and subjectivity implicit in this occupation of tracing one's presence, or rather imaging presence for one's traces, raises the question: What space does the Boone figure, as representative Western subject, occupy? Like the figure in a photographic negative, he is formulated as the interstice between material objects that therefore become his margins, and he theirs. Movement is his condition, and the protean figure takes his limit, his shape, from the matter of forest, as he, mutually, limits it. The oxymoron of this constant negotiation allows the figure to elude figurality, to escape representation; but in so spending himself he leaves behind a streak that articulates the wilderness, maps it with his paths, and draws him in drawing the direction of his desire.

More than anything else, after all, Boone seeks in order to represent himself by virtue of charting his passage. The marks that make him also make the woods, in the interest of reproducing themselves, and it is at this juncture between the initial—and, as it were, accidental—laying down of a mark and the wish generated in this act to remember itself that the character of Daniel Boone functions.

Hawthorne, Emerson, and the Forms of the Frontier

James Barszcz

In the vivid first pages of "The Significance of the Frontier," Frederick Jackson Turner dramatizes his definition of the frontier as "meeting point between savagery and civilization"[1] when he imagines how the wilderness "masters" a settler: "It finds him a European in dress, industries, tools, modes of travel, and thought. It takes him from the railroad car and puts him in the birch canoe. It strips off the garments of civilization and arrays him in the hunting shirt and the moccasin. It puts him in the log cabin of the Cherokee and Iroquois and runs an Indian palisade around him. Before long he has gone to planting Indian corn and plowing with a sharp stick; he shouts the war cry and takes the scalp in orthodox Indian fashion" (Turner, 4). Most readers today, I take it, are embarrassed, at least, by Turner's confident distinctions between civilization and savagery. They might wish to exonerate him by appealing to a general crudity of nineteenth-century views in this regard. But in fact more complicating attitudes had already been expressed in well-established American literary sources, if not historical ones.

Some major works of American literature assume that frontiers, demarcating absolute distinctions between settlements and wilderness, or, more abstractly, art and nature, don't exist or can't be trusted. This is the view proposed in many of Hawthorne's works, for example. When Hawthorne refers to characters living apart from settlements of transplanted Englishmen—Indians, witches, Christians abjuring Puritan doctrines—he usually associates them not with the absence of culture but with an exaggeration or caricature of culture. And as *The Scarlet Letter* forcefully argues, for Hawthorne the human imagination never confronts or even perceives the wilderness directly; no individual nor any group of people lives in a "natural" state, no matter how removed from settlements they may be. Language, metaphor, and custom always mediate relations between individuals and between groups and their environments.

Emerson, too, discredits demographic frontiers, though as part of a naturalizing rather than civilizing project. That is to say, while for Hawthorne an Indian can be as culture-ridden as a European, for Emerson an imaginative city dweller experiences the frontier of consciousness—the frontier most important to Emerson—as fully as a pioneer. In essays such as "Nature," "Self-Reliance," and "The Poet," as well as many of his poems, Emerson reduces the imaginative life to its first principles and finds only subjects perceiving objects. His "objects"—flowers, planets, words, ideas, other people—can be drawn from what seem to be disparate categories, but that hardly matters since they are all available to the perception of "poets." All objects, even other people, Emerson assumes, are "natural," since that term refers to anything outside of the mind. The frontier that matters to him is the one dividing awareness from what awareness is aware of. For writers like Hawthorne and Emerson, the frontier is less a matter of woods than words; it exists at the borders of the perspectives created by language.

1. Hawthorne's Political Frontier

Hawthorne's fiction frequently exposes a unifying element in all social life, "savage" and otherwise. "Main Street," for example, a short story published in 1849, depicts scenes of the main street in Salem as it changes, gradually, from an Indian path to a modern commercial thoroughfare.

The narrator begins by describing a woods where "the white man's axe has never smitten a single tree."[2] And yet "there is already a faintly-traced path, running nearly east and west, as if a prophecy or foreboding of the future street had stolen into the heart of the solemn old wood" (*Snow Image*, 50). The first human figures in the story represent the Indians who created this aboriginal path, and Hawthorne explicitly locates them at the top of political and religious hierarchies. First appears "a majestic and queenly woman, . . . the great Squaw Sachem, whose rule, with that of her sons, extends from Mystic to Agawam. Next to her is her second husband, the priest and magician, whose incantations shall hereafter affright the pale-faced settlers. . . . They pass on . . . holding high talk on matters of state and religion, and imagine, doubtless, that their own system of affairs will endure forever" (*Snow Image*, 51).

Hawthorne's satire, though mild, is defined well enough. In characterizing the conversation of these figures as "high talk on matters of state and religion," the narrator sounds as if he is scoring them for an exaggerated sense of their own importance, though such topics no doubt would be matters of life and death to those over whom they rule. And while there is complacency in the narrator's superior knowledge that the Indians' "system of affairs" will not endure forever, the phrasing also suggests to the presumably white reader that his or her own system will not endure forever either.

This similarity between Indian and white cultures is implied in the choice of the opening scene of the story. By beginning at a time when the path through the woods already exists, the story suggests first that the woods—nature, or the wilderness—is not appropriate by itself, in Hawthorne's view, for literary representation; it becomes suitable only when it shows the shaping efforts of man, or, more precisely, of people, the efforts of men and women creating order for themselves. Also, Hawthorne suggests, the line of development from Indian path to contemporary Main Street is continuous; the entire story is predicated on the continuity, the near-identity, of these thoroughfares. The early one is a "prophecy or foreboding" of the later one. The ominous phrasing expresses an awareness never far from any text by Hawthorne that humans distort and constrict their own lives through the shapes they create. The entire story, especially its opening passages, assumes a conditionality of experience, an inability to get outside of acculturated circumstances to experience an unmediated world or frontier, unshaped by human imagination.

Hawthorne found material for fiction, throughout his career, in characters' attempts to transcend the limits of knowledge and experience, implicit at the opening of "Main Street." One of the most provocative examples is, of course, the scene spanning three chapters in *The Scarlet Letter* when Hester meets Dimmesdale in the forest to the west of the Puritan settlement, a scene which has provoked some of the most influential commentaries on the meaning of the frontier in American literature and mythology. Hester Prynne and, at least temporarily, Arthur Dimmesdale reject the moral and legal codes that Puritan Boston would hold them to. Their ultimate effort to escape fails, of course, but at least while they talk of it in the forest they seem to enjoy the freedom conventionally associated with the wilderness by romantic writers of all eras.

Much critical commentary from the 1950s to the present has emphasized this aspect of the narrative. R. W. B. Lewis, for example, arguing for an absolute disjunction between the city and its wild surroundings, writes that Hester and Dimmesdale meet "to join in an exercise of the will and the passion for freedom."[3] Edwin Fussell, in *Frontier: American Literature and the American West*, compares Hester to Crèvecoeur's archetypal American when she "enters the passes of the dark, inscrutable forest—the West of the human heart—temporarily and magnificently free of ancient principle."[4]

The larger point about *The Scarlet Letter*, made by these critics and others, seems irrefutable: Hawthorne doubts that such moments of freedom can be extended or strung together as an environment for living. But such criticism looks to the overall shape of the plot, the failure of Hester and Dimmesdale to achieve their flight, to find evidence for Hawthorne's skepticism about freedom. This simplifies the meaning created for the frontier in the very moments of supposed freedom or frontier consciousness, for it assumes that the frontier differs, actually and radically, from civilization. As "Main Street" suggests, Hawthorne envisions a radical continuity with the conventionalized life of the city, of people in groups. Within the very moments of the characters' supposed frontier consciousness, they cannot escape—Hawthorne will not let them escape—urges of the will and imagination that have shaped the civilization they would flee.

To estimate the forces at work in the interchange in the forest, we must first look back at earlier conversations in the settlement. In the first scaffold scene, when the Puritan leaders implore Hester to reveal the identity of Pearl's father, Hawthorne specifies vocal influence as the source or sign of political power. In general, Hawthorne's Puritans exercise power through language by assigning single, unequivocal meanings to words, symbols, objects, and even people. So Hester Prynne, in their view, means only "adulteress," until later, after much charitable work, she comes to mean (no less reductively) "able."

Dimmesdale and the Reverend Wilson, more erudite and refined than most of the populace, rely less on allegory than on a subtler power of voice. They utter the common purpose of the crowd; those who echo or harmonize with their representative voices constitute the polity: "The young pastor's voice was tremulously sweet, rich, deep, and broken. The feeling that it so evidently manifested, rather than the direct purport of the words, caused it to vibrate within all hearts, and brought the listeners into one accord of sympathy."[5] Acting treasonably, Hester first spurns their demands to identify her lover. Then she establishes a countervoice, which takes dominion over Dimmesdale, as evidenced by his repetition of the words she enunciates: " 'I will not speak!' answered Hester. . . . 'She will not speak!' murmured Mr. Dimmesdale" (*Scarlet Letter*, 68).

This interchange in the settlement is recapitulated during the later forest scene. Hester crosses the stream that separates the settlement from the woods, ostensibly to inform Dimmesdale of Roger Chillingworth's identity as her husband and his tormentor. But within a few pages, Hester persuades Dimmesdale to flee New England with her and make a new life elsewhere. At several moments in this supercharged sequence, Hester's thoughts penetrate Dimmesdale's mind. Dimmesdale, for example, silently considers the question of fleeing with Hester and concludes his meditation with a prayer:

> "O Thou to whom I dare not lift mine eyes, wilt Thou yet pardon me!"
> "Thou wilt go!" said Hester calmly, as he met her glance. (*Scarlet Letter*, 201)

Hester's words can be read in several ways, all of which show an extraordinary arrogation of power. She might be predicting Dimmesdale's decision or she might be dictating it. Most radically, she might be seen as addressing God, borrowing from Dimmesdale's unspoken thoughts his referent for "Thou," banishing Him from the world she is creating, presumably to leave her own dominance unchallenged. She certainly claims supernatural powers for herself in her subsequent words as she throws off her embroidered letter: "Let us not look back. . . . The past is gone! Wherefore should we linger upon it now? See! With this symbol, I undo it all, and make it as it had never been!" (*Scarlet Letter*, 202).

On the face of it, Hester's homily, which argues that the past can be "undone" and souls be reshaped through human effort, contradicts the moral, social, and religious values of Puritan society. It might therefore be taken as a sign of her liberation from the constraints imposed by that society, an exertion of individual power capable of being expressed only on a frontier beyond the society's limits. But of course calling her efforts a "liberation" begs the question. For at the same time that she counsels Dimmesdale about his power to remake himself and his life, she speaks over, for, and through him. She speaks, that is, like the Puritans who tried unsuccessfully in the first scaffold scene to overwrite her thoughts, substituting for their mode of oppression one of her own.

Hawthorne also qualifies the freedom of Hester's thoughts by pointing out European models for her social criticism. In chapter 13, "Another View of Hester," he places her in relation to political and intellectual revolutions of the seventeenth century: "It was an age in which the human intellect, newly emancipated, had taken a more active and a wider range than for many centuries before. . . . Hester Prynne imbibed this spirit. She assumed a freedom of speculation, then common enough on the other side of the Atlantic, but which our forefathers, had they known of it, would have held to be a deadlier crime than that stigmatized by the scarlet letter" (*Scarlet Letter*, 164).[6]

In addition it should be noted that, while Hester only feels sufficiently free to express her beliefs about individual potentialities when wandering outside the borders of the settlement, she foresees the Old World as the most likely place for their fulfillment. The supposed wilderness cannot support them as well as a community on the European model with institutions of learning. Indians and witches, who appear only glancingly, are perhaps more at home in the forest than Hester is, but as we have seen in "Main Street," Hawthorne suggests that they are no less ritual-ridden and conventional than the Puritans.[7]

The character who imposes no artificial or predetermined shapes on others or on the wilderness is Pearl. Pearl is Hester's "natural child" in two senses of that dated idiom. Not only is she born out of wedlock; she is imbued with a "natural," unformed, or frontier consciousness, at least until her domestication at the end of the book. But *natural* in this second sense means, for Hawthorne, preternatural, freakish, alien, unknowable. She contains or exhibits impulses and desires organized by no recognizably human principles. Although she is the figure most identified with the wilderness, her essential incoherence means that she can hardly be considered a character at all.[8]

So, while *The Scarlet Letter* is frequently cited as a seminal source in the genealogy of the frontier in American literature—the comments of Lewis and Fussell quoted earlier are only two of many examples—the frontier, as commonly construed, scarcely exists in it. Hawthorne imagines two environments for his characters: the settlement, which is already shaped by the human will and which excludes or represses energies or desires that it regards as eccentric; and the wilderness, which is not available "in itself" or "as it is" or "naturally" as a site for social life. Like Wallace Stevens's jar in Tennessee, Hawthorne's characters "take dominion" of their environment, and the wilderness becomes no longer wild. Hawthorne's wilderness serves only as a stage for expressions of human desire that are necessarily indebted to previous expressions and are never new, natural, or free.

By pushing the scene of his fiction to the west, from its implicit origins in England and the Netherlands to the settlement in Boston, and then to the woods beyond that settlement, Hawthorne reduces political relations to their most basic elements. He moves his fiction to the woods, not to escape politics but to distill the essence of politics, the adaptation of one individual to another. Each of these settings is a simplified version of the earlier, much as the Indian path is a simplified version of Salem's Main Street. Seen in this light, Hawthorne affirms what Turner calls the "European" understanding of the frontier as a political boundary (Turner, 3) or "a fortified boundary line running through dense populations" (Turner, 41). Hawthorne slightly alters this European conception, since for him the frontier is the contested boundary between two individuals, rather than between "populations." Nonetheless, his version of the frontier is much closer to this European use than it is to Turner's "American" conception of the frontier as a border between civilized and uncivilized regions, or settlements and wilderness.

Hawthorne's skepticism about the frontier as a fictional environment deserves examination if only because it aligns him with an Emersonian tradition from which he is usually excluded. The American frontier, in Turner's sense of this phrase, cannot serve as a scene for fiction, as Hawthorne practices it. This is because Hawthorne assumes that anything approaching absolute freedom for the self or the imagination requires a solitude that will not bear fictional representation. A consciousness can expand only so long as none other is present. But if none other is present, there can be no social life, no frustrations or conflicts suitable for narrative prose. On the other hand, if another consciousness *is* present, then the border between the two is a contested area (a "European" frontier), and some representable drama can ensue. But, since such a border defines the limits of the selves, freedom in a pure sense is impossible: if one consciousness expands the other one must, willingly or otherwise, contract or submit to penetration or expropriation. An author might avoid this threat to the imaginative autonomy of a character by insulating the character from any contact with others. But this solution entails, in literature, giving up prose fiction grounded in the life of society, and in life, forgoing the enrichment of human contact, including of course sexual experience.[9]

If a sense of freedom in the presence of others exists anywhere in Hawthorne's work it is in the relation between readers and writers. Reading, as delineated by Hawthorne in "The Custom-House" and other prefaces, functions as marriage implicitly does in *The House of the Seven Gables* and *The Marble Faun*: participants enter into a relation by mutual consent, for mutual benefit, and with a minimum of coercion. Although readers and writers depend on each other for their existence, they are present to each other only in an attenuated manner through the printed page. In this pale marriage, speaking and listening are only metaphoric. Print mediates and thereby mitigates the dominance of voice.

2. Emerson's Frontier Within

In *The Scarlet Letter*, characters primarily know themselves, and we as readers know them, when they challenge or are challenged by other characters. While there are no characters in the same sense in Emerson's work, there are frequent references to entities called "man," "people," and "the mind." If, with regard to these images of human experience, we pose the question raised by Hawthorne's works—whom do you know yourself *against*?—we get a crucially different answer. In their most ennobling interactions, minds flow together into a unitary consciousness beyond individuated identities. Still, on the issue of what constitutes civilization and savagery, Emerson and Hawthorne resemble each other more than either of them resembles Turner.

From the outset of his career, Emerson seems to sustain himself as a writer virtually without reference to any exterior human presence. He is his own Other. "The mind goes antagonizing on," as he puts it in "Experience,"[10] meaning that no outside antagonist is needed. He is fascinated by differences within himself, his shifts in mood and judgment, each of which he considers as authentic and justified as moods experienced at any other time.

Such transitions and inconsistencies, as Richard Poirier has recently pointed out, are a primary quality of language for Emerson.[11] It is the office of poets, the archetype of the artist, to expose them to us: "The quality of the imagination is to flow, and not to freeze," Emerson writes in "The Poet," "for all symbols are fluxional; all language is vehicular and transitive, and is good, as ferries and horses are, for conveyance, not as farms and houses are, for homestead" (*Essays*, 463). The literary forms that he is most drawn to—journals, essays, lectures—leave a writer free to follow such shifts. (As practiced by Emerson, essays don't require sequential argument extended beyond a sentence or two.) An author working in these forms seems to write for himself, or, what amounts to the same thing, for the undifferentiated mass of others who might attend a lecture.

For Emerson, at least in some of his moods, the wilderness exists everywhere. That is, things outside the self that call forth wonder, creativity, or manipular power can be found outside of human culture as well as within it. And both the woods and the city at times fail to satisfy his powers of vision, as Sherman Paul has pointed out.[12] As Emerson maintains in his essay "Nature" (originally published in 1836), man's "operations," meaning the cultural artifacts of the species, "taken together are so insignificant . . . that in an impression so grand as that of the world on the human mind, they do not vary the result" (*Essays*, 8). Actually, this particular sentence reverses the usual relation in Emerson between "the world" and the "human mind"; more frequently than being a passive receptor of impressions, the mind, for Emerson, creates, arranges, composes its sense of the world. As a result, Emerson can reach for sublime or radical interpretations of man's place in relation to his environment in response to rather tame settings, neither especially urban nor wild—a bare common, or the view across several farmers' fields.

Although not a novelist, Emerson incessantly analyzes "point of view." He makes himself and his readers aware of the adventitiousness of their particular vantage points and the "horizons" they thereby create.

He thus posits a wilderness or strangeness in any landscape, even the most familiar: "Turn the eyes upside down, by looking at the landscape through your legs, and how agreeable is the picture, though you have seen it any time these twenty years!" (*Essays*, 34). And the pleasing sensation of a new perception uncovers an essential dualism: ". . . man is hereby apprized that whilst the world is a spectacle, something in himself is stable" (*Essays*, 34). As Carolyn Porter has noted, Emerson "constructed a method whose genius lay in its power to penetrate the immediate and show it to be mediated."[13]

In this approach to experience, Emerson recognizes only consciousness, the stable something within, and its objects, the world. Other minds don't pose a problem for him, most of the time: they get subsumed into one of these two categories. In the first instance, mere personalities or social selves are transcended, as Emerson and his companion blend into a larger consciousness or power. Some of Emerson's journal entries on conversations with Thoreau record such confluences even, paradoxically, when the subject of the conversation is solitude: "It would be hard to recall the rambles of last night's talk with H. T. But we stated over again, to sadness, almost, the Eternal loneliness. . . . [H]ow insular & pathetically solitary, are all the people we know! Nor dare we tell what we think of each other, when we bow in the street."[14] The two men seem to talk in unison rather than converse with each other, as they "state over again" the elemental fact of loneliness. But of course their very unity contravenes the loneliness, at least for themselves, and keeps the mood only "almost" sad.

Emerson's alternate move in responding to other people is to turn them into objects, parts of a scene, topics for analysis and speculation, as at the beginning of his poem "Each and All":

> Little thinks, . . . yon red-cloaked clown
> Of thee from the hill-top looking down;
> . . . Nor knowest thou what argument
> Thy life to thy neighbor's creed has lent.[15]

At some moments, Emerson will concede only provisionally that there are other minds out there, separate from him, residing in other bodies: "Let us be poised, and wise, and our own, today," he writes in "Experience." "Let us treat the men and women well: treat them as if they were real: perhaps they are" (*Essays*, 479). For Hawthorne, in his fiction, in his relation with his reader, and apparently in his social life, individual experience only fully knows itself and becomes known in relation to specific others. For Hawthorne, one grows out of solitude into a social self; for Emerson, one grows out of a social self into a transcendent, communal consciousness.

Despite differences like these, the works of Hawthorne and Emerson share a common project: they redefine the frontier as a border, made apparent by language, between consciousness and restraints on consciousness. Both authors attempt to convey an experience of freedom beyond such restraints, though Hawthorne in his unsparing treatment of would-be social reformers had a grimmer view of what happens when you think you've achieved this freedom. Through this redefinition, they allow us to place in the tradition of frontier literature such unlikely works as William James's *The Principles of Psychology* (originally published in 1890). James argues, in consonance with Emerson, that an individual's developing selfhood, especially as it relies on the resources of language, consists in limiting consciousness, in paying attention to some segments of experience while ignoring others. If we think of consciousness as a stream, words tend to freeze it: language sometimes "works against our perception of the truth."[16]

From this perspective, any work dramatizing stylistic freedom can be understood as frontier literature. "Song of Myself" proleptically tests William James's thesis of selection, for Whitman proposes to ignore nothing. In effect, he lops off half of the Emersonian dualism of consciousness and its objects and, the title of his poem notwithstanding, frequently essays to become all Other. Emerson, as we have seen, relegates others to the status of objects or translates himself and his companion to a unifying realm of consciousness where individuated social selves are left behind. Whitman imagines himself, in the first stanzas of his poem, diffused like a gas. He insinuates himself into the everyday lives of people (and animals) throughout the country. He specifies where Emerson generalizes. Identifying himself with myriad individuals, he becomes everyone and no one, recognized best by his constant shifts in diction.

Henry James explores an analogous border between the freedom of unrestricted imaginative potential (Isabel Archer's multivalent "independence," for example) and the fixity of any code, style, or method of expression. He counterposes a desire to be infinitely open to experience (as in Lambert Strether's heartfelt but open-ended advice to Little Bilham in *The Ambassadors* to "live") and the plangent necessity to choose, in social life, one manner of living, which in literature means one manner of talking. Characters like Isabel achieve a stoic nobility when they accept this necessity without repudiating the value of the freedom they give up.

In Turner's version of American experience, individuals crossing the border between settlements and the wilderness transform themselves from one type of person to another, from Europeans to Americans. The individuals imagined by Hawthorne and Emerson cross, or at least survey, an even more basic border, a frontier that runs between the self and whatever is outside the self—other people, "objects," nature. While their chances for success are narrower and the rewards less tangible than those imagined by Turner for his settlers, the frontier they face can never be closed.

Frontier Violence in the
Garden of America

Reginald Dyck

Most searchers for a new life in the garden of America had to take the peaceable kingdom by violence—against the Indians, the land, each other, and themselves. Western writers have presented the violent actions of their characters within the contexts of two apparently contradictory myths: the myth of the garden, which attempts to hide the American legacy of violence, and the myth of the frontier, which celebrates it. Willa Cather and Wright Morris represent two quite different ways that Western writing has presented violence. One is to render it nonthreatening through various narrative techniques; the other is to use it to challenge the validity of these myths by exposing their strategic omission of the possibility of failure. In the latter case violence is either self-directed out of frustration from failure or directed against others as a means of gaining at least the illusion of power and social recognition.

Northrop Frye explains that "myth is the imitation of actions near or at the conceivable limits of desire," although that "does not mean that it necessarily presents its world as attained or attainable by human beings."[1] However, "with an unspoiled hemisphere in view it seemed that mankind actually might realize what had been thought a poetic fantasy."[2] Utopian desires, combined with a deep confidence that they could be fulfilled, became an American formula for frustration and failure that often led to violence.

Richard Slotkin, stating that "myth is the primary language of historical memory,"[3] emphasizes the study of myth for cultural rather than transcultural analysis. The archetypal approach to myth, in his view, ignores the fact that myths are produced or adapted within particular sociohistorical contexts in order to meet the specific needs of a culture. In looking for commonalities among myths of various cultures, the archetypal approach fails to consider sufficiently the significant differences. In contrast, when myth is defined as a pattern of values given metaphorical expression,[4] both the historical and ideological nature of myth become evident since values arise out of historical situations. Slotkin's emphasis on myth as historical memory suggests the role of myth in the interpretation of culture. Mythic patterns are derived less from historical reality than from the tradition of usage (Slotkin 1986, 74); consequently, myth sets forth the expectations rather than the actual conditions of a particular historical situation. The tradition of usage develops out of a culture's need to explain, or more accurately, to cover over contradictions within its values. For example, when the Puritans found that they could not subdue the Indians by converting them, they resorted to violence. Not willing to see themselves as intruders destroying another people for their own purposes, they established a "permissive narrative" or ideological explanation that covered the contradictory need of exterminating the Indians while retaining their Puritan collective identity as "a city upon a hill." Picturing themselves as representatives of godly civilization and the Indians as denizens of the heathen wilderness, they could justify their actions to themselves.[5] Along with the continuing need to maintain an American sense of innocence as more land was usurped and more native inhabitants removed or killed, Europeans who came to America and Americans who moved west had to justify to themselves and to those they had left behind the sacrifices and hardships experienced in leaving the Old World and beginning over again in the New. Therefore, the myths of the frontier and the garden became necessary narrative patterns of value.

Although significant contradictions arise between the two myths, the values they share reflect the way the dominant culture of America wanted to see itself. Together, the two myths create a picture of American exceptionalism based on the land. Early writers such as John Smith praise the natural abundance of America in contrast to the scarcity in Europe. Crèvecoeur, no less enthusiastic, makes great claims for the economic possibilities of the New World; and Jefferson, though more restrained and scientific in his description, also shares their hopes for this new land. These writers exemplify the belief in American exceptionalism underlying the myth of the garden. Frederick Jackson Turner, setting forth his frontier thesis from a retrospective view in 1893, equally asserts American exceptionalism as a result of its land. In both myths the land shaped the unique American character. For example, Crèvecoeur claims for the farmers in the garden that "the simple cultivation of the earth purifies them."[6] Turner states that the frontier "strips off the garments of civilization" and creates a new man—practical, inventive, and full of restless energy—who cherishes individual freedom and builds a democracy of the people.[7] Available land meant that people could escape the corrupting influence of civilization and cities, a significant component in the myths of the frontier and the garden.

Both myths, while accentuating positive values, cover over similar contradictions in American values. Slotkin explains: "The idea of Indian extinction [as a natural occurrence, like growth and decay], the belief that a reservoir of cheap land could buy off class conflict, and the mythologization of figures like Filson's Boone [on the frontier] and the "yeoman farmer" [in the garden] are all fantasies of denial, symbols that wishfully negate real and persistent fears and ideological ambivalences."[8]

First, by emphasizing the negative qualities of the city and idealizing rural life as being close to nature, these myths could hide the cultural losses caused by isolation from centers of Western civilization. These myths provided settlers in America needed reassurance that their losses in emigrating were not higher than their gains.

Second, the myths could hide important consequences of capitalism. The rhetoric of both the virtuous yeoman farmer and the frontiersman fighting against savagery masked the primarily economic motivation behind the conquest of the West. Richard Hofstadter notes, "What developed in America was an agricultural society whose real attachment was not to land but to land values" (41). These myths also asserted individual rather than corporate or governmental effort as the dominating force of development. They denied the crucial importance of eastern capital and markets by emphasizing the significance of free land. They also failed to acknowledge the essential role of the federal government in subduing the Indians and distributing the land.[9] Furthermore, in setting forth the belief in equal opportunity for all and advancement based on personal achievement alone, these myths excluded any recognition of economic injustice or class conflict.[10] The consequence was "the 'fatal environment' of expectations and imperatives in which . . . a whole political culture can be entrapped" (Slotkin 1985, 20). The extent to which writers recognized this danger is an indication of their stance as either supporting or critiquing American culture's use of these myths.

Whether minimizing or celebrating violence, both myths offered Westerners a moral framework for their ventures. American pastoralism promised immigrant farmers regeneration in the moral geography between the savage wilderness and the wicked city. The potential of their new identity as American Adams was to compensate for the actual material and spiritual losses that many suffered. Jefferson, the most revered spokesman for the pastoral dream, presented a vision of the virtuous American farmer owning his own land and thus escaping the corruption inherent in factory-dominated, socially stratified cities. The motivation for following this vision was moral rather than economic. He acknowledged the resulting material losses but believed that the quality of life achieved would more than compensate for the sacrifices.[11]

The myth of the garden necessarily hides the violence that took place as Americans gained access to Eden. But violence erupts from sources within the garden as well. When the dream of the garden failed, the dreamers often struggled with a sense of impotence. They either felt betrayed by the dream or blamed themselves for failing to live up to it. Disillusioned and frustrated, these pioneers often resorted to self-violence. Consequently, writers using the myth of the garden had to either ignore or minimize this violence, or present a critique of the myth itself.

The myth of the frontier also asserts a moral order. Before possessing the land, the new Americans had to wrest it violently from the native inhabitants. Thus the frontier myth originated from the Indian wars of the Puritan era. At first the wars were cast in biblical terms, and though the terms changed from good and evil to civilization and savagery, their clear contrast persisted. The myth, therefore, inextricably connected violence with innocence. It justified the violence on the frontier by directing it against those outside of society. As with the myth of the garden, however, this myth hid the problem of failure and unsanctioned violence associated with its ideology of unrestrained competition, a frontier social Darwinism that took little notice of those less fit. Again, frustration and impotence led to violence that the myth did not legitimate but nevertheless instigated.

When violence enters the garden, the vision of an ideal world explodes unless that violence is carefully controlled. Willa Cather, the prairie writer with the greatest commitment to a pastoral vision, confronts the problem that although the myth of the garden implies the impossibility of suffering, a denial of violence would weaken her fiction's dramatic force and sense of authenticity regarding pioneer life. As Blanche Gelfant has observed, "Violence is as much the essence of prairie life as the growth of the wheat and the blossoming of the corn."[12] Consequently, Cather's narratives, especially *My Antonia*, use various strategies to make violence safe.

One such strategy is to make violence exotic. The story of Peter and Pavel provides an example. Traveling through the cold Russian woods, a wedding party is attacked by wolves. One sleigh after another overturns as the wolves bite at the horses' legs. In order to distract them, Pavel throws the bride to the wolves. Although the action succeeds, the two brothers are driven from place to place by guilt and social pressure.

In another example, a tramp commits suicide by jumping into a threshing machine. Neither of these incidents, however, threatens the sense of safety in the garden. In the first example the setting and action are too remote; in the second the violence seems to occur inexplicably as a curious aberration, and its threatening quality is masked by a discussion of the poem found in the tramp's pocket.

Another strategy for making violence safe is to segregate and minimize the evil underlying violence. Because Cather's pastoral heroes may have weaknesses but no sins, they are sources only of goodness. Antonia confesses, "The trouble with me was, Jim, I never could believe harm of anybody I loved."[13] Although this leads her into trouble with Larry Donovan, she is vindicated in the final section where her only weakness, seen in a better context, becomes a fundamental strength in the haven of family and farm. Cather reduces her violent characters to minor, one-dimensional figures unable to disrupt the force of good. Wick Cutter, an eccentric villain in *My Antonia*, ends his life in a murder and suicide so bizarre that its threat is deflected through caricature. The description of the incident, given to Jim Burden at Antonia's dinner table, creates a seeming incongruity between the harmonious setting and the family's fascination with violence, but the wild story enhances rather than disrupts the meal. The recitation causes the children to giggle in anticipation of the gruesome climax, showing that characters like Cutter are outside of their realm.

An earlier episode involving Cutter has not become a part of the family's stock of stories from the past because it involves attempted rape. Even if repulsed, rape poses too direct a threat to pastoral calm; thus Cather turns the incident into a grotesquerie by having Jim Burden rather than Antonia in the house when Cutter enters. Because Antonia is kept safe, the resulting scene does not threaten the garden with its violence or the evil underlying it.

Ivy Peters fulfills a related, though more central, role in *A Lost Lady*, Cather's next prairie novel. A story of paradise lost, it presents a more complex vision than *My Antonia* by exploring forces within the garden that are more threatening. Capt. Forrester, the aristocratic representative of a pioneer world uncorrupted by modern materialistic values, retires with his young wife to the quiet garden that he has dreamed of while working to develop the West through building railroads. Cather's depiction of Forrester as a hero in the garden (his name reinforces the connection) reveals that her pastoral ideology differs in a significant way from Jefferson's idealization of the yeoman farmer. Writing a century later than Jefferson, she felt disenchanted with the world his "virtuous yeomen" were creating. Consequently, she believed in a moral aristocracy that could stand aloof from the modern materialism and standardization that she saw infecting rural as much as city life. Members of her aristocracy, rich and poor, share a commitment to honor and integrity, a deep love for the land, and a personal strength and determination to face all difficulties.[14]

When the Forrester Eden of good taste and virtue collapses, it is taken over and corrupted by the egalitarian lawyer, Ivy Peters, a young man with snake eyes. His first action in the novel is to slash the eyes of a female woodpecker for the sake of creating a spectacle. This cruelty against nature, representing the modern corruption of the garden, is considerably more threatening than Wick Cutter's violence because it is intended as a challenge to the Forresters' class-based domination. Ivy's cruelty also symbolizes sexual violence, Miriam Forrester being associated with the vulnerability of the woodpecker. Out of economic desperation, she must depend on Ivy's morally unchecked financial dealings. Forced to acknowledge that "we have to get along with Ivy Peters, we simply have to!",[15] she does not resist him or what his actions imply when he "walked up behind her, and unconcernedly put both arms around her, his hands meeting over her breast" (*A Lost Lady*, 169). She must similarly allow his violence against the land. While the Forresters are wealthy, they have the luxury of aestheticizing the land by preserving its natural state. But in the end Capt. Forrester has no protection against severe economic conditions and so must submit to Ivy's abuse of his land and his wife. Thus, in *A Lost Lady* Cather acknowledges that the modern world, represented by Ivy Peters, cannot be ignored or minimized.

Ivy's acts of violence include not only the mutilation of the woodpecker and the economic and physical seduction of Miriam Forrester, but also the draining of Capt. Forrester's meadow so that it can be turned into a wheat field.[16] For the first time in Cather's writing, making land productive is pictured as rape rather than romance. Capt. Forrester and Ivy Peters represent an evolution in Cather's two opposing visions of the land, which generally, although not here, divide according to gender. Antonia and Alexandra (of *O Pioneers!*) love the land and work to make it productive. Although important, economics is subordinate in this female vision; that Antonia remains relatively poor while Alexandra becomes wealthy makes little difference because their success with the land is equal when measured in spiritual rather than material terms. In *The Land Before Her*, Annette Kolodny states that "the prairie . . . spoke to women's fantasies. And there, with an assurance she had not previously commanded [i.e., on the forest frontier], the newly self-conscious American Eve proclaimed a paradise in which the garden and the home were one."[17] The communion that Alexandra experiences with "the Genius of the Divide" and the representation of Antonia as Earthmother when her children scramble out of the fruit cave suggest that these two characters have been able to make the prairie a home rather than a place for conquest.

In contrast, their brothers share Ivy Peters's male-oriented conception of the land solely as a basis for economic power. One imagines Ambrosch treating his land as unfeelingly as he treated Antonia by making her his drudge. Because Alexandra's brothers Oscar and Lou care mainly about status, they see their land primarily as the basis for their position. Their attachment to it is no greater than their concern for Alexandra's welfare. Thus they participate in the abuse of the land that Americans have been crying out against since the eighteenth century, using "images of incestuous impregnation and rape."[18]

However, rather than being widely condemned, conquest of the land was more commonly justified and praised in the metaphors associated with Manifest Destiny. Conquest became a mission, thus masking "the guilt intrinsic to the national errand into the wilderness."[19] Annette Kolodny in *The Lay of the Land* unmasks this guilt by analyzing the imagery used to describe the new land. Her thesis parallels Cather's depiction of the male view of the land as economic power. Both popular and literary writers, picturing the land as feminine, created a vision of a maternal garden providing nurture and abundance. However, experiencing the land as feminine meant more; it was woman as well, "the total feminine principle of gratification" (Kolodny 1975, 4). The dark side of this vision, therefore, was the violence of desire, possession, and dominance. Within a century of European entry into the American garden, a sense of frailty began to characterize the dream.[20]

Capt. Forrester, a participant in the development that caused that sense of frailty, sets aside a garden that preserves a few acres of paradise. Like Jim Burden but unlike Alexandra and Antonia, he has no need to make the land productive. For him the garden does not require cultivation to be aesthetically fruitful. In contrast, dreams of the garden in *My Antonia* and *O Pioneers!* depend on hard work in order to break the sod and farm the land. Forrester illustrates a historical pattern: "The more commercial this society became, however, the more reason it found to cling in imagination to the noncommercial agrarian values" (Hofstadter, 24). Having spent his life pursuing commercial values, he can afford to purchase the fulfillment of his dream, a refined version of the garden that has developed out of his absence from rather than participation in farming. Ivy Peters stands at the same distance to the land, being no farmer either. His stake in it, though, is the opposite; his interest is in real estate. By this more complete polarization of her two visions of the land in this later novel, Cather creates a new definition of violence against the land and sharply emphasizes what has been lost in the modern world.[21]

Whereas *My Antonia* stands at the center of Cather's pastoral vision and *A Lost Lady* adds complexity by exposing the outside forces that destroy the garden, her earlier works explicitly show the violence latent within the pastoral dream itself by presenting the consequences for individuals who find that the dream has failed.

O Pioneers!, the prairie novel that precedes *My Antonia*, presents but then defuses a significant type of violence within the garden. Masked as individualistic passion of revenge, this violence is actually more complex and threatening because it is inherent in the restrictive social fabric of rural life. Unlike *A Lost Lady*, however, this novel does not bring social issues to the foreground. Frank Shabata, the offended husband who murders his wife and her lover, is a city man trapped in the country as a frustrated farmer. Beneath his passionate jealousy is a sense of impotence from being exiled in the garden. Cather controls his threatening vision of the garden as a social wasteland, however, by presenting his failure as a dramatic contrast to the main character's pastoral heroism.

It is in Cather's early short stories written when she was rebelling against her Nebraska upbringing that we find the starkest illustration of Oscar Handlin's statement, "The history of immigration is a history of alienation and its consequences."[22] "On the Divide" places violence at the center of the prairie experience.

> When the yellow scorch creeps down over the tender inside leaves about the ear [of corn], then the coroners prepare for active duty; for the oil of the country is burned out and it does not take long for the flame to eat up the wick. It causes no great sensation there when a Dane is found swinging to his own windmill tower, and most of the Poles after they have become too careless and discouraged to shave themselves keep their razors to cut their throats with.
>
> . . . . It is useless for men that have cut hemlocks among the mountains of Sweden for forty years to try to be happy in a country as flat and gray and as naked as the sea. It is not easy for men that have spent their youths fishing in the Northern seas to be content with following a plow.[23]

Because Cather here is an apprentice writer, she sensationalizes the violence, simplifies its causes, and does not present it as part of a mature vision of the human situation. She does, however, make explicit and central the violence inherent in the dream of finding a rural paradise, and she acknowledges that its causes are not just individual. As she matured as a writer, this understanding becomes less and less evident as pastoral values become central to her vision.

Because Ole Rölvaag's *Giants in the Earth* neither minimizes violence nor simplifies its causes, his critique of the immigrant dream of finding a garden of Eden at the end of a transforming journey is much more troubling than Cather's in her early stories. Vernon Parrington's introduction sums up the novel's historical significance: for the first time in American fiction, we see the emotional costs of settling the frontier, "the appalling lack of those intangible cushions for the nerves that could not be transported on horseback or in prairie schooners."[24] Harold Simonson's *Prairies Within* emphasizes Rölvaag's recognition of the spiritual costs of immigration. The Dakota Territory prairie, rather than a garden, proves to be a wilderness where people suffer from broken connections.[25] The consequence for the character Beret is a terror that has two causes related to the land: "the empty desolation of the prairie" and the change in her husband, Per Hansa (Simonson, 31). Since Beret sees in the garden only what is absent, she retreats into temporary madness. Because there are few landmarks to order space and few institutions to regulate behavior, humans stand more exposed than they can endure.[26] Per Hansa can make the land productive, but his successes isolate him as he pursues the immigrant/American dream with greater and greater intensity, at the cost of losing his spiritual bearing.

Violence in *Giants* is psychological rather than physical. Rolvaag presents this in the madness of Beret's retreat for protection into the trunk she has brought from the Old World and in the madness of the woman who, after being unable to give her young son a proper burial, must be tied down in the family's wagon so that they can continue their westward journey. Both examples show the potential for psychological violence within the male vision of conquest, which places less value on human community than on economic gain or a sense of power in subduing the land. Rölvaag also implicates the harsh land itself; chapter titles such as "Facing the Great Desolation," "On the Border of Utter Darkness," and "The Great Plain Drinks the Blood of Christian Men and Is Satisfied" suggest a biblical apocalypse rather than a pastoral paradise.

Nonfictional accounts corroborate Rölvaag's presentation by describing psychological and physical violence as an inescapable part of life in the garden. June O. Underwood in "Men, Women, and Madness: Pioneer Plains Literature" explains that personality and cultural factors underlie the tendency of the harsh land to produce in the pioneers a loss of control. Triggering events "range from economic frustration, personal displacement and loss of identity, to guilt and isolation."[27] She draws this conclusion: "The diaries and published memoirs show madness as a temporary element in the life of most pioneers. Women became depressed and silent for finite periods of time; men became violent and acted out their rage and frustration and then subsided" (Underwood, 58). Although Western fiction presents considerable self-inflicted physical and psychological violence, nonfictional accounts present madness as both more common and complex; if less dramatic than in fiction, violence for the pioneers was still an "ever-present part of their existence on the Plains" (Underwood, 56, 59–60). Both immigrants and immigrant characters often began their adventure with high hopes but then discovered a dark side to their dream of the garden. For some like Beret and Mr. Shimerda, that is all they found. However, even for those who eventually succeeded, the garden was still a place of violence—against others, against the land, and against themselves. Some could work the land with love and understanding, but many pursued male visions of economic power. They lost much, though, in the pursuit.

A sense of loss or impotence, as much a problem for twentieth-century Westerners as it was for the immigrant pioneers, has often incited those who have failed to achieve the American dream to resort to the type of violence legitimized by the myth of the frontier. Wright Morris explores the problem of acting out this myth in a postfrontier era. His characters hope for what Slotkin characterizes as a "regeneration through violence, not realizing that they are following a pattern that no longer can work."[28] The frontier myth asserts violence as a vehicle for self-assertion and self-definition. As John Cawelti explains, the need for justice and order does not motivate the Western hero; it only provides a socially acceptable opportunity for him to assert himself through violence. "What he defends, at bottom, is the purity of his own image."[29] As the frontier was being transformed into civilization, values were not adequately defined because of the conflicting demands for freedom and order; thus the hero in a time of uncertainty had to assert his own identity through decisive action.

In the modern West of Morris's fiction, characters also face uncertainty, but a sense of powerlessness combined with it results in alienation from society and its system of values. Living in a mass society but psychologically separated from it, his marginal characters possess little personal sense of direction. Other characters accept a place in a peaceful suburban society of comfort and vacuity, but they find that it is also a place of violence.[30] Haunting the background of Morris's *Ceremony in Lone Tree* is a fictionalized account of the 1958 Charles Starkweather murders that terrorized the people of Nebraska. They, like their fictional counterparts, did not dismiss this as exotic violence; they bought more locks and kept their lights on all night. Nevertheless, characters in the novel attempt to maintain the status quo rather than confront this violence with understanding. "You want to know why [he did it]?" teenage Etoile yells at her father. "It's because nobody wants to know why. It's because nobody wants to know *any-thing*! Everybody hates everybody, but nobody knows why anybody gets shot. You want to know somethin'? I'd like to shoot a few dozen people myself!" All her father can reply is, "You want to pour your daddy's coffee, Etoile?"[31] Morris's characters do not want to know the facts about themselves and their society because the knowledge is too frightening. A few days earlier, Etoile's own cousin Lee Roy "gunned down" three high school students with his hot rod.[32] Avoided by sexually electric Etoile and ignored or mocked by the society of his high school, Lee Roy gets a revenge that gives him something he has never had: " 'Lost control of it, eh?' one of them said, but Lee Roy shook his head. No, he hadn't lost control. He had been in control for once in his life. 'F—k the bastards,' he had said, and that was just what he had done" (Morris, 127). In confronting contemporary society with its aimlessness and its violence, Morris demonstrates the inadequacy of following the frontier hero's pattern of self-assertive violence.

In his novel the frontier myth appeals most strongly to society's marginal figures. They resemble those characters in Cather's work who resort to self-violence because they fail to find a place in the rural, agricultural garden. However, the violence Morris's characters commit is significantly different. Violence within the context of the garden myth is generally an admission of personal failure, a last act of hopelessness, whereas violence generated by an attempt to recapture the myth of the frontier seeks to deny failure; therefore it is directed outward and demands recognition by society. It is an attempt to gain at least an illusion of control.

The frontier myth as presented in Westerns often ends with the integration of the hero into society. After defeating the town's enemies with justifiable violence and thereby overcoming the heroine's scruples, the hero marries and accepts a settled life. But postfrontier conditions, which call for conformity rather than individualistic assertion, have inverted the myth. The modern marginal character does not use violence to protect society against threatening individuals but to protect the individual, himself, against a society that threatens because it refuses to give recognition. At the core is the same desire for self-definition by self-assertive violence. However, because its motivation is no longer masked as socially generated, this violence further marginalizes the character involved. For Lee Roy Momeyer it leads to the invisibility of prison life.

Lee Roy states that he is tired of being pushed around; Charlie Munger, the fictionalized Charles Starkweather, said that he wanted to be somebody. The real Starkweather in a sense knew what he wanted and got it. His murders and confessions made national headlines and gave him wide recognition. However, though he became "somebody," his violence brought no social integration. Lee Roy's violence brings him the same result.

Reading the newspaper accounts of Munger, McKee thinks of his childhood friend Boyd, the main character in *Ceremony*. Two parallels exist between Munger and Boyd's situations. First, like the newspaper readers for whom Starkweather/Munger performs, McKee has acted as a witness to certify and inspire Boyd as hero. McKee accepts this responsibility: "Maybe it's as much my fault as it is yours. . . . You'd never walked on that water or squirted pop at that bull if me or Mrs. McKee hadn't been there to watch you."[33] The second parallel follows from this. Boyd, an outsider sharing Lee Roy and Munger's sense of frustration and impotence, also attempts to " 'become somebody' by outrageous, destructive acts" (Machann, 168). The differences are that Boyd is articulate and insightful and that, though he performs for an audience, he turns his violence on himself. Most obviously, he attempts to commit suicide, but his whole life seems a record of self-destruction as he "courted failure like a bride throughout his strangely aimless career" (Miller, 166). His audacious acts, such as trying to walk on water, do not create a new social order. Boyd refuses to accept a place in the banal society of emotionless, clichéd living that has provided the McKees with financial success at the cost of spiritual numbness, but he can neither cut himself off from that world nor create a satisfactory alternative. And in spite of his attempts, neither can he awaken the McKees.

His namesake, Gordon, if no more successful in awakening his grandparents Lois and Walter McKee, does, like Boyd, gain recognition through his violence. Obsessed with guns, he strikes terror in those gathered for Scanlon's birthday ceremony when he plays with his great-grandfather Scanlon's old pistol. Etoile again confronts her elders' desire for avoidance by exclaiming, "What we'll do is wait till the little darling s-h-o-o-t-s somebody" (Morris, 186). When Gordon points the gun at Mr. Jennings, an outside observer, he explains, "You don't need to be scared. I don't shoot men, just wimmen." Threatened by this, his aunt slaps him "hard across the mouth" when he points the gun and screams at her, "*Bang*! You're dead!" (Morris, 187–88).

Thus violence in *Ceremony* erupts not only because of a sense of powerlessness, aimlessness, and failure, but also out of a hatred of women; and the two causes are related. Little Gordon McKee reveals what is not so obvious in the other males. The narrator states that "he hated women like every male member of the family" (Morris, 59), but the situation is not that simple. When Gordon bellows, "*I don't want to play with girls!*", the narrator explains, "There she [Lois] had it. There every living woman had it. All these blessed little boys who were born girl haters would grow up and have to have one around the house to play with" (Morris, 60). Hatred soon becomes inextricably tangled with desire.

Fearful of both male hatred and desire, Lois wishes for a world without guns, "nor anything that you could point at anyone" (Morris, 58). This veiled sexual reference is crucial. A world without sexuality would be a world of emasculated males,[34] which is exactly what men in traditional Westerns have feared. In the mythic frontier world of violence, a gun represents "masculinity and freedom" (Machann, 168). In contrast, "a married man figuratively becomes a gelding. . . . Marriage virtually unmans a Western hero."[35] McKee is that emasculated man who has lost all connection, except suppressed longing, with the frontier pattern of behavior. A believer in peace through avoidance of confrontation (a distinctly feminine attitude in the Western code), he feels that if he "represented Good, like the Gray Ladies on the war posters, then the forces of Evil would carry the day" (Morris, 51). The narrator here associates McKee with women, who threaten the Western code because "they are the harbingers of law and order enforced by police and courts, and the whole machinery of schools and peaceful town life" (Cawelti, 222). Once more, Etoile blurts out the truth. When told to hurry because "you know how your Uncle Walter feels about waiting," she replies, " 'He feels it's what he's supposed to be doing,' . . . since that was all Etoile ever saw him doing. She often saw him, holding pennies in his hand, peering at the needle in the parking meters or circling the block in front of Miller & Paine's, waiting for Aunt Lois to come out" (Morris, 89–90).

McKee has made his peace with women, though it is through emotional avoidance. The other male characters haven't. Their covert as well as overt hatred and violence toward women, which follows the Western tradition,[36] is because women stand for love, forgiveness, and reconciliation, which deny both violence and power. Thus Westerns, and *Ceremony* with its critique of their underlying myth, are "about men's fear of losing their hegemony and hence their identity."[37] Boyd and the other male characters lack the strength of identity necessary to be able to reconcile their masculine sense of self with the values represented by women and with women themselves. For this reason they never mature into adulthood.[38] McKee, in his retreat into conventionality, acts as a foil and an audience for Boyd's audacious gestures that rebel against responsible maturity that seems either deadening or out of his grasp.

Calvin, the novel's modern parody of Western values and dreams, imitates the silent Western hero in his stuttering, which he is told "symptomized . . . his silly rebellion against a world where he couldn't ride horses, shoot guns and live just as he pleased" (Morris, 93)—that is, a world controlled by women's rather than Western values. To gain the world of the Old West, he takes up prospecting with an old-timer, but he continues to forfeit his true self in the process because he is running from the modern world—his own culture—and from the world of relationships with women. Not surprisingly, the frontier world is destroyed for him when it collides with these other two. First the sight of a uranium engineer carrying a geiger counter troubles his dream of the West; then he is pulled away from it, ironically, while back in town for supplies, as he watches a Western movie with a friend. While his partner calls out the names of the mountains on the screen, Calvin becomes transfixed by "the girl who wore pants, rode a horse like a man. . . . and when she swung her long leg over the horse, Calvin felt it in his thighs. . . . It was what his cousin Etoile did when she crawled into her bunk at night after taking a shower. . . . She put one long foot on his berth, and when Calvin opened his eyes, he would see it like a marble column to where it forked at the crotch" (Morris, 100). Etoile and Calvin's elopement, plotted by their mothers, looks more like a bad compromise of the different principles of women and the West than a union that can result in maturity through shared values. The sexual engagement that leads to the elopement is a strategy and an attack on Etoile's part, necessary because the Western hero has desires but stutters as much in his actions as in his speech. Feeling his sense of self in jeopardy, he cannot give up his frightened celibacy and reconcile himself to a postfrontier world of mature relationships.

In contrast to Wright Morris's critique of the frontier myth by exposing the illegitimate violence it produces when its patterns are overlaid on a modern social context, Douglas Unger in *Leaving the Land* transforms the myth's legitimized violence by shifting its dramatic use and reducing it to a cliché. He uses the myth's underlying justification of violent self-assertion and self-definition in a personal rather than social context, which makes violence appealing to more than just socially marginal characters. Unger's novel includes at least ten incidents of interpersonal violence. When his characters become frustrated or angry, they slap each other, shoot at each other, break noses and eardrums, smash chairs, throw ashtrays, and kick cars. In spite of this, the novel's violence does not seem conspicuous because it has become merely a device for marking emotions. Readers and movie viewers, when seeing interpersonal violence, have learned not to think of the pain of the victim—physical or emotional—because violence has been stripped to a clichéd signal telling us that the perpetrator is angry, indignant, or confused. Such a reduction is possible because this violence has no consequences: the gunshot always misses and the broken nose only lasts for a sentence.

This use of the frontier myth creates safe violence, but makes the work to some extent escapist rather than confrontational. However, that it is possible for self-defining violence to become clichéd attests to the continuing force of the frontier myth and the adaptability of its pattern to new contexts. Morris, recognizing that force, instead presents frontier violence in a postfrontier setting as a sign of failure. Characters reduced to using violence as a means of gaining recognition fail to gain social acceptance. Consequently, violence in his work brings the reader into an engagement with problems of society rather than providing an individualistic escape from them.

Each of the myths considered here has given writers two options for presenting violence. Safe violence creates drama that evades rather than confronts social problems. In Cather's pastoral works, violence is controlled through narrative devices so that it cannot destabilize social structures. In contrast, Morris critiques society by depicting violence as an expression of impotence caused by the failure of characters to realize society's dreams. He shows the danger of seeking recognition through violence. Morris also exposes the myths' inability to acknowledge or assuage the problem of failure by demonstrating that socially marginal characters can only gain power through illegitimate violence.

The purpose of myth is to reconcile individuals to a collective identity. The myths of the garden and the frontier combine to allow Westerners, and Americans in general, to picture themselves as innocent and noble farmers harvesting the fruit of a land bounteous toward all, and at the same time see themselves as powerful individualists outside of the group and beyond its censure, yet acting for its good and deserving its praise. Cather and Morris have explored the myths' effects on Americans' individual sense of self and their interpersonal relationships. Whether justifying behavior, criticizing it, or longing for a time when honorable behavior was possible, these writers attest to the force the myths of the garden and the frontier continue to have in shaping our perceptions of ourselves and our world.

Foreign-Born Immigrants on the Great Plains Frontier in Fiction and Nonfiction

Linda S. Pickle

The settling of the Great Plains in the late nineteenth century has been the subject of numerous works of both fiction and nonfiction. Such works have normally focused on the tremendous human costs as well as the ultimate achievements of what is often regarded as the last phase of that most American aspect of our social history, the expansion westward. Most of the actors in this endeavor were ordinary people, many of them foreign-born immigrants, who attempted farming under the marginal conditions of the so-called great American desert. In the crucible of the American melting pot, these immigrants were to make their contributions to the new society. Their trials and triumphs were memorialized in oral traditions and in printed texts, especially in the early decades of this century. Two of the most important novels written about the Great Plains frontier are Willa Cather's *My Antonia* (1918) and Ole Rölvaag's *Giants in the Earth* (Norwegian original, 1924–25; English translation, 1927). In both works, the actions and experiences of foreign-born immigrants are central to the depiction of the Great Plains frontier as the setting for a human drama of a particularly American cast. The New World dream of unending expansion and progress, shared by many of these immigrants, comes up against the limitations of harsh physical reality. The characters' cultural distance from the Great Plains environment is another frontier that they must confront. This inner frontier intensifies the potential, always present in a border situation, for heroic grandeur on the one hand and for horrific alienation and (self-)destruction on the other.[1]

Among the works of nonfiction that deal with much the same material as Cather's and Rölvaag's novels, Mari Sandoz's *Old Jules* (1935) and John Ise's *Sod and Stubble* (1936) are especially compelling. However, these biographical studies of the authors' parents and historical sketches of their home areas in Nebraska and Kansas affect us differently than the two novels. Although all four works are about the same geographical region, the same important period in our history, and some of the European immigrants who played a role in it, the novels are more successful at evoking the timeless, mythic dimension of their material. In part, this is due to the diminished significance attached to the foreign origins of the main characters in their interactions with the Great Plains environment. Much of the power of the novels derives from the exploitation of the theme of ethnicity, from the rich resonance of the age-old situation of the stranger in a strange land. The significance and value of the works of nonfiction are different. They broaden and deepen our knowledge about the cultural and historical meaning of one particular frontier, that of the American West. As literary works, as well as historical documents, they demonstrate the varied legacy of the frontier in our national self-awareness.[2]

The four narratives I will be looking at all chronicle the arrival on the Great Plains frontier of immigrant farmers and others in the 1870s and 1880s and their experiences during its settlement.[3] Geography, climate, and the slim margin for successful farming are central in all four books. The negative aspects of pioneer life—the natural dangers of the prairie (Indians, droughts, storms, prairie fires, snakes, grasshopper invasions), the harshness and poverty of life in the early years, the isolation from neighbors and from settlements of any size with the attendant loneliness and tendency toward lawless behavior, and the resulting psychological stress that drove people to madness and violence—are themes that have a more or less prominent place in each work. The positive aspects of frontier life are also present in each: the beauty and grandeur of the prairie, the generosity people showed each other in times of need, the acts of ingenuity and heroism that necessity called forth, and the proof of perseverance of the human spirit. The raw material of what we might call the American myth of the agricultural frontier is present in all four books.

All four authors were intimately familiar with their subject matter. Sandoz and Ise were the children of the pioneers of whom they wrote and they spent their early lives in the areas depicted in their works. Cather and Rölvaag also lived in the geographic settings of their novels at the end of the frontier period. The two novelists knew people on whom they based some of the characters of their works, and they drew on the stories they had heard about the early pioneering days as well. They did not do the research on the period that Sandoz (*OJ*, ix) and Ise

(*SS*, xi–xii) tell us that *they* did, but we know that Rölvaag was concerned with the factual accuracy of his work and that Cather acknowledged that she owed much to the stories told her by immigrant farm women she knew in Webster County, Nebraska.[4]

The personal familiarity of the authors with the material of their works and with the oral tradition that recorded the events of those early days is the basis, it seems to me, for another quality that the four works have in common: the consciousness of an epic significance to the events they record and consequently the epic tone of their narratives. In his study of the works of Rölvaag, Cather, and John Neihardt, Paul A. Olson defined an epic in this way: "a work in which a heroic person, or people, acts to destroy an old civilization or create a new one, or alternately, one in which he or they act at the request of the transcendent, fail to accomplish these grand deeds, and move inevitably toward destruction."[5] Mari Sandoz wrote that the frontier is "a land of story-tellers, and in this respect remains frontier in nature until the last original settler is gone" (*OJ*, vii). From these storytellers, as well as from her own experience and research, she seems to have gained what we might call an epic understanding of these stories and the actors in them. She wrote what any of our four authors could have written: "These people have endured, and as I review them from the vantage point of twice knowledge my eyes mist. A gallant race, and I salute them" (*OJ*, ix). Each of the works in question is a similar salute to heroic times and figures. Each also implies, although to varying degrees, that the story it imparts has significance, not only for an understanding of the past, but also as a "model for future enterprise" (Olson, 266).

There are structural as well as thematic similarities among the four works. All follow an essentially chronological sequence of events corresponding to the settlement process. Each begins with the arrival on the frontier of the main character or characters: Per and Beret Holm in Dakota Territory in 1870 (*GE*), Henry and Rosie Ise in western Kansas in 1873 (*SS*), Jules Sandoz in northwestern Nebraska in 1884 (*OJ*), and Antonia Shimerda in Nebraska in the 1880s (*MA*). Each ends when the frontier era ends, symbolized by the death or departure of the main character in three of the works—Per Holm in 1881, Rosie Ise in 1910, and Jules Sandoz in 1928—and by the depiction of Antonia's established family and farm in Cather's work, about thirty-two years after the point at which the novel begins. All four stories are strongly focused on the narrative present, and the immigrants' early lives in their home countries are touched on only obliquely, for background. To be sure, how the fictional characters deal with their Old World past determines to no small extent how they confront their frontier experiences. The interplay of European past and American present deepens the significance of their reactions. But it is the American here and now that is primary, just as is the case with the Ises and Sandozes. The close association of the frontier part of the characters' lives with the content and temporal structure of the works indicates that to a large extent the respective authors identified the frontier period with these characters, or with the spirit that they saw incorporated in them.

The narrative techniques of these works are also quite similar. Dialogue is interspersed among descriptive passages, even in the works by Ise and Sandoz in situations where these authors could claim at most secondhand knowledge of such verbal exchanges. Sandoz's own assertion at different times that *Old Jules* is "fictionalized biography" or "fictionalized history"[6] could also be said of *Sod and Stubble*. Three of the four works use the same point of view: Rölvaag, Sandoz, and Ise employ an omniscient narrator who is able to enter the minds of the main characters at times. In *Giants in the Earth*, we often are told the thoughts of Beret and Per. In *Old Jules*, the title figure's perspective predominates in those sections that Sandoz is likely to have known about through her father's stories and letters, while her own or her mother's viewpoint is evident in other parts depicting family life with this difficult man. In *Sod and Stubble*, Rosie Ise's perspective is clearest, which is perhaps not surprising, as her son tells us that it was his mother's stories that first moved him to write the book and her patiently "piecing together the scattered recollections of years now long past" that helped him as he worked on the story (*SS*, xii). Cather's use of a first-person narrator is a significant difference that must be discussed in more detail below in connection with her artistic intention.

Given the long list of subjects and techniques shared among these four books, isolating important distinctions would be useful in explaining the different effects they achieve. To begin with, the nonfiction narratives contain many more details about frontier life in this period. Ise's book, even more than Sandoz's, is a methodical, chronological account of almost all the details and events of any importance in his parents' lives. Most of the material he presents seems to be undifferentiated in significance. The work is structured episodically, as in chapter 28, "The Darkness before Dawn" (*SS*, 260–72), where we read of a poor investment Henry had made of a friend's money, the ending of a drought just in the nick of time, the death of a neighbor youth from appendicitis, visits from members of Rosie's family, Rosie's visit to eastern Kansas along with a neighbor woman, the departure of the two oldest girls to college, and their return at Christmas.

The stringing together of events related mainly through chronology in *Sod and Stubble* is interesting and even moving at times. This same chapter 28 is a good example. The depth of human interest in what Ise relates here is fully explored, so that the details have more than mere informational purpose and value. His discussion of his father's involvement in investing a departed friend's money in a local grain elevator is the occasion not only for telling of that friend's history as a Kansas settler, but also of the Ise family's open criticism of Henry's poor judgment and of Henry's own feelings of failure. The description of the death of the neighbor boy leads into a short discourse on the latter's family, including the story of how his father would play the violin beside his mother as she milked the cow. We get a taste of what visits among large rural families in those times were like from Ise's comments on the visits of his mother's brothers and their families, when as many as twenty children and four adults had to be fed and cleaned up after, with the children sneaking off to play forbidden card games or to go swimming rather than doing their chores, and squabbling among themselves about who got to sit at the first table setting. What is interesting about Rosie's trip across the state to visit her family is that she goes primarily to accompany a neighbor woman, "Aunt" Lisa Meirhoffer, who had pioneered with a brutal, hard-drinking husband and for the first time was allowed to visit a brother in eastern Kansas whom she had not seen since both had left Switzerland many years before. Having read of this life of deprivation and self-effacement, we are as touched as Rosie at Mrs. Meirhoffer's reaction to a Swiss yodel record:

> She dropped into a chair, sobbing as if her heart would break; then, as the falsetto notes of the yodel sounded again she started up and resumed her walk back and forth, waving her hands, alternately crying and laughing hysterically: "Herr Je! Herr Je! Herr Je!"
> . . . Rosie . . . reached for her handkerchief, as she sensed the stark outlines of the picture before her—the picture of the broken old woman, after long, lonely years in her home up in the wind-swept hills of Kansas, hearing again a song of her native Switzerland. (SS, 270)

As is almost always the case with Ise's narrative, it is the human dimension of this episode, in itself so peripheral to the Ise family story, that seems to make it worthy of inclusion.

The final cluster of events narrated in chapter 28 also illustrate this "human-interest" element of the book. The family's sorrow when the two oldest girls leave for college, the preparations for their return for the Christmas holidays, and their joyful welcome home are sketched briefly but with a warmth of feeling that family reminiscences often have. The girls bring back news of a new food, tapioca, and this becomes a favorite family dessert. Such a detail might seem to be significant only to those interested in the factual, historical particulars of American farm family life, and Ise offers many such details, like the prices of grain and goods, that are perhaps valuable in themselves. But what makes them interesting beyond this is the human dimension he lends them through the place they have in his family's oral tradition. He recalls that Henry bought some tapioca "the next time he went to town" and that Rosie cooked a kettle of it "—no, it was two kettles-full, before she was through" (*SS*, 272). He tells us that Rosie sometimes flavored this family favorite with dry fruit, and then relates how one of the little boys, Happy, came running into the house during a hailstorm shouting excitedly: "Ma, Ma! It's raining tapioca!" (*SS*, 272). This anecdote communicates the warmth and closeness in this family, in which everyone—father, mother, older children and younger—contributed to sharing a dish and to relishing the pleasure and excitement that such a mundane thing can produce.

The very wealth of detail and of "human-interest stories" in *Sod and Stubble*—chronicling, year after year, the crops planted and the weather experienced, the joys and the misadventures of the eleven surviving children, the neighbors who gave the family friendship or cause for strife, the domestic animals that were loved and lost, the family and neighborhood activities and the growth of the community—has a cumulative effect that makes the people and times Ise describes live vividly for us. A few pages of chapter 21 illustrate this. The first section of the chapter deals with baby Joe's bout with polio. Then the list of misfortunes of the drought year 1887 continues. The loss of the winter wheat and then of the corn to heat and chinch bugs, the drying up of the garden and the pastures testify to the harshness of the family's physical environment and the vulnerability of their livelihood. But it is through family stories and events that we come to understand the strong bonds forged by the shared experience of these hardships. Ten-year-old Billy is thrown by a colt and recuperates only slowly. While he is still in bed, the remaining horse of Henry's original team, old Sam, has to be killed. Ise's language reflects the gratitude and love that people felt toward the domestic animals on whom they depended for so much.

> All that is loyal and faithful [Sam] had been, and now that he was too old to work, he had been allowed to wander about the place at will, enjoying an old age of leisure. This hard year, though, as the pasture dried up and the feed became scarcer, it seemed evident that Sam might have to go. Neither Rosie nor Henry dared to say it, as across the dinner table they talked over the critical problems of ways and means. Neither had the heart to suggest outright that they should kill the faithful brute; but when all of the horses began to grow thin, and Sam himself began to look gaunt and hungry, standing at the stable door much of the time patiently supplicant for the doles of fodder and oats straw that were sometimes available there, then the problem took on a new aspect. Life was no boon to such a hungry and decrepit animal, tormented by the

heat and flies, and they finally decided to kill him. Henry led him out to the field, tied a gunny sack over his eyes so he might not see, and killed him with an axe. That night supper was eaten in undisguised tears, and in almost reverent silence. (*SS*, 177)

The next paragraph relates the death of another beloved animal in this bad summer. Fanny, the family pet mare, had been sick and given free run of the farm, with no one paying her much heed. Finally, one "scorching day in August," one of the children misses her, and Henry goes to look for her: "He found her down in the cornfield, where she had died several days before, after beating down the corn stalks about her, in vain efforts to get upon her feet. The faithful animal, who had never for a moment neglected any of the children given over to her care, had been forgotten for days by all of them, in her final distress, in the heat of those August days, without feed or water or care" (*SS*, 178). The undertone of love, sorrow, and guilt evident in these passages testifies to the bonds between humans and the dumb brutes with whom they shared this harsh environment. The next vignette, of neighbor Martha Hunker, reveals the care and affection people also felt toward each other. Learning that pregnant Rosie's stomach is upset for a lack of greens and vegetables, Martha brings a basket of lettuce: "On the way over, she found the creek impassable from a rain up north, and had to go two miles out of the way to find a crossing; but she brought the lettuce just the same. Martha was no Venus. She always pinned her scanty hair in a little knot on the back of her head, pulling it so tight that it hurt one to look at her; but she was the kind that would walk four or five miles to bring you lettuce" (*SS*, 178–79). Affection, sorrow, guilt, and gratitude, based in common troubles, speak in these paragraphs. These are the feelings shared by the family and passed on as part of the communal lore of the family group. By the end of Ise's book, after reading dozens of such passages, we can fully appreciate Rosie's anguish at leaving the homestead where she and Henry had experienced so much: "Who would have realized what it means to leave everything you've worked and saved for—everything you've cared for!" (*SS*, 322). As she rides away she asks her son to stop the wagon at the top of the hill. Surveying the valley where she spent so many years, she thinks of all she has experienced in joy and sorrow there, and she remembers the lonely log cabin and stable she came to, "standing out on a treeless and fenceless expanse of waving grass—bare and lonely" (*SS*, 325). The well-tended, prosperous farm she leaves is a memorial not only to her and Henry but to all those who came and endured in Kansas.

We can say that of her son's book as well. As deeply rooted as it is in the particular history of his parents, we come to see them as part of a broader picture, as actors in larger, epic events and endeavors. Henry and Rosie Ise persevere in the face of what often seem to be overwhelming odds and help create a new civilization on the Plains. Rosie, in particular, emerges as an individual of heroic qualities, the strong, hardworking, self-denying center of the family, who "would always be a pioneer, at heart" (*SS*, 306). The epic tone of Ise's narration is achieved partly through the compilation of details documenting this perseverance, its costs, and its rewards. The accumulation of small, ordinary daily actions gives the work a universal dimension. In addition, Ise chooses not to intrude his persona as narrator into his tale, but rather, in keeping with his stated intention of "preserving for the future" (*SS*, xi) the picture of those early times, remains so faceless that we have no clues that he is the little crippled boy Joe of the book. Ise's narrative stance gives his work a broader, more representative tone than it might otherwise have had. Even the personal and family sentiments his text often communicates do not detract from this tone. Indeed, I would argue that they lend the Ise family story a certain representative validity as illustrations of actual, viable subjective reactions to frontier experiences. This grounding in real, personal experiences, along with the completeness of the picture he offers of pioneer life, causes us to feel such a familiarity with it that we accept his particular account as emblematic for what might be told of many Great Plains families who helped change the vistas of prairie sod into the harvested stubble of productive farmland.

Sandoz is more selective than Ise in the information she gives us, although there are certain important similarities. Both works have a fairly straightforward chronological structure, and both contain a good deal of information about frontier community life as well as the particulars of the individual family histories involved. Sandoz's style is somewhat less episodic than Ise's, perhaps because she concentrates more narrowly on her father and on his role in settling the Niobrara Valley. Her chapters are organized primarily around interconnected events that may span several years and that overlap in time with events in other chapters, rather than covering one or two years in chronological sequence, as in *Sod and Stubble*. Therefore we learn less in Sandoz's work about the mechanics of pioneering and more about the dynamics of social life among the early settlers in western Nebraska. This emphasis stems from her father's great passion for social dynamics—not how the land was actually settled (such manual labor he usually left to others), but the relationships among people, and his vision of what the region could become. For example, we feel that it is only because Jules was lamed in an accident digging his well that Sandoz tells us anything about that procedure (*OJ*, 42–44). But she devotes a chapter to "The Niobrara Feud" (*OJ*, 120–47), a three-year dispute involving her father and several other landowners, for this was what obsessed Jules Sandoz during those years, much more than the weather, his crops, or even the relationship with his second wife, who finally had enough and divorced him at that time. As its title indicates, *Old Jules* gives us a more individual, idiosyncratic view of frontier life than *Sod and Stubble*, a view that is dominated by the personality of Jules Sandoz and by his daughter's reaction to him.

Mari Sandoz also offers us a more problematic view of the American frontier because of her main character. Jules had many of the qualities of a frontier hero. He was a crack shot, a friend to the Indians, a claims locator to numerous settlers, a defender of the farmers in their struggle against ranching interests, and a noted horticulturalist. His visionary enthusiasm and hard work mark him as one of those strong individuals who did much to promote the settlement of the West, and his daughter clearly sees him as important in that process. He is an epic figure in her treatment of her material. But the negative aspects of the frontier also come out through her father: its lawlessness and violence, and the assertion of extreme individualism to the detriment of others.[7] Jules Sandoz was a brutal husband and father, an irascible man constantly embroiled in disputes with others. His relationship to his children, and how it marked them, is indicated by what seems to be Mari's earliest memory, that of being struck repeatedly when she was three months old for waking Jules in the night (*OJ*, 215–16). Another childhood memory also stayed with her and is transmitted in all its force to us: her mother trying to take strychnine after Jules beat her with a wire whip, the bottle knocked from her mouth by her own mother, while Mari and her two brothers cowered under the bed "like frightened little rabbits, afraid to cry" (*OJ*, 230–31). Such pictures temper our perception of Jules as frontier hero in such later scenes as his standing up to the cattlemen, and his courage in "shooting off" rattlesnake venom from a bite in his hand (*OJ*, 329–35).

Mari Sandoz's acknowledgement of the negative aspects of her father's character are part of her general tendency to explore the dark side of the frontier experience. The human costs of settlement are made very clear, especially in the lives of women. Mary Sandoz, Jules's third wife and Mari's mother, is the most immediate example. She was prematurely aged by work, poor nutrition, and childbearing, and she was tyrannized and unappreciated by her husband. But worse things than this happened on the frontier. Women went mad, killed their children and themselves, and were murdered by their husbands.[8] People suffered not only physical privations but spiritual and cultural ones as well. Mari Sandoz was not sent to school until she was nine, and she and her brothers attended very intermittently after that because they were needed to help their parents farm. Men lived lonely lives, or married hastily and unhappily, because of the scarcity of women. Intelligent, decently educated women like Jules's second wife Henrietta and his last wife Mary suffered from the lack of civilized contacts and the necessity of leading lives of drudgery. Mari Sandoz's biography of her father and historical study of the region and era he lived in is a fascinating account of the role played by an exceptional person in the settling of one small region of the Great Plains. It acknowledges the heroic qualities of such people and times. But *Old Jules* also illustrates that prairie fires, blizzards, and cattle barons were only outer, readily identifiable dangers to the agrarian settler. The real West had other very real dangers hidden in the human heart, dangers that became visible in a frontier community unfettered by the traditional forces of civilization and culture.

Ole Rölvaag's novel also is concerned with the opportunities and dangers of the frontier experience. *Giants in the Earth* begins by telling us about concrete realities of life on the early Great Plains frontier. In the first pages we learn what an immigrant family caravan looked like, what the daily routine on the trip was, and how the wagons were loaded. Every step of the process of making a home on the prairie follows: the proper way in which a homestead claim was filed; the building of a sod house, even to the details of the arrangement of the furniture and, later, the formula of the mixture used to whitewash the interior walls; breaking the sod and sowing and harvesting the first crops; the hunting of game to increase the sparse and monotonous diet. But concerned as Rölvaag seems to have been about historical accuracy, and dependable as his descriptions of pioneer life are, we come to feel that this realism is secondary to the author's primary interest in this subject matter: the positive and negative challenges to the human spirit.

On the surface, Per Hansa seems to meet these challenges in an appropriate and admirable fashion. His grand feats in building a larger sod house and breaking more land than his neighbors, his early planting of the wheat, and his netting of fish and ducks for winter stores are all examples of the accomplishments to which his pride and ambition drive him. Per comes to see himself in heroic terms, and is viewed in that way by his neighbors as well, especially after he befriends the Indians and then finds the small community's strayed cattle. But he is a rash and impulsive man of action, as well as a superior husbandman.[9] When he acts singlehandedly to destroy the Irishmen's claim stakes, he wants to defend his friends' interests, but he does this by taking advantage of the absence of established legal limits on actions on the frontier. Although he happens to be in the right about the stakes, he does not know this, and so as a kind of justification of his actions, he envisions himself a hero in a fight against the trolls of Norwegian folklore: "How would it turn out when the trolls came? Would he be able to hack off their hands and wrest the kingdom from their power? . . . It might happen that he would be going about with some object in his hand, and would suddenly grip it hard; all his strength would be needed to wield the enchanted sword. . . . For these would be archtrolls, no less" (*GE*, 121). His actions, positive in their effects as they usually are, nevertheless are flawed by hubris. Even his loyal, phlegmatic friend Hans Olsa senses this when he wonders why Per Hansa would have kept the secret of whitewashing sod walls to himself. He gently admonishes Per: "You shouldn't be vain in your own strength, you know!" (*GE*, 197).

It is precisely this vanity and the destructive aspects of Per's ambitious, ruthless frontiersman personality that alienate his wife. Beret comes to feel that he is no longer the same man she loved and married in Norway. When she learns that the Irishmen's claim stakes were not lawful, her anguish at Per's actions is not diminished: "But suppose it had been otherwise—would he have done any different? . . . Was this the person in whom she had believed that no evil could dwell? . . . Had it always been thus with him?" (*GE*, 148). This is to her the ultimate proof that men cannot live on the prairie, that they lose their human, civilized qualities in this empty landscape: "The explanation was plain; this desolation out here called forth all that was evil in human nature" (*GE*, 148). Her alienation from Per is as important a cause for her descent into madness as is her alienation from her environment. As one critic has noted, Beret's deterioration can be seen to have a mythic dimension similar to that noted for Per.[10] The balance and mutual completion between Beret (Freya) and Per (Frey) is lost away from their Norwegian homeland. But also on the most concrete, practical level, Beret cannot rejoice in Per's exploits, for she recognizes in them an adventurism and self-aggrandizement that estranges him from his past and from her. The outer dangers that Per overcomes, Rölvaag shows us, are nothing compared to the inner ones to which he succumbs: the concentration on material gain, competition with his neighbors, the rejection of the old system of values and with these the wife he loves, who clings to them.[11] Rölvaag reveals, in the conflict between between Per and Beret, the spiritual costs of gaining the American dream of materialistic progress by severing cultural ties. Thus the details of this frontier progress are not merely informational but also cautionary.

Rölvaag's intention in dealing with this material is revealed by the structure of the novel, which on the surface seems to be straightforwardly chronological, following the development of the theme of material progress. But underneath this, Beret's descent into madness parallels her husband's economic and social ascent. In the first three-fourths of the novel, Beret's growing depression and paranoia are presented in an almost clinically realistic fashion. The symptoms of her growing mental disturbance—sleeplessness, loss of appetite, atypical slovenliness in her appearance, loss of powers of concentration (*GE*, 174, 202–204)—abate when her son is born the first Christmas on the Plains. Indeed, we are told: "That winter it was *he* who saved people from insanity and the grave" (*GE*, 245). But this is only a temporary respite. Beret's horror of the landscape, which takes on literally monstrous features for her, so that she covers up the windows to prevent it from seeing her (*GE*, 103–104, 180–81, 321–22); her conviction that moral, civilized human beings cannot survive life on the Plains; and her belief that she and all others on the frontier are being led astray by the Evil One for their sinfulness climax in her complete breakdown during the grasshopper plague in the middle of book 2 (*GE*, 331–39). The five years that follow bring material prosperity to Per Hansa, but Rölvaag tells us this only after the fact. We learn that Per has acquired two more quarter sections of land and is considered the richest man in the neighborhood, but the relative insignificance of such acquisitions is brought out by the author's acknowledging them only in passing. The last half of book 2 instead turns to Beret's recovery and Per's final defeat. She is healed by two things: the assurance of God's love and forgiveness through the itinerant minister (*GE*, 400–402), and the words of love and self-blame she overhears Per speaking to Hans Olsa (*GE*, 403–405). In addition to the minister's sermon, several other things are catalysts in her recovery: that the first church service in the community was held in her sod house; that Norwegian hymns had been sung, "yet no harm had befallen the house on that account" (*GE*, 401); and that her ancestral immigrant chest, the same chest she had planned to be buried in when she feared she would die in childbirth and in which she had hidden during the first grasshopper plague, had been used as the altar. These things sanctify a connection between the Old World and the New that finally reconciles Beret to her life on the Great Plains. She feels that she has come home (*GE*, 408).

The fact that Beret is a foreign-born immigrant has a great deal to do with her experience of alienation on the frontier. Per's accomplishments are those of any aggressive frontiersman, but Beret's madness is largely culturally motivated. It is not only the physical emptiness of the landscape that terrifies her but its cultural and communal emptiness as well. She and Per battle over cultural issues. She objects to the taking of American-style names, for example (*GE*, 277), and she is horrified by Per's breaking the Norwegian taboo of tampering with another man's property markers (*GE*, 140–50). To her, rejections of the old ways are rejections of civilized, human behavior as she knows it. In both *Sod and Stubble* and *Old Jules*, the fact that the main characters are also immigrants plays a much less significant role. It is simply a given in their lives that influences certain of their attitudes, but it is not a prime determining factor in either their experience of the American frontier or in their children's portrayal of them as pioneers. In *Giants in the Earth*, Beret's ethnic alienation is not only an important element in the plot of the novel, but it functions also both as a symbol for the general alienation of any immigrant from new, unformed, empty land and as a vehicle to criticize the reckless behavior that a frontier can call forth in the best of settlers. Rölvaag's use of ethnicity as symbol and as matrix of behavior is one of the most important qualities of his work that distinguishes it from the biographical, historical narratives discussed above.

Willa Cather does not focus as intently on the early years of settlement as Rölvaag, but she, too, is intrigued by the universal, even mythological significance to be found in the settling of the Great Plains. To explore this significance, she uses some of the same means as Rölvaag: ethnicity, the hardships of the early days, and the landscape of the Plains, but to quite different purpose. Let us examine her use of ethnicity first. Cather, through her narrator Jim Burden, presents ethnicity primarily as a source of strength rather than of pain in the frontier experience. If Beret Holm is a misunderstood Cassandra, admonishing those about her of their errors in neglecting the old ways, Antonia Shimerda becomes a founder of a new race on the frontier, able to transplant old values in the soil of the New World. Cather gives Antonia the immortal, universal quality of myth: "Antonia had always been one to leave images in the mind that did not fade—that grew stronger with time. . . . She lent herself to immemorial human attitudes which we recognize by instinct as universal and true. . . . [She] had that something which fires the imagination, could still stop one's breath for a moment by a look or gesture that somehow revealed the meaning in common things. . . . She was a rich mine of life, like the founders of early races" (*MA*, 353). Antonia's role as mythic founder of a new race on the American plains is evident in the final scenes of her with her children. She is portrayed as an Earth Mother, surrounded by the bounty of her nurturing activities.[12] Beyond what we might see as her ability to succeed on the frontier through her maternal nature, her ethnicity makes her, in Cather's view, more suitable to help found the new American society there. Lives like Antonia's contain the past within the present, as her memories of Bohemia and of her educated, artistic father show, and so the roots she sends down in American soil have a depth and a strength that make them a superior foundation for the new society.[13] Immigrants were not merely "more successful" in material terms, because they brought with them a greater hunger for land and the willingness to have their daughters work for the family good, as Jim Burden thinks (*MA*, 198–200). They were also better suited to found a new American people and culture from the fertile soil of the varied heritages of the Nebraska immigrants. Thus Antonia uses her memories of her childhood in Bohemia to enrich the lives of those around her: first Jim, then the Harling children, and finally her own children. Unlike Beret, she does not find it hard to make connections between the old and the new, as when the cracked chirping of the little green insect reminds her of the old beggar woman Hata (*MA*, 39).

She passes on her language and her ethnic heritage to her descendants, as she does her father's violin to her son (*MA*, 347).

But Antonia is also able to integrate new elements with the old. Her experiences growing up on the Nebraska plains become "the family legend" (*MA*, 350), and the people she has known and the knowledge she has gained become the foundation on which her children's lives, and so also American society of the present and future, rest. The interconnectedness of past and present, and with this the intermingling of various cultural heritages in the lives of individuals and peoples, is the main theme of the novel. Willa Cather presents Antonia and the Nebraska frontier as parts of the long, continuous history of humankind. Cather establishes this continuity symbolically and structurally by presenting the same situation at several points in the novel: a feeling of transcendent bliss, of being at the center of a golden circle of nature, which always takes place at sunset. The Great Plains landscape is anything but hostile in *My Antonia*. Rather, it is the background and even the foundation of a sense of oneness of the individual with nature, with the past, and with others. The first time this happens is soon after Jim's arrival in Nebraska, when he sits in the center of his grandmother's garden under the sun and feels "like the pumpkins, . . . entirely happy, . . . dissolved into something complete and great" (*MA*, 18). Here it is the connection of humankind with that which came before, the earth and its creatures, that Cather celebrates: the waving red prairie grass that seems to cover galloping herds of buffalo, the badger that watches Jim's grandmother work, the insects and plants around him (*MA*, 16–18).

Related incidents follow throughout the novel, and each establishes a connection between the present and the prehistory of the Plains and their inhabitants. Jim's first meeting with Antonia takes place in "a nest in the long red grass" where it was "wonderfully pleasant" (*MA*, 26) and where he teaches her her first words of English. Then on a late fall afternoon Jim and Antonia meet in his grandmother's garden for a reading lesson. It is here that she finds the little green insect that reminds her of the old storyteller Hata in Bohemia. On the way home they see the figure of a man walking dejectedly, outlined against the sunset sky. It is Antonia's father, full of sadness for his old life, who promises to give Jim the old Bohemian gun with which he subsequently commits suicide (*MA*, 38–42). Later, after Jim and Antonia are in town, there is the memorable picnic they go on with Lena Lingard, Tiny Soderball, and Anna Hansen. They are outside town in the sheltered bed of the river. Again it is sunset, and this time the grand mood of the time and place is brought vividly to life by the picture of the plough silhouetted by the sun (*MA*, 245), an image that Jim comes to see as symbolic of "the places and people of [his] own infinitesimal past" (*MA*, 262). The conversations among the young people that precede this vision are important, for they, too, link the past and the present of the Plains and those who dwell there. The scent of the elders reminds Antonia of Bohemia and her father (*MA*, 235–37), and then each of the girls speaks about her immigrant family and its links to the Old World (*MA*, 239–42). Late in the afternoon the conversation turns to Coronado, the Spanish sword turned up by the plow of a Nebraska farmer, and the sorrow that killed the explorer when he did not find the Seven Golden Cities (*MA*, 243–44). The memory of Antonia's father resonates here, both in the figure silhouetted against the sunset sky as well as in the unhappy Coronado, destroyed by the failure of his dreams. Mr. Shimerda's memory is also immanent the next time Jim and Antonia meet, years later, after she has given birth to her illegitimate child. The setting is again the prairie at sunset, this time by her father's grave, where Jim feels "the old pull of the earth, the solemn magic that comes out of those fields at nightfall." He wishes he could be a boy again, and he vows to himself to carry Antonia's face with him forever, "the closest, realest face, under all the shadows of women's faces, at the very bottom of [his] memory" (*MA*, 322). It is remembrance that Jim and Antonia speak of here, the remembrance of people and times past, and the way these attain a kind of transcendent immanence through acts of memory (*MA*, 320–21). The chain of related moments has its high point in the beautiful scene of Jim and Antonia together in her farm orchard, which "seemed full of sun, like a cup" (*MA*, 341). The talk here, too, is of the past, as it is later that evening in Antonia's parlor, with its photographs of her Bohemian village (sent to her by Jim, visual proof of the extent to which her past has become part of his) and of people from her life in Nebraska and the sounds of her father's violin and of her children speaking "their rich old language" (*MA*, 349).

Cather's novel ends with a summation of the theme of remembrance, of the connectedness of past and present set against a background of untouched nature. Jim leaves Black Hawk at sunset after a disappointing day there (disappointing because so much of what he cherished in it is now gone) and walks onto the rough pastures north of the town. There he comes upon the last vestiges of the old road "which used to run like a wild thing across the open prairie." He is overwhelmed by "the sense of coming home to [himself], and of having found out what a little circle man's experience is" (*MA*, 371–72). The repeated evocation of the past within the present in this and similar scenes throughout the novel has a cumulative effect that causes us to feel that the work is only incidentally "about" the Great Plains frontier, and that it actually has as its subject matter the preservation and the celebration of "the precious, the incommunicable past" (*MA* 372) of human history.

Tracing this elaborate pattern of repeated, related events in Cather's novel helps us see the conscious structuring of fiction in comparison to the linear, episodic structure of the biographies. The reality of events is less important than what their underlying pattern communicates about the common human experience of remembrance and nostalgia. This theory of event patterns also helps explain why Cather is much more selective in what she tells us about actual frontier life than our other authors. At first glance, this lack of detail might seem to be because Jim Burden, who comes to the Nebraska frontier as a young boy, notices and remembers only those things a child might. We learn almost nothing about the mechanics of pioneering, and we hear mostly indirectly about its hardships. One of the few exceptions is the scene depicting the miserable dugout in which the Shimerdas spend the first hard winter. But this scene is there, we feel, primarily to show us what drove Mr. Shimerda to suicide rather than to tell us about pioneering as such. And this early scene reverberates in our minds in the last book when we see Antonia's well-stocked fruit cellar, the dugout transformed, as it were, and feel the earlier atmosphere of poverty and misery obliterated by the dizzying sight of her children bursting joyfully forth from the dark womb of the earth. Indeed, it is only through the latter scene in Antonia's orchard that the dugout episode gains its full significance as an example of "the little circle of man's experience."

Other bits of early frontier life in *My Antonia* also serve the purpose of connecting past and present, rather than the purpose of completing a biographical picture of frontier life. Examples are the Indian circle in the grass (*MA*, 62); the combination of Virginian, Nebraskan, and Austrian elements in the Burdens' Christmas preparations (*MA*, 81–83); and the story of the evil deed done on the Russian steppes that haunts Pavel and Peter on the Nebraska plains (*MA*, 53–61). The same might be said of the religious, ethnic, and superstitious considerations that prevent Mr. Shimerda from being buried in the Catholic or the Norwegian cemeteries and lead to his burial at the crossroads, only to have the American road curve ever after around the spot and create a kind of shrine to his memory in its untouched oasis of prairie grass (*MA*, 111–14, 119). Another episode in the first book of the novel, Jim's killing the rattlesnake at the prairie-dog town, also seems to be included because it would stick out in a boy's memories of his youth. But there are other, more important literary reasons. The snake is connected with the presettlement past of the prairie, "left on from buffalo and Indian times," and even beyond this, is associated with "the ancient, eldest Evil" (*MA*, 47). There are human rattlesnakes in the book, as well: Krajiek, who cheats the Bohemian family when they arrive, continues to live off them during the first winter (*MA*, 32), and even encourages them to eat prairie dogs (*MA*, 71); and Wick Cutter, the Black Hawk moneylender, who also lives off his fellow humans and whom Jim fights, albeit unwillingly (*MA*, 278–79). The interweaving of the past in the present and the foreshadowing of future events in such episodes of pioneer life make *My Antonia* more than a novel "about" the Great Plains frontier. It is a novel that mythologizes that frontier, placing it in the eternal, because ever-recurring, pattern of human history.

Such patterns comprise one of the most important differences between this novel and the biographies discussed earlier. In spite of the linear chronology of the plot, the underlying structure of *My Antonia* is circular. The work begins on the Plains, and it ends there, with both Antonia and Jim affirming their allegiance to their early experiences there. The intervening sections lead them away, but only so that they may return all the more completely. The second book, which takes place in Black Hawk, is their introduction to the wider world. It is a world that holds both rewards and perils for the two young people: the expansion of their interests and experiences, with the danger of losing their connection with their past and thus with their true selves. In the third book, we lose sight of Antonia completely, but what Jim experiences during this period is parallel to what she is going through as well. In Lincoln, Jim grows intellectually and emotionally through his friendship with Gaston Cleric and his affection for Lena. He gains an understanding of his past through these experiences and can go out into the world armed with this self-knowledge. In the meantime, Antonia learns much the same thing through her misplaced love for Larry Donovan. In the last two books, Antonia shows her acceptance of who she is by her treatment of her illegitimate child and the way in which she and husband build their life together.[14] Jim's way back to his past is slower. He first must forgive Antonia for having betrayed the image he had built up around her. Then, as he writes, "life intervened" (*MA*, 327), and it is only twenty years later, after a successful career with the railways and what seems to be a sterile and disappointing marriage (*MA*, ii), that he returns to her and to his own past in the fullest sense. The manuscript Jim writes and presents to the author of the introduction is a personal reappropriation of the past, a subjective view of the wider significance of one life (therefore the possessive of the title, *My Antonia*): "More than any other person we remembered, this girl seemed to mean to us the country, the conditions, the whole adventure of our childhood" (*MA*, ii). Antonia Shimerda becomes representative of the Great Plains frontier experience for Cather's readers as well. And this is so not in spite of, but precisely because of, the fundamentally biased view of Antonia and of (immigrant) frontier life that Jim Burden's narrative communicates.[15]

The four works under discussion prove to be quite unlike each other in spite of superficial similarities in subject matter and technique. The outer fictionlike qualities of *Old Jules* and *Sod and Stubble* (that is, the attributing of undocumented dialogue or thoughts to the main characters) are merely stylistic conventions intended to increase the realism and immediacy of events. In their biographies, Ise and Sandoz depict the reality of the Great Plains frontier as they and their parents experienced it, as a record for the future and as a salute to the endurance and heroism of the early settlers. Their works are essentially chronological, episodic, and linear in structure, as ordinary human life seems to be. Indeed, I would argue that the episodic style of *Old Jules* and *Sod and Stubble* is related to what Albert J. von Frank has identified as one aspect of an American frontier consciousness. This consciousness is in part a reaction to the constant attention to circumstances that a new and often hostile environment demands: "Constant attention to the environment diffuses the unity of the perceiving mind, breaks up impressions, fragments identity, and undermines belief in larger meanings."[16] The resulting fragmentation is mirrored in the surface fragmentation of style. This effect is particularly clear in *Sod and Stubble*, but it is also evident in *Old Jules*. Ise and Sandoz, so close to the frontier experience themselves, would have found it difficult to banish the disjunctive experience of frontier reality from their writing style. This is not so with Cather and Rölvaag, who could distance themselves from their subject. Yet they exhibit the other quality typical of a frontier consciousness, as Frank defines it, the turning toward tradition to provide unity and a larger meaning. We find this in *Giants in the Earth* and *My Antonia*, both in regard to content (Beret's clinging to Old World traditions, for example) and symbolic import (the mythological references in both works). Thus outer differences in style between the biographies and the novels spring from inner, yet related, differences in frontier consciousness that are very much a part of a long American literary tradition.

Similar though the biographies are in their style and structure, they do differ in the narrative stance that their authors take toward their subject. Ise retains the most distance, which helps give his story of the very individual fate of a frontier family a representational significance that it otherwise might not have. Sandoz also seeks to maintain a detached presentation of the facts of her story, but a sense of a personal coming-to-terms with these facts often shows through her narrative. The complex and seemingly contradictory nature of her title character and the often negative experience of frontier life that his nature created for his family cause Sandoz to open to our view not only the devastating physical hardships of the frontier but its psychological and social costs as well. Her work is perhaps the most personal of those discussed here, but it also places her father and his surroundings in the wider historical picture.[17] Yet it does not convey the tragic or elegiac mode found in the novels discussed here. Although both Ise and Sandoz communicate in their texts the extent to which they view the people of whom they write as actors in grand and epic events, they do not attach a symbolic or mythic significance to them. They also display this tendency in regard to their ethnicity. Part of the truth of the lives of Henry and Rosie Ise and of Jules and Mary Sandoz was their general acceptance of their foreign origins. They felt neither crippled by cultural alienation nor exalted by their ties to older European civilization.[18] In writing their accounts of their parents' frontier lives, Ise and Sandoz could not truthfully use their ethnicity in order to symbolize or intensify the alienating aspects of frontier existence. The Ises and the Sandozes attained the American Dream of relative material success that had brought them and many other immigrants to the frontier. The friction between themselves and Anglo-American neighbors is relatively minor and does not inhibit their frontier progress. The costs of pioneering, in terms of physical hardship and threatened breakdown of codes of morality and civilized behavior, are evident in both works. These and similar works of nonfiction can provide a "corrective" to romantic notions about the frontier that may have taken root in American literary and cultural heritage.[19] A Jules Sandoz or a Rosie Ise may help us decide whether the American Dream could be truly fulfilled in the harshness of wilderness life, whether even such materially "successful" pioneers were "diminished in the genuine stuff of life."[20] But the dominant message is conveyed by the parallel resolutions: the price paid by the first settlers bought a decent living for their descendants and a new, civilized society.[21]

Both Rölvaag and Cather use their subject matter in order to communicate more than factual or historical knowledge about the Great Plains frontier. Rölvaag is most interested in the spiritual and cultural dangers of leaving an old society and entering an environment void of the accustomed moral framework. The contrasting structural lines of material progress versus spiritual jeopardy discussed above reveal this interest. His novel was intended first for a Norwegian audience, and this explains to some extent his choice of subject matter, the profusion of factual detail, and the focus on cultural alienation. But his deeper intentions in dealing with this material transcend any national identity. We cannot forget that Per, the heroic frontiersman, dies at the end of the novel, and that his wife is driven by cultural alienation into a narrow religiousness that distorts all her human relationships. The tragic reverse side of attaining the American Dream is central to the novel. Rölvaag was fascinated by and convinced of the cultural and spiritual perils of the westward expansion into the uncivilized void. It is this that makes *Giants in the Earth* one of the great American frontier novels and that makes ethnicity so central to his work.

Cather recognized cultural alienation as a danger on the American frontier, as Mr. Shimerda's fate shows. But she chose to concentrate on the gains brought to that frontier and to any "new" land by the heritages of its immigrants. Her novel is about the continuation of human history and the mutual enrichment of culturally varied individual lives within society. There is very little "information" about the Great Plains frontier in her novel that does not contribute to that theme. As we have seen, the fundamentally circular structure of her novel also reveals her certainty about the interrelatedness of people and events in a meaningful world. Her literary intention is made clear in the narrative perspective she chooses to communicate this sense of personal and communal enrichment. And in spite of our awareness of the subjectivity of Jim Burden's narrative, Antonia and the frontier world she represents for him become for us, too, through Cather's nostalgic lyricism, an "essential aspect of the American experience."[22]

The most striking difference between the novels of Rölvaag and Cather and the works of Ise and Sandoz is the extent to which the former employ various devices to endow their subject matter with a sense of universality and of epic and even mythic significance. Both Rölvaag and Cather refer to mythic models in the shaping of their characters and events, as we have seen. And they both use symbols to enhance and crystallize the significance of people and events. Per's trolls, Beret's immigrant chest, Mr. Shimerda's grave, and the plow silhouetted against the setting sun are images that have no equivalents in the works of Ise and Sandoz. The wider human significance of the story of the Great Plains frontier is indicated in such images. And in these works of fiction, ethnicity becomes central to the depiction of the meaning of the frontier in American cultural history. Ethnicity is deeply connected to long-standing American ideals about the frontier: the social melting pot, and the possibility of material independence and a life of dignity for all. The emphasis on ethnic identity in *Giants in the Earth* and *My Antonia* intensifies the potential for grandeur and for tragic failure inherent in this American Dream of the frontier. For it is fiction's particular province to put such historical material in a timeless context and thus deepen and enrich our understanding of it.

Part 2

Exploring New Territories

Mary Jemison and the Domestication of the American Frontier

Susan Scheckel

On 29 November 1823, James E. Seaver, a retired physician living in Genesee County, New York, spent three days interviewing Mary Jemison, a white woman then in her eighties who had spent much of her life among the American Indians. Captured by the Senecas at age fifteen, she was adopted into the tribe, married two Indian husbands (in succession), and lived at the time of the interview with her family of half-blood children on her own farm situated between the Indian village and the white town. From his introductory comments, it is clear that Seaver believes he is presenting just another typical example of a genre that is by now quite familiar to his readers: the Indian captivity narrative. He places Jemison's narrative in the context of "the stories of Indian cruelties which were common in the new settlements" and hopes that it will, like most captivity narratives, reinforce the values of white civilization, "increas[ing] our love of liberty" and "enlarg[ing] our views of the blessings that are derived from our liberal institutions."[1] But Jemison's narrative, with its sympathetic account of Indian life and her willing accommodation to it, is hardly what Seaver's introduction would lead the reader to expect.

Nevertheless, American readers were ready for the sort of narrative Jemison had to offer. The book was immediately a best-seller at a time when the captivity narrative was, according to Roy Harvey Pearce, far past its height in popularity.[2] As Pearce observes in his classic study of the genre, "It becomes apparent that towards the end of the eighteenth century American readers were not taking the captivity narrative very seriously. Even for a popular genre, it was quite old and quite tired."[3]

Pearce describes three major phases in the development of the Indian captivity genre: the earliest examples were primarily religious documents, presenting the experience of captivity as parallel in many ways to religious conversion as envisioned by the Puritans; in the mid-eighteenth century, especially during the French and Indian wars, the captivity narrative served as a vehicle of propaganda; by the beginning of the nineteenth century, when Indian wars and the Puritan model of religious conversion were no longer pervasive concerns for most Americans, and when the genre was becoming quite formulaic and stylized, captivity narratives were no longer taken seriously as culturally significant or historically accurate documents.

But the Jemison narrative brought something new to this "old" and "tired" genre, something that appealed powerfully to American readers at the dawn of the Jacksonian era and throughout the next century as the book went through twenty-two editions in 100 years. Although Seaver introduces it in quite conventional terms, the narrative is actually quite unconventional—not simply because of Jemison's sympathetic view of the Indians, but, more significantly, because of the unusual structure and resolution of the captivity experience as represented in the narrative.

While it is difficult to speak of a "typical" captivity narrative, most of them do have a general three-part structure. The narrative begins with an act of separation, when the captive is forcibly removed from his or her familiar world. This removal is followed by a "liminal" phase, during which the captive exists between two worlds; having left the security and familiar customs of his or her own culture, the person lives for a time among the Indians, according to *their* customs, yet never fully belonging or locating his or her identity in this world. Finally, the narrative ends with reincorporation or restoration, when the captive returns to his or her own world transformed by the captivity experience. Several critics have discussed ways in which the captivity narrative, with its three-part structure, enacts an archetypal pattern of initiation or rite of passage. Richard Slotkin, in *Regeneration Through Violence*, describes the Indian captivity narrative as "a variation on the great central myth of initiation into a new world and a new life that is at the core of the American experience." In further defining the kind of initiation represented in the captivity narrative, Slotkin focuses on the final step (restoration) that completes the process: "The captive is not initiated into an entirely new way of life; rather he is restored to his old life with newly opened eyes."[4] Critics Alden T. Vaughan and Edward Clarke note the "danger in focusing too intently on the initiation ordeal and overlooking the significance of the much longer and equally profound captivity experience itself." They discuss the meaning of the captivity narrative in relation to Victor Turner's three-stage model of *"rites de passage,"* which, they believe, allows a broader focus on the central, "liminal" stage of captivity.[5] But in each of these approaches, the final resolution and meaning of the captivity experience derives from the captive's reincorporation, since it is this step that completes and gives value to the experience as a process of initiation. The captive's restoration is further emphasized by the fact that, almost by definition, the narrative is told from the perspective of the reincorporated captive, since the captive must return in order to tell his or her story. In fact, the act of communication itself becomes part of the process of reintegration, for it involves an implicit assertion that the captive's experiences in the liminal realm beyond the boundaries of his or her own culture, and the transformations that have resulted from these experiences, are meaningful and valuable to that culture.

The resolution of the Jemison narrative differs in several ways from that of the "typical" captivity narrative. Instead of being reincorporated into the white culture, Mary Jemison remains permanently in what can be compared to the liminal stage of the initiation process, the state of being between two well-defined social positions. Living on the frontier between the Indian village and the white town, Mary Jemison has settled and made herself at home in this liminal realm between white and Indian worlds. Even narratively, Jemison does not enact the reintegration that usually occurs when the captive finally offers an account of her experience to the community she returns to: Jemison does not offer her story to the white community; instead, Seaver goes to her, to solicit and take the account from her.[6] Thus, Mary Jemison's narrative, removed from the frontier realm she still inhabits, enters the white world without her.

But even as it enters the white world, the Jemison narrative, in a sense, carries the frontier with it, for the text itself becomes a sort of frontier—a narrative space upon which two world visions and two narratives meet.[7] It is not strictly Jemison's narrative, since Seaver shapes her oral account into the written text the reader encounters. But neither is it entirely Seaver's narrative, since he must work with the material Jemison provides, which may not always fit neatly into his own vision of her experience. In the preface, Seaver insists that he is simply a faithful recorder of facts: "No circumstance has been intentionally exaggerated by the paintings of fancy, nor by fine flashes of rhetoric; . . . Without the aid of fiction, what was received as a matter of fact, only has been recorded" (*Jemison*, v). At times, however, it is clear that Seaver is not simply reporting the facts as Jemison presents them. At one point, for instance, Seaver feels the need to insert a long account of the wartime exploits of Jemison's husband, Hiakatoo, complete with the customary descriptions of the Indian warrior dashing out the brains of an infant and "thirst[ing] for the blood of innocent, unoffending, defenseless settlers" (*Jemison*, 108). In a footnote, Seaver admits that he had to go to sources other than Mary Jemison for this information, which, to him, seemed crucial to her story. At other points, Seaver does not openly admit that he has shaped Jemison's account, but there are inconsistencies that suggest the presence of two different voices. For example, near the end of the narrative, Jemison is supposedly summarizing the meaning of her captivity experience: "The bare loss of liberty is but a mere trifle when compared with the circumstances that necessarily attend, and are inseparably connected with it. It is the recollection of what we once were, of the friends, the home, the pleasures we have left or lost; the anticipation of misery, the appearance of wretchedness, the anxiety for freedom, the hope of release, the devising of means of escaping, and the vigilance with which we watch our keepers, that constitute the nauseous dregs of the bitter cup of slavery" (*Jemison*, 140). This passage, with its conventional sentiments and phrasing, is hardly remarkable. It might be imagined as appearing in any number of captivity narratives—just about any narrative, in fact, except this one. Mary Jemison, far from anxiously seeking to escape her captors, actually praises her life among the Indians and repeatedly refuses to return to the white society, even when encouraged to do so by members of her adopted tribe.

It becomes clear, then, that we cannot look to the Jemison narrative for a reliable account of how Mary Jemison envisioned herself and her experience. What we can find there, however, is a complex text produced by the interaction of two narrative visions—Jemison's story of her experience and Seaver's notions of what kinds of stories can encompass such experience. Because of the gaps between these two narrative visions, the Jemison narrative achieves a certain openness. Because there is no single author in control, some of the conventions that would ordinarily govern the construction of a coherent narrative are relaxed. For example, the Jemison narrative includes within a single text material that could not easily originate from a single perspective, and presents this material without tightly weaving it into a single logically consistent story line. In its openness, the text embodies narratively some of the conditions that Victor Turner associates with the social condition of liminality. According to Turner, the liminal situation is characterized by a suspension of customary laws and normative social structures; it represents "a free and experimental region of culture, a region where not only new elements, but new combinatory rules may be introduced."[8] I believe that this liminal quality of the narrative contributes to its power, just as Mary Jemison's liminal position, between two worlds and in neither, contributes to her power as a frontier hero.

By representing Mary Jemison comfortably "at home" between two worlds—and by embodying within the text itself a narrative space where different world visions and narrative perspectives meet—this unusual text offers the white culture that appropriates it a way to stabilize and symbolically enter into the frontier realm that Jemison inhabits. Here the frontier is not simply an ever-shifting physical or conceptual boundary between opposed or conflicting worlds; nor is it simply a threshold (or "limina") to be crossed in the process of initiation into a new position in the old social order. Rather, it is a space to be inhabited: a space in which a variety of attitudes and experiences arising from the contact between white and Indian, between progress and wilderness, can be examined, tested, and played with; a space in which to explore new ways of imagining and dealing with the issues and challenges associated with the American frontier during the Jacksonian era.

One of the central challenges associated with the frontier at this time was the "Indian question": what to do about the Indian tribes east of the Mississippi River who stood in the way of America's ever-more-rapid westward expansion. With the Louisiana Purchase of 1803, Jefferson had hoped the problem might be solved by persuading the Indians in the East to exchange their holdings for unoccupied land west of the Mississippi. Jefferson, and others, further justified removal on philanthropic grounds, arguing that the Indians needed to be isolated from the vices of white civilization while they gradually acquired its virtues. Thus, removal was presented as a temporary stage of protective isolation to be followed by the eventual integration of fully "civilized" Indians into American society.

There were, however, serious contradictions undermining this vision of Indian removal. As Roy Harvey Pearce points out, in *The Savages of America*, the removal policy was actually premised upon an idea of "savagism" that precluded the possibility of ever "civilizing" the Indian. Defined as the antithesis of the "civilized," the "savage" belonged to a completely different order, with its own set of virtues and vices, and thus could never be incorporated into the "civilized" order. Removal or destruction were the only logical consequences of such a vision.[9]

The contradictions in American Indian policy were becoming increasingly apparent by the mid-1820s, when the Jemison narrative was published—especially in states such as Georgia, where the Cherokees had succeeded in becoming quite "civilized" where they were and refused to exchange their prosperous farms for vacant lands west of the Mississippi. At the same time, Georgians were becoming impatient for the federal government to fulfill a promise it had made to Georgia in 1802 to extinguish Indian title within the state as soon as possible. But this promise conflicted directly with promises the federal government had made to the Cherokees as part of treaty agreements.

As tensions steadily mounted, it became increasingly difficult to avoid facing such contradictions in American Indian policy and to preserve the nation's moral self-image. According to Philip Fisher, one response to experience that is contradictory, or difficult to accept, is to stabilize that experience within the familiar narrative structures of popular literary forms, in which predictable, often formulaic, narrative conventions help to make complex issues seem simple and new experience seem familiar.[10]

The Jemison narrative, published in 1824, as the tensions that finally led to the Removal Bill of 1830 steadily mounted, offered readers the very familiar framework of an "old" and "tired" genre within which to contain and stabilize the complex and contradictory experience underlying the "Indian question." Although, no doubt, it is not the story line Jemison herself would apply to her experience, it is possible to see in the narrative a reassuringly positive and simplified account of Indian-white relations and Indian removal. Because Seaver and subsequent generations of editors commented extensively upon the Jemison narrative, we have a detailed record of how one set of readers responded to the narrative. These responses are especially important because they became part of the framework through which other readers would approach the text. Through a careful examination of this extensive editorial apparatus, we can begin to understand how readers could find (or create) in the figure of Mary Jemison a frontier hero embodying American values and serving American goals.

Crossing the Line: Outlaw or Hero?

In many ways, Mary Jemison seems an unlikely candidate for a heroic role as harbinger of American values, in spite of Seaver's insistence that the narrative will "enlarge [the white readers'] views of the blessings that are derived from our liberal institutions" (*Jemison*, vi). One might more readily expect the Jemison narrative to be somewhat unsettling for its white audience, since it seems to reinforce some of the deepest cultural fears represented by the captivity experience. Far from affirming the superiority of the white culture, Jemison enjoys her life among the Indians and chooses to remain with them rather than returning to the "blessings" of white civilization. Furthermore, she consummates her alliance with the Indians through marriage, thus permanently crossing the physical boundary between races.

Anxiety regarding sexual violation of women captives was pervasive throughout the history of the captivity narrative. Although there was no ethnological evidence that northeastern Indians raped women prisoners, popular writing and art often suggested that a large part of the perceived threat to women captives was sexual. Female authors of captivity narratives often felt a need to defend their sexual conduct to avoid suspicions that might prevent their full reacceptance into the white society they returned to (Vaughan and Clarke, 14). Writing in 1872, Col. Sheridan reveals that fears concerning the sexual violation of female captives persisted far into the nineteenth century. Supposing these women would have been raped by their Indian captors, an event he describes as "a fate worse than death," he suggests that it would be better for the women and their families if they were never recovered, preferably perishing by murder, suicide, or the stray bullet of a would-be rescuer.[11]

Mary Jemison not only violates racial boundaries but even praises her Indian husbands. This aspect of her story might add to her interest for readers as an outlaw figure who ventures into forbidden territory and enjoys personal freedoms beyond those generally available or permissible according to mainstream social conventions.[12] But how, then, do we explain Seaver's unambiguously positive portrait of Mary Jemison as a model of conventional virtue and heroism? The editor of the twenty-first edition articulates the message conveyed in the first edition: central to Jemison's "elevated character" and heroism is the fact that "amidst the hardening surroundings of barbaric life, she preserved the sensibilities of a white woman" (*Jemison*, h).

In the introduction to the first edition, Seaver strongly emphasizes qualities that identify Jemison with the white world and its values. He notes that she speaks English well (with a slight Irish accent)[13] and that "her complexion is very white for a woman of her age" (*Jemison*, x). He makes a point to mention details that would identify her as a properly feminine and sentimental woman: "Her passions are easily excited. At a number of periods in her narration, tears trickled down her grief worn cheek, and at the same time a sigh would stop her utterance" (*Jemison*, xi). When she refuses to give him the information he desires regarding the wartime "atrocities" of her warrior husband, Seaver makes up his own explanation for her reticence, in keeping with the delicate character he has assigned to her: "The thoughts of his deeds probably chilled her old heart, and made her dread to rehearse them" (*Jemison*, xiv). Seaver also identifies her with American values, such as industry (*Jemison*, xi), and he praises her hospitality and charity (described in very Christian terms):

> Although her bosom companion was an ancient Indian warrior, and notwithstanding her children and associates were all Indians, yet it was found she possessed an uncommon share of hospitality. . . . Her house was the stranger's home; from her table the hungry were refreshed;— she made the naked as comfortable as her means would admit of; . . . she became celebrated as the friend of the distressed. She was the protectress of the homeless fugitive, and made welcome the weary wanderer. Many still live to commemorate her benevolence towards them, when prisoners during the war, and to ascribe their deliverance to the mediation of "The White Woman" (*Jemison*, viii–ix).

In this description of Jemison's character, Seaver sets up a rhetorical opposition between her hospitality and her association with Indian culture. This opposition is especially striking since hospitality was, during the nineteenth century, among the traits commonly identified with "the Indian character." Throughout this passage, Seaver's repeated use of qualifying terms betrays his difficulty in reconciling the white traits and values he ascribes to her and the Indian world with which she is associated. A few pages later, he points out traits that identify Jemison even more explicitly with the Indians: "Her habits are those of the Indians— she sleeps on skins without a bedstead, sits upon the floor or on a bench, and holds her victuals on her lap, in her hands. Her ideas of religion, correspond in every respect with those of the great mass of the Senecas" (*Jemison*, xiv). Seaver does not attempt to reconcile these conflicting elements in Jemison's character; nor does he establish a clear relationship between them, with one set of traits in full authority over the other. Instead, he simply suggests the conflict and leaves the two elements juxtaposed, combined but not blended.

In her rather equivocal cultural identity, Mary Jemison resembles James Fenimore Cooper's Natty Bumppo, the frontier hero with the habits of an Indian and the values of a white man, who is enlarged rather than contaminated by his contact with the Indian culture.[14] While Natty exhibits many Christian virtues, he is not a practicing Christian; but neither does he embrace the Indians' religion. While he has friends among the Indians, his allegiance to his own race remains pure: he never fights as an Indian (taking scalps) or with the Indians against white Americans. Natty participates in both Indian and white worlds, embodying elements of each, without belonging entirely in either one. Such a position, located in two worlds and in neither, gives him an unusual power to negotiate between Indian and white worlds without ever being defined as a threat to white culture—either through his absolute opposition to it or by bringing into white society unacceptable attitudes or experiences produced by his close association with the Indians and the wilderness.

Likewise, much of Jemison's power, and the power of the narrative, arise from her simultaneous identification with the opposing perspectives and sets of values associated with white and Indian worlds. For example, she is able to act as mediator interceding among the Indians on behalf of white prisoners because of her double identification: while her racial identity underlies her compassion for the white prisoners, her present connection to the Indians gives her influence among the Indian captors. Jemison mediates between white and Indian worlds in another way by interpreting the Indian world to her white audience—mapping the geographic world the Indians inhabit, describing daily life among them, explaining Indian rituals and customs—providing knowledge accessible only to one who lives as part of the Indian world from a perspective that white readers can trust and identify with: the perspective of a white woman adhering to "civilized" values. Seaver's inclusion of an appendix, almost one-third the length of the narrative itself, containing additional description of Indian life and customs, based on Jemison's testimony, suggests that he expects such information to be a strong focus of readers' interest.[15]

While Jemison's identification with white and Indian worlds is important, her power as frontier hero, like Natty Bumppo's, derives equally from the fact that she does not fully belong in either world. If Jemison were seen as locating her loyalties and identity entirely in the Indian world, she would be considered either an outlaw, whose transferance of racial allegiance would make her opposed to white values, or an outsider, whose severence of all ties to the white world would make her irrelevant to it. On the other hand, if she actually tried to reintegrate into white society, her experiences among the Indians—especially her violation of racial and sexual boundaries—well might cause some difficulties.

To understand better the significance of Jemison's position between worlds and in neither, it may be useful to compare her story with that of John Dunn Hunter, whose experiences are in many ways similar to Jemison's, but whose position in relation to white and Indian worlds is quite different. Like Mary Jemison, Hunter was captured as a child and, after brief stays with the Kickapoo, Pawnee, and Kansas tribes, was adopted by an Osage family, with whom he lived happily until a white–Indian conflict disrupted his life among them. At age nineteen, after learning of his tribe's plan to attack a local trader, Hunter decided to warn the trader and thus save him. Unable to face the Indians he had betrayed, Hunter returned (reluctantly) to white society. In 1823, just one year before the Jemison narrative, he published the story of his adventures. Like Jemison, Hunter gives a sympathetic account of Indian life, rich with ethnographic information. But unlike Jemison, Hunter, while living among the Indians, located his identity more firmly in the Indian world: whereas Jemison kept alive her memory of and fondness for her former life, even naming her children after her white family members, Hunter, who was younger when captured, remembered none of the details of his former life in the white world. Hunter's position after leaving the Indian world again differed significantly from Jemison's: whereas Jemison left the Indian village to establish a life for herself in an entirely new position between Indian and white worlds, Hunter returned to the center of white society, where his Indian loyalties became dangerous.

Upon his return, Hunter went to England, where he and his book attracted much attention and became the center of ongoing debates regarding American Indian policy, which encompassed deep national rivalries. In this position of prominence, Hunter's narrative, expressing condemnation of American treatment of the Indians, became a threat to America's vision of itself and its values—and, perhaps even more importantly, a threat to America's national image abroad. In defense, America rallied its strongest forces to crush Hunter. Lewis Cass and Thomas McKenney, two of America's most respected and influential authorities on Indian affairs, published scathing attacks discrediting Hunter and his narrative while English writers rallied to his defense.[16] As Richard Drinnon notes in his book-length study of Hunter, the narrative became the battleground between two nations, with the American national character and pride at stake.[17] By assuming a position opposing America's national interest, Hunter, in effect, was fighting on the side of the enemy—one of the clearest and most abhorrent marks of "Indianization"—making him an outlaw rather than a hero of the American frontier.

Even more threatening than his reentry into white civilization carrying his Indian loyalties with him was Hunter's attempt to bring the Indians themselves into white society. Hunter was not content simply to denounce America's past treatment of the Indians; he proceeded to devise a new plan for the future that would integrate the Indians genuinely and permanently into American social and economic reality. After studying Robert Owen's model factory villages in England, Hunter developed a practical plan for saving and civilizing the Indians by building utopian farming communities on Indian land, making the Indians "red yeoman who would turn Western America into a 'blooming garden'" (Drinnon, 40). But white Americans did not want such an alternative economic system nor a new line of American yeomen within its boundaries; it wanted the riches of the American garden for itself, not the Indians. Hunter's efforts to test his new model Indian community failed when he arrived in Arkansas too late, after the Quapaw Indians there had just ceded their land to the United States government. He died in Mexico still trying to find a place for the Quapaws and Cherokees to settle, his narrative discredited and largely forgotten.

While Hunter's attempt to bring his Indian loyalties (and the Indians themselves) into American society made him a threat to white society, Mary Jemison's position, frozen between worlds, contributes to her heroic role. By identifying with Jemison, Americans could share in her sympathetic response to the Indians, but she offers no vehicle—practical or symbolic—to incorporate the Indian into American society, and even claims, on the contrary, that all efforts to civilize the Indians are futile. Jemison's words, in fact, echo common justifications for Indian removal: "The attempts which have been made to civilize and christianize them by the white people, ha[ve] constantly made them worse and worse;

increased their vices, and robbed them of many of their virtues; and will ultimately produce their extermination" (*Jemison*, 48). The Indians remain, in the vision presented in the Jemison narrative, safely located, like Jemison herself, between worlds, belonging in neither.

At Home on the Frontier

In addition to the power that Jemison acquires by virtue of her location in two worlds, her ability to be at home in such a position contributes another dimension to her role as frontier hero.[18] In a figurative sense, the fact that she is at home amid diverse elements, bringing together in one coherent figure opposing perspectives and sources of identity, stabilizes those elements in the text. In more literal terms, the fact that Jemison makes herself at home on the frontier in the capacity of a mother, struggling to find a home for her family, lends to her character certain powers (and stabilizing limitations) implicitly associated with mothers in the context of American domestic ideology during the nineteenth century.

Jemison's story is presented in a way that emphasizes the significance of home and domestic values. Providing a wealth of biographical detail unusual in the genre, the narrative begins with a lengthy account of Jemison's family history and childhood home. The frontier home of Jemison's youth is described in terms that reflect popular nineteenth-century notions of the domestic ideal and call forth the image of the home as center of earthly bliss: "Health presided on every countenance, and vigor and strength characterized every exertion. Our mansion was a little paradise" (*Jemison*, 20). When the Indians intrude upon this "little paradise," destroy the happy family, and carry Mary Jemison into the wilderness, we might expect the experience of captivity to be described as a kind of hell (as the Puritans represented it) in contradistinction to the "paradise" she left behind. What we find in the Jemison narrative, however, is not a vision of unremitting chaos and loss, but rather the discovery of a new social order, the establishment of a new home and family, leading to a new vision of paradise within the wilderness.

After her adoption into the tribe, Jemison becomes part of a new social order and begins to feel at home among the Senecas. Immediately after her account of the adoption ceremony, Jemison goes on to describe her situation in terms of her new domestic role: "Being now settled and provided with a home, I was employed in nursing the children, and in doing light work about the house" (*Jemison*, 39). Soon Jemison takes an Indian husband, admitting, "Strange as it may seem, I loved him!" (*Jemison*, 44). By her fourth year with the Senecas, she seems to locate her social and personal identity among them: "With them was my home;

my family was there and there I had many friends to whom I was warmly attached in consideration of the favors, friendship and affection with which they had uniformly treated me from the time of my adoption" (*Jemison*, 46). Jemison's new home in the wilderness, like her former home upon the frontier, is described as a sort of paradise: "No people can live more happily than the Indians in times of peace. . . . Their lives were a continual round of pleasures. Their wants were few, and easily satisfied; and their cares were only for today. . . . If peace ever dwelt with men, it was in former times, in the recesses from war, amongst what are now termed barbarians" (*Jemison*, 64). But this paradise, too, is disrupted—this time by white civilization. When American soldiers, during the Revolutionary War, destroy her tribe's winter provisions, Mary Jemison "immediately resolve[s] to take my children and look out for myself" (*Jemison*, 74). Thus she leaves the wilderness behind to find yet another home for herself and her family.

When Jemison arrives at Gardow Flats, she enters the frontier: the land has already been cleared and two runaway slaves are farming there.[19] She comes to the frontier as a mother motivated by the need to protect her children from starvation, and she succeeds in building, with her own hands, a new home there. The remainder of the narrative (almost seventy pages) focuses on Jemison's struggle to raise a family on the frontier. Her Indian husband, who lives with her for much of this time, is hardly mentioned; the domestic drama centers upon mother and children. At the end of the book she is pictured as a matriarch sitting surrounded by her children, a picture which, as Richard Slotkin notes, calls to mind popular visions of Daniel Boone as patriarchal hero of the frontier (Slotkin 1973, 450).

There is, however, a significant difference between Boone and Jemison: whereas Boone was father to a new line of American frontiersmen, Jemison's children are half-blood Indians.[20] It is precisely this fact that makes Mary Jemison an important cultural hero for Jacksonian America, for it lets readers envision within her story one of the central issues facing Americans in the nineteenth century: how to locate the American Indians in white America's vision of itself—its past, its future, and its present national identity, an identity premised upon westward expansion.

Mary Jemison and the Domestication of the American Indians

During the Jacksonian era, the disappearance of the Indians was considered by most Americans to be a foregone conclusion, a mere footnote in America's already "manifest" destiny. According to Brian Dippie, the theory of "the vanishing American" assumed its full-blown stature and general acceptance as natural law during the second decade of the nineteenth century.[21] After the War of 1812, with the American claim to virtually all land east of the Mississippi secured, fears of a significant Indian threat to American sovereignty diminished and the Indians were no longer seen as a determining factor in America's destiny. In addition, the Indians' recent alliance with the British was seen as an act of treachery and a sign of the Indians' innate depravity and unworthiness of survival. Even missionaries, who had been among the most adamant in their determination to "save" the Indians began to share the widespread conviction that their disappearance was inevitable. As one anonymous religious writer commented in 1830, "There seems to be a deep rooted superstition . . . that the Indians are really *destined*, as if there were some fatality in the case, never to be christianized, but gradually to decay till they become totally extinct" (Dippie, 10).

Once Indians were no longer seen as a threat, they increasingly came to be viewed as powerless and like children. In a report to the Speaker of the House in 1818, John C. Calhoun, Secretary of War, noted that "helplessness has succeeded independence" among the tribes on the western frontier. "The time seems to have arrived," he continued, "when our policy toward them should undergo an important change. They neither are, in fact, nor ought to be, considered as independent nations. Our views of their interest, and not their own, ought to govern them" (Dippie, 8). Such thinking formed the basis of Jacksonian Indian policy, according to which the American government assumed the role of the "Great White Father," firmly insisting that his Indian "children" remove to lands west of the Mississippi "for their own good."

As Michael Rogin argues, in *Fathers and Children: Andrew Jackson and the Subjugation of the American Indian*, this paternal model of Indian–white relations tends to include an element of violent, forceful domination, which arises in part from the psychological dynamics of the relationship between father, child, and mother. Francis Parkman, writing in 1851, reflects a popular vision of the Indian as a child of nature, who resists growing up (i.e., becoming "civilized") because of an excessive attachment to his mother: the Indian is the "irreclaimable son of the wilderness, the child who will not be weaned from the breast of his rugged mother."[22] White civilization, imagined as "The Great White Father," would be completely excluded from and threatened by this intense mother-child relationship. From the perspective of the excluded father, then, efforts to "civilize" the Indian would require intervening with paternal authority forcibly to break the Indian's excessive, even unnatural, ties to his mother (Rogin 1975, 208). This is precisely the course that Jacksonian policy followed with the forcible removal of the Indian from his land.

In Mary Jemison's story of a white mother's efforts to raise her

Indian children, the American public could see an alternative model for its attempts to "civilize" its Indian "children." That a mother should be represented as a civilizing force is quite consistent with nineteenth-century conceptions of women's role in society. The influence of women—especially mothers—was envisioned at the core of American civilization, since it was the mother's responsibility to produce good citizens by instilling American values in her children. As Nancy Cott explains in *The Bonds of Womanhood*, "The purpose of women's vocation was to stabilize society by generating and regenerating moral character."[23] It would not be a far step for nineteenth-century readers to envision a white woman performing a similar role within Indian society. By regenerating Indian character in accordance with white values, Mary Jemison, the white mother, could be imagined as civilizing the Indians—conceivably without the element of violent domination implied in the paternal model and characterizing actual Indian–white relations under the influence of Andrew Jackson. In the maternal model, white civilization represented as a mother could be envisioned stepping in gently to replace the Indians' wilderness mother. Americans could then hope that the Indians would willingly accept their new mother and learn from her to act in accordance with the values and goals of white civilization.

The 1842 editor shows that this hope is central to his vision of the significance of the narrative when he adds material tracing the civilizing influence of Jemison upon her Indian descendants. He notes that "several of the grandchildren of Mrs. Jemison, now living, are highly respected in their nation. . . . They have acquired the use of the English language sufficiently to speak it fluently, and have adopted the dress, habits, and manners of civilized society" (*Jemison*, 197). The editor goes on to express his hopes that the descendants of Mary Jemison "will, undoubtedly, ere long, take their departure from the land of their fathers, and assume important positions in legislative and judicial stations in the new Indian territory west of the Mississippi" (*Jemison*, 197). Discussing removal in terms of a shift in filial loyalty—from the lands of their Indian fathers to the civilized values and policies associated (by the editor) with their white mother—tends to smooth over the radical violation of the Indians and their way of life implicit in the act of removal.

The 1877 editor makes even more explicit Jemison's maternal role as civilizing force by adding a long chapter describing her grandson Buffalo Tom as the ideal of the civilized Indian. He is honest, industrious, thrifty, and the owner of a prosperous farm and a home that "differs little from the ordinary abode of well-to-do farmers in the New England or Middle States" (*Jemison*, 204). Tom's white grandmother is imagined as the direct source of his civilized virtues: "In fact, it would seem that the virtues which adorned the character of the grandmother, after lying dormant for one generation, had blossomed into rarer beauty in the next" (*Jemison*, 204). Like his grandmother, Tom becomes famous for his hospitality. While Mary Jemison provided food and shelter for whites venturing into the wilderness, her grandson provides hospitality to the wave of westward emigrants who flow steadily past his reservation home. According to the editor, his home becomes "a vision of beauty to the wayward pilgrims passing by, on whom it beamed a smile of welcome" (*Jemison*, 203). Just as the 1842 editor ends his account of Jemison's civilizing influence with an appealingly positive vision of Indian removal, the 1877 editor ends with a similarly positive vision of Indians in the context of American westward expansion. The image of the Indian at home on the reservation, embracing the values of white civilization, offering a smile of welcome to the settlers as they move further west to claim what was recently Indian land, would most likely have been quite appealing to a nation that spent most of the nineteenth century seeking to "civilize" and find an appropriate new home for the dispossessed Indians.

Such ideal visions of Mary Jemison as white mother leading her Indian children on the path to civilization are sadly inconsistent with the historical reality of Indian–white relations during the nineteenth century. There are clues within the editors' optimistic accounts that betray the truer, darker reality: the fact that the editor consistently refers to Jemison's descendants simply as "Indians" and locates their sphere of influence entirely within the "Indian territory west of the Mississippi," and the fact that the success of the civilizing process seems to be measured by the Indian's acceptance of the need for their physical exclusion from white society, suggest that the influence of the white mother is not meant to carry the Indian toward genuine integration; the final step in America's benevolent plan to "civilize" the Indians is never meant to occur.

While the maternal model might be less disturbing to whites than the paternal, both visions entail the destruction of the Indians, for both define the Indian as a child, and the logic of natural law insists that childhood is a temporary stage, which every being who continues to live and grow must leave behind. But to grow up, according to the symbolic system whites employed, is to become white. As Michael Rogin concludes in his study of Jacksonian Indian policy, "In the white scheme, civilization meant, no less than death, the disappearance of the Indians. They could not remain Indians and grow up."[24]

Thus the Indians were frozen in a liminal position: forever in the *process* of being civilized; forever children who could never grow up; forever ghosts hovering between the past, where Americans were so anxious to embrace them as relics of the national history they longed for, and the present, where they could be located neither entirely within nor outside of American society. Americans would not allow Indians an independent identity—neither as a threatening force opposing American destiny, nor simply as separate sovereign nations following their own destinies within the boundaries of the American nation. At the same time, Americans would not grant Indians full membership in American society, with the rights of American citizens. Judge Marshall's decision, in 1831, regarding the legal status of the Cherokees, reflects the Indians' liminal position: Marshall ruled that the Cherokees should be considered neither as subjects of the United States nor as a separate sovereign nation, but as a "domestic dependent nation."[25] The exact definition—and legal rights—of such an entity remained vague. The policy of Indian removal translated into historical fact the implicit meaning of the Indians' position in Jacksonian America. In 1824, Secretary of War John C. Calhoun developed his plan (endorsed a year later) for a "permanent Indian frontier." Forcibly removing the Indians to this permanent frontier disrupted the integrity of native cultures by breaking ties to ancestral lands, altering means of livelihood, and subjecting the Indians to white laws and policies. At the same time, it kept the Indians "permanently" on the margin, or "frontier," of American society.

Like the frontier upon which Mary Jemison resides, the "permanent Indian frontier" is not a line nor a threshold meant to be crossed, but a space to be inhabited; it is a transitional, liminal phase in a rite of passage (from savage to civilized condition) never meant to be completed. The story of Mary Jemison struggling to raise her Indian children on her farm midway between Indian village and white town symbolically locates the Indians precisely where Americans wanted them to remain: suspended between two worlds, belonging in neither. Thus, Jemison achieves her full stature as frontier hero through her capacity to encompass symbolically, within a stabilizing framework, issues of central importance to American culture.

Representing the transformation of the Indians from members of independent social orders to disempowered, liminal figures in American society in terms of a frontier mother's struggle to find a home for herself and her children confers a sense of comfortable familiarity upon what is actually a complex and potentially disturbing process of change. Similarly, the narrative conventions of the Indian captivity genre stabilize this process of change by making what is radically new seem, instead, like a restoration of the old order. Like the traditional captivity narrative, the Jemison narrative ends with a vision of the family united around the captive, who is, once again, at home. On the surface, it seems that the conventional resolution through restoration has occurred. But here the social unit that was disrupted by the captivity experience has not been restored. Instead, the original family has been replaced by an entirely new kind of family configuration—a configuration that now includes the American Indians. The familiarity of the conventional closing scene of the united family would make the reader less likely to question exactly what kind of family configuration this is or to examine very carefully the true nature of the Indians' new position in the American family. Thus, those elements of the new vision that might be disturbing easily could be overlooked.

Like the fictional frontier hero Natty Bumppo, who moves ever farther west, carrying with him the very civilization he seeks to escape, Mary Jemison finally falls victim to her own heroic mission. As a white woman, Jemison can be embraced by white readers as a hero carrying the values of white civilization into the liminal realm she inhabits. But just as America can embrace Indians only by pushing them away—into the past, onto the "Indian frontier"—Mary Jemison must maintain a certain distance from white civilization to remain its hero. Thus she is undermined by the very forces of civilization she symbolically serves. As the 1842 editor informs the reader, when the advance of white settlers leads the Senecas to sell their land and move to the Buffalo Creek Reservation in 1825, Mary Jemison finds herself "surrounded by whites in every direction" (*Jemison*, 194). Again Mary Jemison is made captive—this time by white civilization. In 1831, she finally abandons the middle ground between the white town and the Indian village, upon which she had built her frontier home and spent most of her life, to find yet another home among her "kindred and friends" on the reservation. Ironically, the final act of this frontier hero, who offered Jacksonian Americans a way to imagine a positive vision of Indian removal, is to enact her own removal.

Catharine Maria Sedgwick's *Hope Leslie*: Radical Frontier Romance

Carol J. Singley

Hope Leslie, published in 1827, was Catharine Maria Sedgwick's third and most successful novel. A historical romance set in the early colonial period, it centers on the adventures of a spirited, independent young woman, Hope Leslie, who energetically resists traditional conventions imposed by her Puritan world, yet who ends the novel in the most typical of ways, married to the young colonial hero, Everell Fletcher. Like many American novels of its time, *Hope Leslie* has a convoluted, somewhat contrived plot, with many doubling structures, cliff-hanging chapter endings, and narratorial intrusions. The novel primarily focuses on three issues: the friendship, romance, and eventual marriage of Hope to her foster brother and childhood friend, Everell Fletcher; a rigid and intolerant Puritan system, intent on order and suppression of women and Indians; and the complex relationship of settlers, land, and Native American culture, represented chiefly through Magawisca, the young Pequod woman who risks her life to save Everell's and who forms an indissoluble bond of friendship with Hope.

As historical romance, *Hope Leslie* combines mythic aspects of the American frontier, a fictional marriage plot, and historical accuracy. Several events in the novel—the Pequod attack on the Fletcher family, Magawisca's rescue of Everell, the villainy of Tory sympathizer Sir Philip Gardiner—are based on documented historical data that Sedgwick culled from her reading,[1] but the novel is primarily fiction, intended, as Sedgwick says in her preface to *Hope Leslie*, to "illustrate not the history, but the character of the times" (*HL*, 5). The novel has from the very beginning been compared with the frontier romances of James Fenimore

Cooper. Sedgwick's contemporary, Sarah Hale, called *Hope Leslie* Sedgwick's "most popular tale; and indeed, no other novel written by an American, except, perhaps the early work of Cooper, ever met with such success" (quoted in Foster, 95). Reflecting the biases of the day, one reviewer noted that Sedgwick "had fallen into the error, so apparent in the works of Cooper . . . that have anything to do with Indians" (*HL*, x), but most applauded Sedgwick's depiction of American Indians, some granting that Sedgwick's novel contained "pictures of savage life more truthful than that of Cooper" (quoted in Foster, 95). Transcendentalist Margaret Fuller, noting Cooper's faults, also praised his fiction for its "redemption from oblivion of our forest-scenery, and the noble romance of the hunter-pioneer's life," and in her next paragraph gave Sedgwick— the only American woman novelist she ever cited by name—tempered praise for writing "with skill and feeling, scenes and personages from the revolutionary time." Sedgwick's work, Fuller wrote, "has permanent value."[2] Alexander Cowie, indicating the direction that critical opinion of Sedgwick would assume by the end of the nineteenth century, compared the fiction of the two writers, implying that Sedgwick "modestly" and wisely did not try to compete with Cooper.[3]

Despite Sedgwick's extraordinary popularity, by the end of the nineteenth-century she was practically unread, excluded from the anthologies that canonized Cooper and formed the literary myths of Adam in the New World—the "melodramas of beset manhood," as Nina Baym has called them.[4] We have little trouble recognizing this process of marginalization. At one time thought to be *the* American literary form, the historical romance gave way to the more imaginative, abstract romances of Cooper, Hawthorne, Melville, and other male writers. Men's narratives assumed the status of the universal while the domestic novel became associated with the particularized, narrow interests of "scribbling women." By 1936 Van Wyck Brooks could write of Sedgwick, "No one could have supposed that her work would live."[5]

But live it has. Newly reprinted and accessible to a new generation of readers, *Hope Leslie* stands ready to take its place in the American literary tradition. I argue here that Sedgwick deserves as prominent a place in an American canon as Cooper, not only for the comparable literary value of her fiction—after all, the same "threadbare formulas" and assortment of escapes, rescues, and pursuits that Robert Spiller cites in Cooper's fiction are no more egregious in Sedgwick's novel,[6] and, furthermore, Sedgwick's prose is often cleaner and clearer in expression than Cooper's (Foster, 94)—but for the alternative vision of the American woman, American culture, and the relationship to nature that she provides. While following romantic conventions, Sedgwick in fact undercuts many of the assumptions upon which the romance is organized. Also, while apparently obeying the moral and literary dictum that literature teach by adhering to the facts of history and by depicting authentic characters and events—Gov. and Margaret Winthrop, the Reverend John Eliot, the Pequod Chief Mononotto, for example—Sedgwick provides an alternative literary history, one that exposes injustice against women, Native Americans, and the land. Finally, while Cooper works in the realm of the abstract, indulging the masculine fantasy of escape into some past golden age or into timelessness,[7] Sedgwick engages both the social and the natural realms, suggesting a transcendental ideal achievable in society as well as nature.

Critics of American literature have persistently favored a mythology that David Levin has described as "a movement from the 'artificial' toward the 'natural.' "[8] This practice celebrates the individual white man either alone in nature—whether he be Natty Bumppo, Ishmael, Thoreau, or Huck Finn—or in union with a same-sexed other.[9] For example, writing about the second of Cooper's *The Leatherstocking Tales, The Last of the Mohicans*—the novel in which the hero, Natty Bumppo supposedly "matures"—D. H. Lawrence is exuberant: "In his immortal friendship of Chingachgook and Natty Bumppo, Cooper dreamed the nucleus of a new society . . . A stark stripped human relationship of two men, deeper than the deeps of sex. Deeper than property, deeper than fatherhood, deeper than marriage, deeper than Love."[10] With its "wish-fulfillment vision" (Lawrence, 73) and yearning for escape, the male-defined mainstream American romance has been constructed around impossibility. Sedgwick shows us the damage that results from insistence on this impossibility: the very fabric of society and nature itself is jeopardized. Order turns to confusion; America's promise is unfulfilled.

Because Sedgwick utilizes the conservative form of the romance—the so-called "woman's novel"—readers have generally read her fiction as reinforcing the conventional nineteenth-century notions that woman's fulfillment is found in the domestic sphere[11] and as validating the notion of the progress of history (Bell). Only recently has attention been given to the deeply critical qualities of Sedgwick's novel. Sandra Zagarell, for example, reads Sedgwick's treatment of women and Indians as two sides of the same repressive Puritan coin, noting not only Sedgwick's domesticity but her concern "with the foundations and organization of public life."[12] Contrary to critical consensus, *Hope Leslie* is not "an extraordinary conventional novel" (Bell, 213–14), nor is its comic marriage plot, as Frye explains, one "that brings hero and heroine together [and] causes a new society to crystallize around the hero."[13] Despite the conservative requirements of its genre, *Hope Leslie* exhibits signs of its own unraveling, as if to suggest the unworkability of its own romantic conventions. The novel replicates the chaos and contradiction inherent in the Puritan conception of its "errand in the wilderness," addressing problems that fall outside the accepted sphere of historical romance. It also posits a heroine who resists what Leslie Rabine calls the "totalizing structure" of romantic narrative, and who struggles, valiantly and sometimes successfully, to sustain herself as an autonomous subject rather than become absorbed into the male quest for identity and mythic unity with himself.[14]

On some levels, Catharine Maria Sedgwick and James Fenimore Cooper have much in common. Both choose fictional contexts to express concern over the rapid, careless encroachment of civilization on the wilderness and the extinction of the Native Americans. Both also depart from their privileged, Federalist backgrounds to advocate egalitarian notions of democracy. We see important differences, however, when comparing *Hope Leslie* with a Leatherstocking novel written just one year earlier, during a period when the Jackson Indian Removal Policy had effectively cleared the eastern United States of Native American presence. *The Last of the Mohicans*, published in 1826 and set in 1740, is only tangentially colonial in that it depicts a chapter from the nine-year French and Indian War. In contrast, *Hope Leslie* focuses specifically on a nine-year colonial period from 1636 to 1645 and, as Mary Kelley notes in her introduction, explores "the roots of American moral character" (*HL*, xiii). Cooper's characters seldom leave the forest or evince concern with the political, economic, or social aspects of the law; Sedgwick's characters directly confront Puritan social, religious, and legal systems, finding in them the basis for discord and injustice. In Cooper's novels, the American hero can thrive only outside the constraints of civilization. Sedgwick addresses questions both of culture *and* nature, criticizing the "Law" of the Founding Fathers that enforces policies of actual repression and thereby fosters patterns of imaginative escape.[15]

If the character of Hope Leslie can be read as the "spirit of American history" (Bell, 221), it is history with a revisionary spirit. Hope's adventurous and generous nature contrasts with the repression and self-absorption of the Puritans; her many "doubles" in the novel challenge dichotomous views of womanhood and warn of the fragmented nature of the American psyche, split in such ways that fusion of the individual, nature, and society is impossible.

The force of Sedgwick's critique is suggested by her biography as well as by her fiction published before *Hope Leslie*. "The country is condemned to the ministration of inferior men," she wrote in a letter to her brother Robert in 1814.[16] In 1821, Sedgwick changed her membership from the Calvinist to the Unitarian church. Her first novel, *A New England Tale* (1822), is a blatant attack on Puritan hypocrisy; after venturing into a novel of manners with *Redwood* (1824), she returns to a critique of Puritanism with *Hope Leslie*, this time linking the present-day concerns about American expansion to the original project of the Puritan founders. Feeding the nation's appetite for historical fiction, *Hope Leslie* became an instant success. But it is by no means a book of reconciliation or progress. Below its seemingly accepting surface are deep fissures that throw into question not only the American project in the new land but also the romance literature that since Richard Chase has been synonymous with the American project.

The novel opens in England with a tale of thwarted romance—that of Hope's mother, Alice, and Alice's liberal-thinking cousin, William Fletcher. Alice's father, also named William Fletcher, prevents her from eloping to the New World with her cousin. Under pressure from her father, Alice marries Charles Leslie instead, but when her husband dies, she sets sail for the New World on her own. She dies at sea, leaving her two daughters to the guardianship of her former lover William Fletcher, who has since married a "meek" and "godly maiden and dutiful help-mate" (*HL*, 14), followed John Winthrop and John Eliot to America, and settled on the western frontier near Springfield, Massachusetts. When Fletcher meets the two orphaned girls in Boston, he renames them Hope and Faith, and sends Faith on ahead to Springfield. In a surprise Pequod attack on the Fletcher homestead, Faith and the Fletchers' son Everell are captured, Mrs. Fletcher and her infant son are killed, and two Indian children, Magawisca and Oneco, captives from a previous battle, are reunited with their tribe. Hope and William Fletcher, some distance away, are spared. The Pequod chief, Mononotto, intends to kill Everell, but Magawisca heroically saves his life and effects his escape; Faith, however, remains a captive, eventually converting to Catholicism and marrying Oneco.

As their names suggest, religious "Faith" of the Puritans is lost to the Indians, while the more secular "Hope" remains to confront the Puritan intolerance and repression spearheaded by Gov. Winthrop and his docile, subservient wife. And although the younger William Fletcher embodies a more liberal Puritanism than his stern elders, he is by name indistinguishable from the authoritarian uncle he has left in England. With this naming, Sedgwick suggests that Old World repression is simply transferred to the New World, at least so far as Native Americans and women are concerned. Themes of imprisonment, captivity and family disruption, rather than the comic restoration of social order associated with romance, pervade the novel. And despite epigraphs from *A Midsummer Night's Dream* and *As You Like It*, in *Hope Leslie*, unlike in Shakespearean romantic comedy, there will be no return to a green world at the end of the story. Society is not rejuvenated.

After the Pequod attack and escape sequence, Sedgwick resumes the narrative nine years later. Everell is being educated in England; writing to him, Hope describes her own "education" in nature as well as an incident in which an Indian woman, Nelema, saves her tutor's life by curing a snakebite. The Boston authorities respond to the news of

Nelema's kindness by imprisoning her for witchcraft and removing Hope from Fletcher's custody so that she can profit from the more or- dered training at the Winthrop residence. Here Hope shares a room with Winthrop's newly arrived niece, Esther Downing. Undaunted by Puritan restrictions, Hope manages to free not only Nelema but Magawisca, who has been imprisoned as a result of a scheme by Sir Philip Gardiner to overthrow the Puritan government. The plot then follows a comedy of manners formula, with Hope escaping the seductions of Gardiner and his hired sailors and finally marrying Everell after predictable mistaken identities and confused affections. At the end of the novel, Esther returns to England and Magawisca to the forest.

Although Sedgwick bases the major elements of her narrative on documented history, it is not her adherence to facts but her departure from them that is so intriguing. Sedgwick's subject, set in "an age of undisputed masculine supremacy" (*HL*, 16), attempts an alternative history from a woman's perspective, a perspective also sympathetic to the plight of the Native American, whom she sees in an oppression parallel to woman's. This woman's history, which as Rabine tells us, takes place outside "dominant frameworks," is deeply critical and seeks "to subvert romantic ideology" (107). Thus, while the Springfield settlement is historically accurate, Sedgwick dramatizes with particular sensitivity the vulnerability of Margaret Fletcher and the children as they sit helpless and ignorant on the porch while the Pequods stealthily plan their attack. Women, the scene demonstrates, are powerless pawns in masculine battles. Whereas in the annals of history, Philip Gardiner's mistress lives on to marry, Sedgwick has her die in a fiery explosion, graphically depicting society's intolerance of sexually experi- enced unmarried women. And while no exact historical figure exists for Esther, Sedgwick invents her as the submissive, dull counterpart to Hope, a model of passivity that only a masculinist ideology like Win- throp's could endorse.

Sedgwick's rewriting of the Indian attack is most telling. The attack on the Fletcher homestead is preceded by a narrative by Magawisca, in which it is clear that the Puritans—not the Indians—precipitated the violence by first attacking the sleeping, unsuspecting Pequod village. During this brutal raid, the Indian children Magawisca and Oneco are captured and their mother and brother killed. The structural symmetry of the two attacks—in each battle a mother and son are killed and two children are taken captive—renders the acts of male violence morally indistinguishable and underlines the falsity of assigning blame to the Indians. The one inescapable difference, however, is that in the end the Puritans will prevail and the Indian tribes will be eradicated. Reinforcing this imbalance of power, Sedgwick depicts Magawisca raising and losing her arm to protect Everell from her father's axe, and noting later in the novel that the Indians cannot "grasp in friendship the hand raised to strike us" (*HL*, 292).

The parallel massacres by the Puritans and the Pequods—the first a "ghost chapter" in the novel—haunt the narrative, undermining dreams of harmony and unity that sent the Puritans to America. Kelley writes that the romance "is interwoven with the narrative of Indian displacement" (*HL*, xxi). In fact, the massacre threatens to displace the romance altogether, just as role inversions in the novel subvert the gender system in which the male provides and protects and the female submits and obeys. The Indian attacks actually set into motion an alternative narrative of redemption, not through Calvinist devotion to doctrine but through the wits and magnanimity of the female characters. Hope and Magawisca, more generous in spirit than their male counterparts, attempt to undo the wrongs of their male leaders, fundamentally challenging the precepts upon which the Puritan, male world is constructed. They do not offer a Cooperian escape or romantic/comic affirmation.

Like Natty Bumppo in *The Leatherstocking Tales*, Hope takes "counsel from her own heart" (*HL*, xxiv), but her independence is unlike his because she is female. Hope's power extends beyond domestic morality and the woman's sphere. And if she exemplifies the selflessness that Kelley associates with nineteenth-century femininity (*HL*, xxiii), she also embodies the traits attributed to men, acting on behalf of her own advancement as well as others'. Hope, as Bell remarks, "seems to specialize in freeing Indians" (216); this observation is true both in the terms of the novel's plot and Hope's larger project of social justice. An "unfettered soul," Hope does not hesitate to commit "a plain transgression of a holy law" (*HL*, 280, 311).

If Hope stands for the white woman's resourcefulness and defiance of male restrictiveness, Magawisca represents the integrity of the Native American woman. But unlike Natty Bumppo's noble savages, who slay in order to achieve peace, Magawisca engages in no violence, whatever the personal risk. Foster (77) and Bell (216–17) speculate on Sedgwick's use of local town history for Magawisca's amputation, with Bell suggesting a source in the Captain John Smith—Pocahontas story. But Sedgwick tells us in her preface that with respect to Magawisca, "we are confined not to the actual, but the possible" (6). Magawisca, her Indian double, Nelema, and her white double, Hope Leslie—all of whom save lives even when it means their own captivity—are Sedgwick's "hope" for a revised American history and new literary mythology. The magnitude of their heroism is Sedgwick's version of what Levin calls the movement from the "artificial" to the "natural." In Sedgwick's view, society should move away from the "artificial" imposition of violence and oppression and toward the "natural" coexistence of peace and mutuality.

Despite Hope's rebellions, the novel ends in the heroine's marriage to the young Puritan Everell Fletcher, seemingly validating Rabine's observation that women's protests and assertions occurring in the middle of romances are often negated by their endings. Marriage is an outcome Cooper assiduously avoids for his own heroes, but a more realistic Sedgwick reminds the reader that no matter how independent the heroine, marriage is not easily renegotiated.

Family is the mainstay of the woman's romance as well as the "familiar" domain appropriated by American male writers to contrast with the fears and unknowns of the American wilderness. And the family, Gossett and Bardes assert in their study of *Hope Leslie*, is the central building block of a democratic republic. Although Sedgwick's reputation rests on her domestic writing, and Kelley describes her as "a divinely appointed reformer within the confines of domesticity,"[17] in *Hope Leslie* no home is glorified. The Fletcher homestead is exposed and vulnerable, the Winthrop home is repressive, and Digby's parlor is the setting for mistaken identities and mismatched lovers. Families are repeatedly torn apart in this novel; women and children are not protected by men but become victims of their battles. Home, then, is not a comforting haven, with "good living under almost every roof," as de Crèvecoeur would have it,[18] but a precarious site of danger.

Ann Snitow notes that the "one socially acceptable moment of transcendence [for women] is romance;"[19] that is, conventional love between men and women leading to marriage. As her name implies, Hope Leslie is "hopelessly" committed to this bourgeois romantic ending. Yet Hope is also an individual—a "pathfinder" in her own right, to use Cooper's term, and through her, Sedgwick goes farther than most previous American writers in exposing Puritan hypocrisy and affirming the value of Native American and female culture. Hope breaks the boundaries of normal expectation for young women as she treks through nature, befriends Indians, frees political prisoners, and eludes drunken sailors. Her most inspiring and affecting experience is not marrying Everell but climbing a mountain with her tutor to survey an expanse of undeveloped land. "Gaz[ing] on the beautiful summits of this mountain," Hope writes in a letter to Everell, who is receiving his education in England, not in nature, "I had an irrepressible desire to go to them" (*HL*, 99). Hope resists romantic seduction, political captivity, and traditional domesticity throughout the novel; she will not become a Mrs. Winthrop, who "like a horse easy on the bit . . . was guided by the slightest intimation from him who held the rein" (*HL*, 145).

Forever the adventurous youth, never the adult, Hope not only challenges conventional notions of what it means for a woman to grow up; she also resists Puritan mandates to be "hardened for the cross-accidents and unkind events . . . the wholesome chastisements of life" (*HL*, 160). Hope, in fact, achieves a fantasy of indulgence *and* sacrifice, of selfishness *and* doing for others, proving as she moves undaunted through one escapade after another that, contrary to Calvinist doctrine, good deeds on earth *can* bring joy. Emerging from virtually every situation unscathed, Hope subverts Puritan ethics and behavior; and although she marries Everell at the end of the novel, the major events in her life revolve not around romance but around nature and the sense of fair play.

Neither is Everell Fletcher romantic or heroic in the traditional sense. Well-meaning but weak, he is an example of the dilution of the bloodline that so worried the Founding Fathers, a parallel to that most famous of feeble Puritan sons, Arthur Dimmesdale. Everell has more tolerance than his stern male forebears, but he lacks vision and capability to put thought into action. His capture during the Pequod raid of the Fletcher farm inverts the traditional female captivity narrative: a white man, he must be saved by an Indian woman. Everell's significant instruction comes not from the Bible or England, but from Magawisca's narrative about her own people's plight. When Magawisca later is imprisoned because Puritan officials mistakenly think her guilty of inciting an attack on Boston, Everell fails to free her because of his fears: the hapless young man struggles outside the jail with a ladder while Hope successfully schemes for Magawisca's release. Passive and ineffectual, Everell is the hero because he marries the heroine.

The true bond—and the real romance—in this novel is between Hope and Magawisca. It is a same-sex bond that Fiedler has found essential to American romance. In constructing same-sex friendship between Magawisca and Hope, Sedgwick creates a parallel of the relationship between Natty Bumppo and Chingachgook in *The Leatherstocking Tales*—but with a difference. Doubles throughout the novel, Hope and Magawisca are drawn together by, and in spite of, the destructive acts of their fathers. Both have lost their mothers through war, both are torn between obedience to their fathers and the dictates of their own minds, and both oppose Puritan law, finding inspiration and guidance in nature or their own consciences. In prison the two learn the meaning of trust and betrayal, and in a secret meeting in a cemetery—symbol of death by male order—where their mothers are buried, they seal their bond: "Mysteriously have our destinies been interwoven. Our mothers brought from a far distance to rest here together—their children connected in indissoluble bonds" (*HL*, 192). The union of Magawisca and Hope represents the waste caused by masculine violence as well as the need for feminine healing—a healing not between the Old World of England and the New World of America, as traditional American romances have it, but between the original world of the Native Americans and the new, intrusive world of the Puritans. Unlike Natty and Chingachgook, Hope and Magawisca do not retreat into nature together, isolated but free. They participate in society, serving as its critics, mediators, and healers. When their relationship is sundered, Hope's marriage to Everell can only be a partial substitute.

Women, Sedgwick suggests, must play active and essential, not passive or secondary, roles in American society. In Cooper's fiction, in service to the American Adam mythology, women are rendered dichotomously. As Fiedler notes (21), Cooper establishes the "pattern of female Dark and Light that is to become the standard form" in American literature: an innocent, passive woman juxtaposed with a vibrant, sexualized one, whether Alice and Cora in *The Last of the Mohicans*, Hetty and Judith in *The Deerslayer*, or Inez and Ellen in *The Prairie*. While women in nature figure as tokens of exchange in elaborate captivity sequences engineered by men in *The Leatherstocking Tales*, Cooper fundamentally endorses the standard nineteenth-century view of separate spheres for men and women, with women "the repositories of the better principles of our nature."[20] This dichotomous view of women has its corollary in the male view of nature: a lone male figure either seeks a lover's alliance in nature as replacement for the relationship he fails to achieve with woman, or he views nature as a fearful object he must conquer or destroy in order to validate his own existence.

Sedgwick rejects these dichotomies for her female characters. Magawisca and Hope are as capable as their male counterparts of participating in nature and society. As sisters, Hope and Faith represent active and passive aspects of the female principle, but this distinction is never expressed in terms of sexual and spiritual purity or innocence. No female in *Hope Leslie* exhibits the "yearning felt by a presumably experienced woman to return to the pristine state of the innocent virgin" that Porte finds in Cooper (21), a view that incidentally reads all female sexuality as a fall into sin requiring redemption or escape. Faith, on the one hand, not only marries, she marries a "red-blooded" Native American; Hope, on the other hand, a virgin throughout the novel, romps from adventure to adventure unaffected by salacious sailors and villainous seducers. And Magawisca, who according to the Cooper paradigm must be "wild and dangerous" because Indian (Bell, 218), is, in fact, peaceable and socially oriented. Only Rosa, seduced and abandoned in the New World, appears as a stock character—a desperate reminder of romance's failure to accommodate women's sexuality. A prototype of Bertha Rochester, she takes vengeance on her oppressor, destroying herself in the process. Rosa gives angry expression to the female energy that her more socially integrated counterpart, Hope, channels into minor rebellions.

Hope Leslie forbids a reductionist view of women and the romance. It rejects patriarchal concepts of female submissiveness and purity, instead presenting women as complex models of democracy, adventure, mutuality, and sympathy. Sedgwick, in fact, presents not just one double of Hope, but many, demonstrating multiple rather than dichotomous ways of womanhood. Hope, Magawisca, and Esther all love Everell, but Magawisca and Esther give him up. Hope marries, but her union with her foster brother is more a friendship than a romance, modeled perhaps on Sedgwick's own relationship with her brothers.[21] Esther's single status endorses autonomous womanhood: "Marriage is not *essential* to the contentment, the dignity, or the happiness of woman," Sedgwick writes in defense of Esther's decision (*HL*, 350, italics in original), and her own life is testimony that a single woman can find satisfaction as friend or sister.

The doublings become uneasy where Native Americans are involved, however. By eschewing a retreat into nature that Natty Bumppo achieves with Chingachgook, Sedgwick emphasizes the crucial difference between the races: the inevitable decimation of the Native American to make way for white expansion and greed. "We are commanded to do good to all," Hope explains to her tutor as she works to free Magawisca (*HL*, 312). But she cannot prevent the inevitable. Esther, prevented by Puritan conscience from helping Magawisca escape from prison, essentially gives herself up to the rigid law-of-the-father; and Magawisca, "first to none" (Kelley 1978, 224), returns to a nature that is blighted and a people "spoiled." Dichotomies reemerge with Magawisca's declaration, "The Indian and the white man can no more mingle, and become one, than day and night" (*HL*, 330).

In *The Prairie*, published in 1827, the same year as *Hope Leslie*, Cooper uses a tree as a symbol to describe the natural cycles of growth, ripening, and death, comparing the monumentality of nature to the works of humans: "It is the fate of all things to ripen and then to decay. The tree blossoms and bears its fruit, which falls, rots, withers, and even the seed is lost! There does the noble tree fill its place in the forests. . . . It lies another hundred years. . . .[22] Sedgwick also presents such a Pantheistic notion of nature, giving Magawisca words that fuse the natural and the human: 'The Great Spirit is visible in the life-creating sun. I perceive Him in the gentle light of the moon that steals through the forest boughs. I feel Him here,' she continued, pressing her hand on her breast" (*HL*, 189). But this notion of nature has been negated by white encroachment. Sedgwick uses the familiar nineteenth-century symbol of the blasted tree, which Mononotto points to as representative of his race at the hands of the white men, to signify not only the decimation of the Native Americans but also the assault against women and nature. Thus Magawisca's body, the right arm missing, is truncated like the blasted tree. Hawthorne uses the same symbol in "Roger Malvin's Burial" to convey the guilty conscience of Reuben, who fails to send a rescue party to his dying father-in-law. Hawthorne's message, anticipated by Sedgwick, is that the strong and able have responsibility to succor those in need.

Hope's sister Faith, another double, also goes off into the wilderness, married to chief Mononotto's son Oneco in one of the few cases of miscegenation in early American fiction—certainly one that Cooper disallows in *The Last of the Mohicans*. The relationship of Faith and Oneco is mutually loving, gentle, and respectful. The bird imagery associated with the couple throughout the novel communicates a spirit of openness and freedom in nature. But just as Magawisca is mateless, the marriage of Oneco and Faith has a sterile, frozen quality about it. Faith speaks no English, and the couple is without children.

Constrained by her own position in history, Sedgwick perhaps could not conceive of an ending that both subverts and rewrites the white patriarchal plot. Were she able to do so, the pressure to produce salable fiction most likely would have prevented its articulation. Nonetheless, *Hope Leslie* strains against its conventions as surely as its female characters struggle against unjust imprisonment.

Hope Leslie is discomfiting for literary critics and readers who prefer retreat into a fantasy world where one can ignore the injustices to nature by escaping further into the wilderness. In this novel, the frontier myth does not seem to be, as Annette Kolodny has outlined it in *The Lay of the Land*, a fantasy of the land as a domesticated garden.[23] It is, to some extent, what Leland Person suggests in his essay on miscegenation: a successful intermarriage of races, an Eden where the white woman is included and the white man excluded.[24] The point is not that women ultimately prove superior—as they inevitably do, both in romance and in this novel—but that the pact with power engineered by men has jeopardized men, women, and nature. Cooper's paradisiacal wilderness is a profound and evocative symbol in American literature, but Sedgwick, while valuing nature, forbids an egocentric or overly romantic view of it. She does not let us forget that we are usurpers and that there will be no regeneration through violence. Her view more closely resembles what David Mogen calls "a gothic tradition of frontier narrative" that expresses, among other meanings, "despair about our history and our future."[25]

The American literary hero feminizes the land, seeking in it a validation of his own creative principle. He wants to be the sole possessor of the virgin soil, which he penetrates with axe or gun and seeks to make pregnant with unresolved possibility.[26] Sedgwick tells us that this pregnancy is a false one and that woman/land will not be reduced to a medium for man's self-glorification. The white man will, like Everell, inevitably find himself its captive rather than its victor. A possessive relationship with the land only results in estrangement from it. Thus Fussell writes, "Cooper's heart was in his writing," but a "habitual need for recessive withdrawal . . . sprang from [his] fundamental alienation from his country" (28, 29).

If the male fantasy is escapist, the female fantasy is integrationist, inclusive of the whole of woman's traits—religious, sexual, adventurous, heroic. Without this integration, there can only be fragmentation. Governor Winthrop's household "move[s] in a world of his own" (*HL*, 301), cut off from the very unity of nature, God, individual, and society that it seeks.

This transcendental vision of unity, suggested in Sedgwick's historical and romantic critique, is developed some years later, not in the individualistic transcendentalism of Ralph Waldo Emerson, but in the social transcendentalism of Margaret Fuller. Like Emerson, Fuller embraces the ideal of the individual in nature, but while valuing the abstract, she also advocates social awareness. Looking out at the western territory near the Great Lakes in the summer of 1843, Fuller seeks "by reverent faith to woo the mighty meaning of the scene, perhaps to foresee the law by which a new order, a new poetry, is to be evoked." Hope enjoys this same personal and transcendental relationship when she visits Mount Holyoke with her tutor and Nelema. But Fuller's fantasy is modified by the "distaste I must experience at its mushroom growth": development "is scarce less wanton than that of warlike invasion," and the land bears "the rudeness of conquest." Emerson sought to unify technology and transcendental philosophy into a seamless fabric of hopeful expansion, but Fuller notes not transcendental insight but blindness: "Seeing the traces of the Indians . . . we feel as if they were the rightful lords of the beauty they forbore to deform. But most of these settlers do not see at all" (Chevigny, 318, 322).

The first writers, as Fussell notes, gave the West its mythology, finding in it their own dreams of possession and control. For women, identified with and through nature, the myth spells death and defeat. Sedgwick quietly but radically alters that mythology, transcending the limits of romance and history to establish her own yearning for social and natural unity.

Southwest of What?: Southwestern Literature as a Form of Frontier Literature

Reed Way Dasenbrock

Southwestern literature has not attracted a great deal of analytical commentary, at least partially because the term—in naming the literature by reference to a region—immediately places it in the tradition of American regionalism. This identification has not been adequately thought through. There are some links between Southwestern and other regional literatures, as Southwestern literature was first talked about with some seriousness in New Mexico in the 1920s and 1930s in the heyday of American regionalist culture.[1] Yet Southwestern literature is quite different from American regionalism as we see it in Sarah Orne Jewett, Hamlin Garland, or the Southern Renaissance. The key difference is in the stance taken by the writer towards the region. Traditional regional literature is—or represents itself as—the discourse of the insider about his or her own region, a celebration of the local. Hamlin Garland, for instance, defines local color writing as having "such quality of texture and background that it could not have been written in any other place or by anyone else than a native."[2] Traditional Southwestern literature is just the opposite: it is the discourse of an outsider, not a celebration of the local but a celebration of the exotic.[3]

To ask what Southwestern literature is, one must first ask, What is the Southwest? For whom is it the Southwest? What is the Southwest southwest of? These are not questions we ask very often, even though—or perhaps because—the answer is so obvious. The Southwest wasn't the Southwest for its original inhabitants, Native Americans of whatever nation or people. It was the center of their world. Just as clearly, it was

123

not the Southwest for the successive waves of Spanish (and Mexican) travelers and settlers. It was the north. People who live in Ciudad Juarez or Hermosillo aren't southwesterners; they are *norteños*.

So for whom is it the Southwest? For the Anglo, whose first penetration into the area was down the Santa Fe Trail, heading southwest. And it is easy enough to see how the term *the Southwest*, in naming a region according to its direction away from the centers of power and population, is a perfect representation of the dependent status of the whole area. Once an area to which statehood was long denied because of a fear of Hispanic political representation in Washington, and now an area whose economy is dependent on the military who love having big open spaces to blow things up in, the Southwest has been treated virtually as a colonial possession by those it is southwest of.

And we should be able to see how the classic Southwestern literature is a perfect part of this axis of penetration from the northeast, even where it may disagree with the military's "land-use plans." Although a good deal of Southwestern literature is historical fiction, such novels are rarely set before the first American incursions into the area. A majority of Southwestern writers have come from places to the northeast, from Josiah Gregg through Willa Cather, Mary Austin, and Mabel Dodge Luhan, to Edward Abbey, William Eastlake, and John Nichols. More important than their places of birth is the fact that their work recapitulates and represents this voyage into the area. Lawrence Clark Powell begins his *Southwestern Classics* with Josiah Gregg's *Commerce on the Prairies*,[4] an 1844 book about the Santa Fe Trail. *Commerce on the Prairies* was written while Gregg was back in the United States after many years as a Santa Fe trader, but one would never know this from the book itself. It tells in quite detailed terms the story of his voyage across the prairies, but nothing about the voyage back. The same is true of Susan Shelby Magoffin's slightly later narrative, the aptly titled *Down the Santa Fe Trail and into Mexico*, a diary of a trip made in 1846–47. The movement in both books is into Mexico, into the Southwest, from the outside. Gregg sets the pattern for this; and the shape of his work—moving us into the Southwest from the outside, but never bringing us back—becomes characteristic of subsequent Southwestern writing.

It is probably no coincidence, then, that the very term *the Southwest*, according to Powell (44), comes from a work of Southwestern literature, *The Land of Poco Tiempo* (1893), by the Massachusetts-born Charles Lummis.[5] Lummis is a key figure in the development of Southwestern literature because he transforms the Anglo voyage into the Southwest narrated in the early works into a thematic opposition between the newcomers' energy and the passivity of the indigenous inhabitants. The *poco tiempo* (or "pretty soon") of the title characterizes the Southwest for Lummis, as even "Nature herself does little but sleep, here."[6] This indigenous idleness seems contagious, according to Lummis. Hispanic New Mexican culture is figuratively asleep: "the Great American Mystery—the National Rip Van Winkle" (*Poco Tiempo*, 1). Lummis represents New Mexico as having been conquered by the Spaniards in one brief "unparalleled blaze of exploration" (1), after which they "went to sleep" in an eternal "after-nap" (2). Activity thus is European; sleep or indolence, *poco tiempo*, is indigenous. According to Lummis, the energy of the first colonizers gave way to lethargy, and though he presents this indigenous lethargy as attractive, he explicitly contrasts it to the values of energy represented by the new outsiders—the new colonizers—such as himself. Lummis's thematic opposition here establishes the paradox that is at the heart of all classic Southwestern literature: the Southwest is presented as the Other, and its interest lies in that otherness, in the landscape and the earlier inhabitants, both Native American and Spanish-speaking. That otherness is celebrated and is clearly what has brought the writer to the region, yet it is also being canceled and presented as something that must give way.

As Gregg and Lummis began, so later writers have continued, thematizing an opposition between the Anglo writer and society and the indigenous Other, yet representing that opposition in a narrative that depicts the transformation of the Southwest by the energetic newcomer. Willa Cather's *Death Comes for the Archbishop* (1927), for example, opens in Rome, with a group of clerics deciding to take advantage of the recent American conquest of the area by sending someone to bring the Southwest under more direct control from Rome. Father Latour is sent on that mission from the American Midwest. We never return to Rome or the Midwest, so Cather's narrative design recapitulates the voyage into the area portrayed by the earlier narratives. More importantly, the story she has to tell is congruent with this external framing, this presentation of the Southwest from the outside. Cather picks an outsider as her protagonist and sympathetically presents his efforts to introduce (or impose) external standards on the area. The two events on which the narrative of *Death Comes for the Archbishop* turns are Father Latour's struggle with and ultimate victory over the unruly, polygamous, and politically active Father Martinez of Taos, and his replacing of an adobe church with the stone cathedral of French design still standing in Santa Fe. These struggles are parallel aspects of the same historical process.

The traditional cultures of the Southwest are represented in *Death Comes for the Archbishop* as the past, and the past—however charming—must give way to the increasingly Anglo-American future of the railroad, ranching, and participation in the national economy. Cather disguises this somewhat by choosing a French protagonist for her story, but Bishop Lamy historically and Latour in her novel are clearly part of the American penetration from the northeast. Lamy historically was the key person who replaced the indigenous hispanophone priesthood in New Mexico with an anglophone (initially largely French, later largely Irish) priesthood necessarily much farther removed from their Spanish-speaking parishioners. Mary Austin is said to have been cross with her houseguest Cather for picking a French instead of a Spanish priest for her protagonist (Powell, 100, 132). And in this disagreement we have two competing interpretations of what Southwestern literature can be: a representation of the original, or at least prior, culture of the region, or a representation of the process of its transformation from without. One's instinct might be to side with Austin here, but Cather was probably more perceptive in realizing that she couldn't represent the culture from within, that her work was part of—and therefore should represent—the Americanization of the area. Nonetheless, her idealization of that historical process takes her in the same thematic direction as Lummis: the outsider, the transformer, is the figure of energy with which the author comes to identify, and the indigenous inhabitants are presented simply as resisting that change and holding onto the past, not as possessing their own competing vision of the future.

That this choice of protagonist and perspective is not simply a matter of Cather dramatizing her own outsider status but a matter of the dynamics of Southwestern literature can be shown by the novels of Harvey Fergusson. Although Fergusson was born and raised in New Mexico, he makes precisely the same choice of protagonist in his novels: the outsider who is part of the American transformation of the area. This choice can be seen throughout his career, in an early novel such as *Wolf Song* (1927) just as clearly as in his last two novels, *Grant of Kingdom* (1950) and *The Conquest of Don Pedro* (1954). *Wolf Song* is a conventional mountain man novel for much of the narrative: the protagonist, a young man from Kentucky named Sam Lash, joins a group of mountain men, goes West, attends Rendezvous, and does the things every mountain man does. But then he goes to Taos, falls in love with an upperclass Spanish woman, Lola Salazar, and carries her off to Bent's Fort. The narrative of *Wolf Song* is not simply one of Anglo conquest, for her family kidnaps her back and Lash has to convert and take Mexican citizenship to be reunited with her. Yet at the very end the young couple are given a tract of land east of the mountains and go off to settle it. Finally and explicitly, American initiative triumphs over Latin passivity, as this land has long been in the family but no one has had the enterprise to occupy it. Lash says to himself at one point: "He had to go! He clung desperately to his resolution. He was a mountain man, a trapper, not a squaw-man. . . . Even if they went back to Taos together, even if her family took him in, he could not sit around like a greaser against a wall. He would rot on a Mexican life of idleness. . . ." (ellipses in the original)[7] And though her family does take him in, he does not "sit around like a greaser" but sets out to conquer a new kingdom. Fergusson's subsequent *Grant of Kingdom* continues this story, with the French-American Jean Ballard as the protagonist instead of Sam Lash. Ballard thinks of himself precisely as a figure of energy in contrast to the Mexicans: "That wavering look he had seen in the eyes of many Mexican men in recent years. They were being overwhelmed by a rush of energy from the East, which they could neither stop nor deal with, and they were losing confidence."[8] And Ballard, as part of that rush of energy, marries the daughter of the Spanish *rico*, takes her east of the mountains, and singlehandedly settles his empire, the kingdom of the title, which no one in the family before him has had the energy, the courage, and the desire to conquer.

A generation later, the same contrast prevails in the lower Rio Grande Valley in *The Conquest of Don Pedro*. Don Pedro is "a half-deserted place asleep in the sun and falling to pieces"[9] that at the time of the American conquest has long settled into a traditional feudal pattern of agriculture, a virtual barter economy, and domination by one rich family. The protagonist of the novel, the conqueror of Don Pedro, is an itinerant Jewish merchant, Leo Mendes, who by opening a store in the town opens it to commerce, modern goods, and a cash economy. And though, like Latour and Ballard, Mendes might seem because of his ethnic background to be somewhat apart from the postconquest Anglo-Latino confrontation, his "conquest of Don Pedro" is nonetheless implicitly the Americanization of Don Pedro. Despite his unusual refusal to carry or even to know how to use a gun, Leo feels a kinship with the Texan cowboy Coppinger because both "belonged to the future and were engaged in destroying the past. Both were vaguely aware that they didn't quite belong in this lost fragment of the Middle Ages" (*Don Pedro*, 162). But Leo adapts himself to the "Middle Ages" well enough, and the novel ends, a little abruptly, when Mendes realizes that while he has been Americanizing Don Pedro, it has been Hispanicizing him. The railroad arrives in New Mexico, and on a visit to Las Vegas, the railroad boom town of the era, Leo felt "suddenly that he was an old-timer, a part of the past, confronted by challenge and disturbance" (*Don Pedro*, 207). And this past has precise ethnic associations: "He stood on a street corner and stared, like any bewildered Mexican. Wasn't he more a Mexican now than anything else? He understood for the first time how completely he had become a part of the slow-moving, soft-spoken life that lived in the quiet adobe towns, in the old recumbent houses, the life of the long siesta and the leisurely meal, a life that had gaiety and passion about it but no hurry at all and little violence. This new life had come to destroy the old one and the whole push and weight of an expanding world was behind it" (*Don Pedro*, 207). A friend offers him a partnership in his business connected with the expansion of trade brought by the railroad. When Leo hesitates, his friend tells him: "I think you've gone native down there—too much poco tiempo, too much siesta, no competition. It happens to lots of good men. You better dig yourself out before it's too late" (210). And Leo does dig himself out; recalled to his purpose in life, he leaves Don Pedro to travel north. By doing so he avoids the fate of Jean Ballard in *Grant of Kingdom*, who with the coming of the railroad loses control of his empire to new speculators, to a new wave of Anglo energy for whom Ballard now represents the old, slow-moving indigenous way of life. To "go native" is ultimately to be destroyed, to be swept into the dustbin of history. This has—according to all these works—been the fate of the first wave of European settlers, the Spanish, and it is being depicted as a possible—but not desirable—fate for the second wave.

However, these novels are not simply the propaganda for American commercial prosperity that a plot summary makes them seem. Fergusson, like his protagonists, is in love with the Hispanic culture that gives his novels their setting. But there is a contradiction between the affective disposition of the novel and the narrative movement. Each novel presents Hispanic and Anglo culture as opposites, the one representing passivity and the past, the other activity and the future. Fergusson, like Cather, is emotionally caught between the two: his narrative instantiates the Anglo values of activity and change, but these novels are written and are likely to be read because they present the values of the setting. Finally, however, this seeming structural ambivalence is tilted, for these are Anglo writers presenting what they see as attractive features of the indigenous culture. It does not seem to have occurred to writers of Cather's and Fergusson's generation to wonder if their representation of Hispanic culture as attractively indolent was likely to be accepted by Hispanics themselves.

However, with the emergence of writing by Chicanos and Native Americans, these representations have been sharply challenged. The historical record tells us that the cliché that New Mexican culture had sunk into indolent passivity before the coming of the Americans is simply not true. Fergusson has to invent a Don Pedro settled for two hundred years in the lower Rio Grande, as that area north of El Paso was in fact newly settled just before the American conquest, with the founding of the village of Dona Ana in 1839. And many Chicano novels subtly but directly challenge the stereotypes that have been established: Rudolfo Anaya's *Bless Me, Ultima* is set east of the Rio Grande Valley (though south of the area Sam Lash settles in *Wolf Song*), and Anaya lets us know that the area was settled by Hispanic pioneers moving east before Anglos got there going west. Nash Candelaria's *Not By the Sword*, a novel about a young priest in the Albuquerque area around the time of the 1846 conquest, shows the priest trying to reform the Church in ways that deny Cather's picture of an utterly corrupt Church before the arrival of

Lamy/Latour.[10] Short fiction by Fray Angelico Chavez disputes in a variety of ways the received vision of the Church as sunk into corruption before 1846. Thus, though a full discussion of this assertion would take a separate essay, Chicano novelists simply do not accept the Anglo characterization of their own culture as a wave of European energy that turned passive and then was inert in the face of historical change brought from the outside by the second wave of European settlement.

Despite this challenge to received stereotypes, however, contemporary Anglo writing about the Southwest is still caught up in the old system of representation, as we can see from the work of Edward Abbey and John Nichols. Both writers are, of course, not native to the region, and they dramatize this in various ways in their novels. Abbey's *Fire on the Mountain* (1962) is told by a twelve-year-old boy from Pennsylvania visiting his grandfather's ranch near Alamogordo, and the figure of the grandson enables Abbey to picture the Southwest for outsiders such as he initially was. Similarly, of the four ecological bandits in *The Monkey Wrench Gang* (1975), only one, Seldom Seen Smith, is from the area in which they are operating. Hayduke is a Vietnam veteran who has just returned to Arizona; Dr. Sarvis and his nurse Bonnie Abbzug—originally a New Yorker—live in Albuquerque. Abbey records these characters discovering the desert as they come into it from the outside. Nichols's densely populated *The Milagro Beanfield War* (1974) has no single protagonist, but time and again across the novel, Nichols will tell the story of an Anglo character—the lawyer Charlie Bloom, the rancher Ray Guysdorf, the VISTA volunteer Herbie Goldberg, Ladd Devine's aide Horsethief Shorty, etc.—who has moved into the area from the outside. For each, the Southwest is a place to come to, not a place to be from.

Moreover, both Abbey and Nichols thematize this aspect of their narrative in just the way Lummis, Cather, and Fergusson do: the Anglo coming into the outside is represented as the figure of dynamism, opposed to the passivity of the area. It is the Anglo who is transforming the landscape, turning the Southwest into part of the modern industrial, technocratic machine. The earlier writers' ambivalence about this process of modernization is replaced in the work of both writers by an explicit critique, but the system of representation is still the same. For Nichols, the opposition to that transformation is still put up primarily by the indigenous peoples of the area: indolent Hispanic is transformed into Chicano activist, but the two do much the same, which is to throw a wrench into the works of the American technocratic economy, mostly by staying faithful to their own different traditions. Nichols has a problem in that many Chicanos clearly have done nothing of the kind and instead are eagerly joining the economic transformation he attacks, but his Marxist class analysis allows him to write them off as *vendidos*, a *comprador* class, and to see the Hispanics nonetheless as generally a working class, united (if only through their cultural difference) against the process of Anglo development. This viewpoint is close to Fergusson's vision in *The Conquest of Don Pedro*, except that the complexity of a Leo Mendes is never found in the caricatured Anglo capitalists like Ladd Devine and Rodey McQueen who populate Nichols's work.

Abbey is perhaps more honest or more desperate in that he realizes that he cannot idealize the indigenous peoples of the Southwest as any kind of barrier to Anglo activity. This is probably not a response to the Chicano and Native American rebuttal of the received clichés, because he seems to have nothing but scorn for Native Americans because of their acceptance of Anglo ways: "The real trouble with the goddamned Indians, reflected Hayduke, is that they are no better than the rest of us. The real trouble is that the Indians are just as stupid and greedy and cowardly and dull as us white folks."[11] Although these are the reflections of one of Abbey's characters, they match Abbey's views as expressed in his nonfiction. Here is the voice of a disappointed romantic, who somehow expected the Indians heroically to oppose Anglo development in the area.

But this pessimism is built into the received system of representation both Abbey and Nichols are working within: energy is going to win out over passivity every time. And this helps create the elegaic tone of both these writers' work. They reserve the romantic spirit in which a Lummis or a Cather had approached landscape and indigenous inhabitant alike for the landscape alone, singing of the glories of the landscape that are passing away. *If Mountains Die* is the title of Nichols's first work of nonfiction and landscape writing; in exactly the same vein, one of the epigraphs to *The Monkey Wrench Gang* is a quotation from Richard Shelton, "Oh my desert, yours is the only death I cannot bear." This stance of keening over the landscape closely resembles the earlier generations' keening over the passing away of the indigenous cultures under Anglo influence. In *Death Comes for the Archbishop*, for instance, Cather has Latour anachronistically visit the declining Pecos Pueblo and lament its passing away even though she herself informs us in a footnote that "the dying pueblo of Pecos was abandoned some years before the American occupation of New Mexico."[12] Part of Hayduke's scorn for the Navahos is their refusal to go into a comparable decline; the lines immediately preceding the passage quoted above read: ". . . the tribe is spreading, fruitful as a culture bouillon: from 9500 in 1890 to 125,000 today. Fecundity! Prosperity! Sweet wine and suicide, of thee we sing" (*Monkey Wrench*, 25). Only what is in decline can be the subject of elegy. And one way of regarding the environmental writing of Abbey and Nichols is that they are works of Southwestern literature in which nature itself is given the part once assigned to the Hispanic and the Indian: a passive remnant of the past valued for its difference and in decline, nostalgically preferred to Anglo values of activity and economic development.

But neither writer really wants to write elegy or admit defeat, so neither Abbey nor Nichols assigns all of the energy to the side of development in these environmental "Southwesterns." At times, the landscape is even given a power to oppose the Anglo development machine, as Abbey delights in telling his readers that the Glen Canyon Dam will silt up and be destroyed in three hundred years by the actions of the river itself.[13] But elsewhere Abbey and Nichols assign people to speak for that which is in decline, to articulate its values. These figures—John Vogelin, the old rancher in *Fire on the Mountain*, the Monkey Wrench Gang in the novel of that name, all the people who fall in love with the mountains in *The Milagro Beanfield War*, April Delaney in *The Magic Journey*—are always Anglos. They oppose the new forces of activity, but they do so with stereotypical Anglo energy, verve, and organizing zeal. And the irony in this is that they come to resemble their opponents more and more closely, though they cannot see this, until there is no significant difference between the energetic Anglo despoilers of the land and the equally energetic Anglo wreckers of the despoliation. The members of the Monkey Wrench Gang are more and more technological in their sabotage until they seem as caught up in technocracy as what they oppose. It is only because they are so complicit with the system that they have the resources and know-how to oppose it and that they are treated so lightly when they are caught. In the same way, Nichols's Anglo activists from the outside—heroic figures for the author as surely as are Abbey's "eco-raiders"—by importing techniques of political agitation from the East change the Chicano culture they seek to preserve as inexorably as Ladd Devine and the developers. But Nichols doesn't seem to see any resemblance between the Anglos he attacks and the ones he praises.

Abbey seems no more aware of the contradictions in *The Monkey Wrench Gang*, but it is to his credit that in his earlier work, *Fire on the Mountain*, he could see some of this and could subject his protagonist to ironic scrutiny. When John Vogelin is defending his claim to the land and his desire to preserve it by saying that it is his, his friend Lee Mackie reminds him that his grandfather took it from the Apaches: "Does the land belong to anybody? A hundred years ago the Apaches had it, it was all theirs. Your father and other men like him stole it from the Apaches. . . . Now the Government is going to steal it from you."[14] As part of the Anglo development of the area, he has no logical ground on which to criticize that development. He was to the Apaches what the government is now to him, and this is close to the dilemma faced by Fergusson's protagonists, Jean Ballard and Leo Mendes. Faced with the bustle of Las Vegas, Leo Mendes reflects: "He resented the change, and yet he already had a part in it" (*Don Pedro*, 207). And perhaps this is the best summary of the situation of the Southwestern writer: all the Anglo Southwestern writers resent the change they depict, yet they all have a part in it.

The tone of this literature is therefore generally elegaic, not just because each writer portrays what is dying but also because each writer is in on the kill. What is prized in each case about the Southwest is its difference, its isolation from Anglo notions of hurry and energy. But the narrative movement of the novel always instantiates the hurry and energy that is transforming the Southwest. This is just as true of those later novels committed to an explicit critique of that energy as it is of the more ambivalent earlier works, for the very energy with which the novelists and their protagonists oppose what they see as Anglo energy shows how these writers remain part of what they oppose. I think the classic Southwestern writing of an earlier generation is to be praised over the contemporary work if only because the contemporary writers seem so much less self-aware. The earlier writers recognized their complicity with what they deplored, as Abbey himself did once. But Abbey in his later work and Nichols think of themselves as somehow different from the Anglo in-migration and development of the area, even though they are participants in it. This is also one reason why contemporary literature by Chicano and Native American writers is so much more significant than contemporary Anglo writing in and about the area.[15] The Chicano and Native American writers are faced with a set of historical and social stereotypes they can oppose with vigor. And though I would want to praise the Anglo writers for their engagement with history and society, they seem not to have freed themselves from the traditional stereotypes the other writers are opposing, possibly because they haven't yet thought through their position (and the implications of that position) in the history and society they depict. If major writing about the Southwest is to emerge from Anglo writers as well as Chicanos and Native Americans, then the first task is a more critical examination of the received notions about the Southwest than any of these writers have undertaken so far.

From the Wild West to the Far North—Literary Representations of North America's Last Frontier

Aron Senkpiel

When cold and dark followed the clouds, the rain became snow and the water ice. That is why the world is the way it is.
—Ikpakhauq and Uloqsaq[1]

The "North" is not merely a point on the compass. It has filled our minds for thousands of years. . . ."
—Louis-Edmond Hamelin[2]

It is a truism that Canada is a northern nation. From the perspective of most Americans, all of Canada is "up there," a distant place far to the north that is often seen as a geographical as well as cultural wasteland: North America's own Siberia. Canadians and Americans alike even joke about it, often together. On "SCTV," for example, one of the more popular comedy routines had two "eh"-saying, beer-drinking brothers sitting in front of a map of Canada that was an expansive void marked "the Great White North." Viewers were never certain which was emptier: the area represented by the map or the area between the two fellows' ears. For many Americans, says Margaret Atwood, "Canada is just that vague, cold place where their uncle used to go fishing."[3]

From the perspective of most Canadians, who live within spitting distance of the forty-ninth parallel, the North is not viewed much differently. It's just closer; it begins a few hundred miles up the road. Most of the provinces have a community or two that boast to be the "gateway

133

to the North." In Manitoba it's the Pas. In Saskatchewan it's Prince Albert. In Alberta it's Fort McMurray. In British Columbia it's Prince George. If these are the cities beyond which the North lies, they are also the places beyond which few Canadians travel. While the North may be a place many dream about, few choose to visit and fewer choose to stay.[4]

Despite the imprecision that characterizes many Americans' and Canadians' knowledge of the North, they seem to agree on a number of basic points. Asked to point northward, most will turn in a direction roughly approximate to the line of a compass needle and say it's "somewhere up there" or "somewhere out there," where houses and paved highways give way to trees and gravel roads.

Not everyone is so imprecise. The noted Canadian geographer Louis-Edmond Hamelin wrote that if he had to accept a "single human factor . . . to define and delimit the North" he would use "the northern fringe of the continuous ecumene."[5] However, when he developed his northern index, he decided on "a family of ten significant, converging factors" that allowed him to quantify a particular place's "nordicity" (*Canadian Nordicity*, 17). Six are "physical": latitude, temperature, cold, presence of ice, precipitation, and ground cover. That is, the higher the latitude, the colder and icier and more barren the place, the more northern it is. But of more significance to us are the four that are, in geographical terms, "human": accessibility, air service, population, and level of economic activity. That is, the less accessible a place, the sparser the population, the smaller the economy, the more northern a place is. In short, using the measurement tools of the geographer, Hamelin quantified—empirically validated in space and time—the artist's notion of the North as a vast, remote area lying just at the edge of most people's experiences. Shelagh Grant, for example, notes that "the North is often referred to as 'wilderness,' a place beyond southern civilisation, agricultural settlement, or urban life."[6] From a Canadian perspective, quantifiable fact confirms the reality of the North. Quite simply, it exists; not only can you read about it, you can walk into it.

Admittedly, it's getting harder to step out the door and amble northward because the North, like all frontiers, is shrinking. Toward the end of the last century, for example, the "southern boundary of the North [was] at the 49th parallel" (*Canadian Nordicity*, 35). Now, a hundred years later, it has receded northward several hundred miles. However, about 70 percent of Canada remains "northern." As Northrop Frye mused in his influential conclusion to *A Literary History of Canada*: "One wonders if any other national consciousness has had so large an amount of the unknown, the unrealized, the humanly undigested, so built into it."[7] Importantly, then, the "frontier was the immediate datum of [the Canadian's] imagination, the thing that had to be dealt with first" ("Conclusion," 221). Most Canadians, therefore, "believe that the North has somehow imparted a unique quality to the character of the nation" (Grant, 13).

But the North has not just shaped the country's past. For Canadians, it has to be contended with in the present and—in a deterministic, even fatalistic way—in the future. Shelagh Grant notes that "since the time of Confederation, the people of Canada have looked upon their North as a symbol of identity and destiny" (13). "In the North," writes Thomas Berger, "lies the future of Canada."[8] It is a statement that has been made many, many times.

Given the contiguity of the northern wilderness to the experiences of Canadians, it is not surprising that it has had a special, formative impact on their identity, particularly as it has been developed through their literature. Indeed, the North and its exploration—in both geographical and psychological terms—are fundamental, even definitive features of Canada's national identity. In her classic thematic study of Canadian literature, *Survival*, Atwood suggests that in Canada "the answer to the question 'Who am I?' is at least partly the same as the answer to another question: 'Where is here?' 'Who am I?' is a question appropriate in countries where the environment, the 'here,' is already well-defined. . . . 'Where is here?' is a different kind of question. It is what a man asks when he finds himself in unknown territory."[9] So we discover that the quest for the North is, in Canadian terms, also the search for a meaningful identity. That search, which began several centuries ago in a "north" that we now think of as eastern and southern Canada, is not only recorded by but continues today in Canada's literature.

This literature is, if not the lineal descendant of the frontier literature of the American West, its first cousin. What Frye has said about the "Laurentian" movement in Canada—which he mistakenly calls "western" rather than "northern" as Hamelin properly does—echoes what has so often been noted about the westward expansion of the United States: it "has attracted to itself nearly everything that is heroic and romantic in the Canadian tradition" ("Conclusion," 217). Romantic in its language and epic in its proportions, this literature describes an imaginative realm often searched for but rarely found.

It is history, more than geography, that separates the frontier West from the Far North. This is important. When the last corners of the West were surveyed and fenced, it could no longer support the wild fantasies and utopian dreams it had sustained for so long. Therefore, as several contributors to this volume suggest, enthusiastic dreams about the "Wild West" have given way to wistful regard for the "Old West." What "was"—rather than what "is" or "could be"—now fuels speculation about the West. Today, cowboy boots are a fashion statement one is apt to see on city sidewalks, not a practical response to the need to keep one's feet firmly planted in a saddle's stirrups. The West, as frontier, quite simply no longer exists except, of course, as one of America's most potent imaginative constructs.

Thus, there is a correlation—if not a causal connection—between the waning of the Wild West and the rise of the Far North. The North is to the twentieth century what the West was to the late eighteenth and nineteenth centuries: a place with more future than past, more unexplored reaches than carefully mapped topography. Even today the North, especially the Far North, is a region suited to the grand speculations of the romantic as well as the matter-of-fact observations of the chronicler. Whereas a century ago, young men may have been urged to "go west" to make their fortunes, today they are often urged to turn north. In doing so, they often not only follow routes first traveled by the early northern explorers but model habits borrowed from them.

As *A Literary History of Canada* attests, many of the early explorers' accounts offer compelling personal narratives. Some, such as Radisson's *Voyages*, are badly written blends of "truth and fancy."[10] Others, such as Samuel Hearne's *Journey from Prince of Wales's Fort in Hudson's Bay to the Northern Ocean*[11] and John Rae's *Narrative of an Expedition to the Shores of the Arctic Sea in 1846 and 1847*[12], offer at times profound observations about the landscape, its original inhabitants, and the physical and psychological challenges frequently faced by the travelers. Taken together, their work is of great importance; as Victor Hopwood suggests, the origins of a Canadian, as distinct from British or American, literature can be found in the writings of these often solitary Europeans who moved out into what the French called *"le pays d'en haut"* and what the English came to call, with the founding of the Hudson's Bay Company in 1670, "Rupert's Land": "The proto-form of our still largely unwritten foundation literature is of necessity the record of our explorers, fur traders and pioneers. The transformation of such material has already begun" ("Explorers By Land," 19). There are now numerous examples— some successful, some not—of that transformation. Some events and characters have particularly attracted the attention of Canadian writers. For example, Albert Johnson's efforts to elude the Royal Canadian Mounted Police in the western Northwest Territories, which earned him the epithet "mad trapper," have been the subject of countless articles and several novels. Two of these—Wiebe's *Mad Trapper*[13] and York's *Trapper*[14]—are rightly considered "northern" classics. As well, countless stories have been written in an effort not just to retell but to reevaluate the contribution of the "giants" of the exploration of the Northwest. Brian Fawcett, for example, adopts a style and diction reminiscent of Mackenzie's own to create "The Secret Journal of Alexander Mackenzie." In it the narrator describes his discovery of a previously "lost" manuscript that shows the explorer "close to the very core and home of the continent's savagery."[15]

But as Fawcett's rather Conradian tale suggests, this preoccupation with things northern goes beyond the simple recasting of familiar northern historical events and personages in modern literary terms. The North has, in the last century, become the favored imaginative terrain across which an individual can travel, usually alone and facing great odds, in search of wealth and knowledge.

This oft-told story of the individual's quest northward is, I believe, reduced to its bare essentials in J. Michael Yates's "The Hunter Who Loses His Human Scent."[16] The story begins with a quotation from the writings of Sono Nis, Yates's alter ego, who suggests that some men are instinctually driven north:

> . . . we come then to the polar particle adrift somewhere in the chromo-somes of the equatorial man—that atavism (auxin in the plant, Man, which causes its leaves to bear around toward a small high window through which—it knows or dreams—sunlight streams) which brings few, nearly no men north. Figuratively, it is possible to say that all of us are born at the equator. Order there is other than north. Most live out their lives at the equator. Those who vanish one day—frequently with promises of return—become regarded, finally, as lost souls. As if in defiance of all human gravities, they go up and do not come down. ("Hunter," 52)

The hunter in the story has been "moving north through the south of the northern hemisphere . . . always" ("Hunter," 52). His travel is made difficult—"his way north labyrinthine" ("Hunter," 53)—by the distractions and obstacles of a "civilized" south: "There are the other impediments—museums of natural history, municipal administration offices, baseball diamonds, and cemeteries which appear suddenly to turn the streets or truncate them altogether" ("Hunter," 53). The pattern is one not of investiture but of divestiture. He travels north first by "public conveyances," then by hitchhiking and finally by foot; he finds walking "a relief." He travels north from a comfortable home to a series of one-room cabins and finally abandons even them for the wide open. He travels north from the humidity and heat of summer to the dessicated air and the cold of winter. Finally, he divests himself of everything, pack, rifle, snowshoes, even his human scent. And it is then that he symbolically "arrives" in a state of pure, simple existence.

Yates, an expatriate American, clearly views the North as the last place in North America where one can psychologically as well as geographically free oneself from the civilized, "equatorial" world of the South and, no longer encumbered by its materialism, find oneself. Thus, the journey north becomes for the individual in search of self-knowledge—Yates's symbolic hunter—a "hunt in an unmapped interior."[17]

Yates's work is characteristic of the Thoreauvian turn that "mainstream" northern Canadian writing has taken in the last several decades. For writers like Margaret Atwood, Aritha van Herk, Robert Kroetsch, and M. T. Kelly, the North represents a last chance to escape the errors and terrors of the "civilized"—that is, industrialized, polluted, and overpopulated—south. It offers a last chance to find a simpler life in a purer world. In van Herk's *No Fixed Address*, the northern Yukon is called "the ultimate frontier, a place where the civilized melt away."[18] In *Surfacing*, Atwood's heroine returns north—to her "home ground, foreign territory"[19]—in an effort to heal the psychological wounds acquired from too much city living. M. T. Kelly's autobiographical main character in *A Dream Like Mine* travels north to Kenora where he is kidnapped by a couple of Indians who carry him into the wilderness where he experiences something akin to a revelation.[20] According to Allison Mitcham, "the pattern of northward flight in pursuit of a utopian dream is clearly a dominant pattern in contemporary Canadian fiction."[21]

While the "frontiersman," that man with Hercules' strength and Odysseus's wit, was traditionally a trapper or factor or missionary or outlaw or even a policeman, today he or she is just as often a writer. As we look more closely at modern exempla of northern quest literature, we discover that they do not merely recount a character's northward search for self-knowledge, but proceed from a prevalent view among contemporary Canadian writers that in the North can be found what has so often eluded them in the South: inspiration. Indeed, over the last three decades the quest for a "voice" has, in contemporary Canadian terms, almost always been northward. The "trip north" has almost become an obligatory rite of passage. Almost every major contemporary Canadian writer has made the pilgrimage. A surprising number of modern Canadian classics are, consequently, "northern." Three—Al Purdy's *North of Summer*[22], Atwood's *Surfacing*, and M. T. Kelly's *A Dream Like Mine*—come immediately to mind. So pronounced is this northward-looking imagination that Allison Mitcham speaks of a distinctive, modern "northern imagination" (9). She notes that "many contemporary Canadian novelists—French and English—[focus] on the northern wilderness in the [continuing] belief that it is what makes Canada distinctive and original" (17).

Just as the literature of the western frontier is largely an eastern creation, the literature of the northern frontier is largely a southern one.[23] It has been written largely outside the area of study, first in Europe and more recently in the United States and southern Canada. At best, writers working within this tradition have made occasional forays into the North, usually returning south to turn their field notes into finished productions destined for a largely southern readership. This pattern was also set by the early explorers and factors. While they wintered in the North, they went "outside" to sell their furs and to Europe for their vacations and retirement. Robert Service, who perhaps more than any other writer popularized the Yukon, did much the same, moving out as soon as his income allowed him to.[24] And the pattern continues; today, however, many writers journey north with the assistance of Canada Council's "Exploration Grants" and the logistical support of the Continental Polar Shelf Project.

Despite the number of literary texts that comprise this literature, only a limited and very imperfect criticism has grown up around it,[25] which has more often than not enthusiastically adopted a "frontier" perspective and perpetuated the frontier myths rather than challenged them. Nevertheless, what many critics have said about the North is validated by many southern Canadians' imaginative perceptions of the North, if not by most northerners' firsthand experiences of it. And, as should now be clear, the south-north axis along which so many of Canada's writers are moving has all the historical and imaginative impetus that the east-west axis did a century ago.

So far, we have looked northward, adopting a national, pan-Canadian or North American perspective, looking up from the South. But there is a small handful of people for whom the North is not "up there" but "right here." When asked to point at a boundary, a line of demarcation, they will do so by turning south and pointing "down there" or "outside." Clearly, the first group is separated from the second by more than a geopolitical boundary, the timberline, or the line of discontinuous permafrost. They are separated by their experiences of the North and, consequently, by how they think and write about it.[26]

Despite the difficulty of drawing a precise boundary between the sparsely populated north and the settled south, we must make a fundamental distinction between "here" and "there"—that is, if we are to differentiate critically among the vast number of texts about the North. While there has been at least one recent attempt to classify the types of northern literature,[27] we in fact need to distinguish between two literary traditions, both of which are about the North but each of which reflects a fundamentally different relationship with or stance toward the North. So far we have, as I have suggested, looked at a tradition that, while imaginatively focused on the North, is written and read largely outside it and that is preoccupied, ultimately, with the North as a frontier. But there is another tradition we need to examine, one which focuses on a fundamentally different north: the one that Justice Thomas Berger first brought to the public's attention when he said he wanted Canadians to learn about a north that was not the south's frontier but an ancient homeland.[28]

For several decades these two views of the North have been colliding violently. They have collided in virtually every arena: politics, history, economics, and even religion. Out of this collision a new literature of the North is beginning to emerge. Protean as it is, this new regional literature has many identifiable and unique features. The most important, perhaps, is that it is, to use Reed Way Dasenbrock's phrase, "the discourse of the insider about his or her own region,"[29] and much of its impetus comes from a desire to confront, even repudiate, what Dasenbrock appropriately calls the "received notions" of traditional "northern" writers. For example, a recent publication of the Dene Cultural Institute reexamines Alexander Mackenzie's accomplishments; its title alone announces the challenge it intends to conventional thinking about the exploration of the North: *Dehcho: Mom, We've Been Discovered!*[30] Such works, on the one hand, challenge the romantic notions of the South's northern imaginings and, on the other, take inspiration from the North's oral traditions. Even when they are not especially good, they are provocative. As Frye suggests, "It is much easier to see what literature is trying to do when we are studying a literature that has not quite done it" ("Conclusion," 214).

If the accounts of the early explorers and traders represent the protoform of the frontier tradition, then the protoform of this emergent tradition is provided by the oral tales of the North's indigenous peoples. Once passed by mouth from generation to generation, they have been written down by anthropologists and, more recently, by a new generation of native writers. These tales document a world much different than that found in the frontier literature of the North. In them one crosses no frontier (unless it is that which lies between the physical and spiritual worlds) and gets lost in no northern "wilderness"—a word with no counterpart in any Athapaskan dialect.[31] Rather, one walks across a familiar, even comforting landscape called quite simply "the land" or "home." In this literature, which is so intimately tied to the northern landscape, the northern frontier, as Anglo-and Franco-Canadians think and write about it, has no existence, except occasionally as a target for satire.[32] Indeed, from an Inuit perspective the great unknown lies south of the tree line.

Elsewhere, I have discussed the gradual evolution of oral material from unattributed quotation scattered in anthropologists' writings into mature, "authored" texts.[33] This foundation-building process continues. Two Alaskans—Nora Marks Dauenhauer and Richard Dauenhauer— are, for example, editing *Classics of Tlingit Oral Literature*, the first volume of which, *Haa Shuka, Our Ancestors*, appeared in 1987.[34] In Canada, *North-*

ern Voices: Inuit Writing in English[35] has recently been published by the University of Toronto, thus making easily available a wide range of Inuit writing for the first time. Despite the great distance that separates the Tlingit and Inuit cultures, these recent works express remarkably similar attitudes about the land, ones diametric to a traditional European, frontier attitude.

At the same time that native people in the north are authoring their own texts, a number of northern anthropologists are producing texts that are consciously "literary" in that they mix traditional scholarship and personal narrative. In Hugh Brody's *Maps and Dreams*, chapters of personal narrative alternate with chapters of conventional scholarship.[36] Similarly, Robin Ridington has said that his *Trail to Heaven* describes "moments in the life of a northern Indian community. . . . from the point of view of my own involvement with the community and its people." Moreover, he says that it is "to the best of [his] ability, a true story and a very personal one."[37] Clearly, such texts are mapping a new literary territory, not just thematically but structurally as well.

While these efforts first occurred outside the literary world as narrowly defined, they are now clearly having an impact on mainstream Canadian writing. Richard Davis writes: "Many Canadian writers are today recognizing that the oral legends and myths of Chipweyan, Cree, Montagnais, Inuit, Algonkian, and other indigenous cultures—which were here long before Europeans "discovered" North America—have immense relevance to Canada, and modern authors are drawing from this rich well of Canadian "stories" that pre-date even the records of the first European explorers" ("The North in Canadian Literature," 14). One of the most impressive recent examples of this recognition is to be found in Rudy Wiebe's *Playing Dead: A Contemplation Concerning the Arctic*. In it, we see, for the first time perhaps, a Canadian writer of considerable stature turning his attention away from the grand names and events of northern exploration and focusing on a more immediate and, somehow, more truly northern world.

Quite simply, the North confronts him. "When one personally goes to the Mackenzie Delta," says Wiebe, "Franklin and Richardson seem amazingly irrelevant."[38] Even when Wiebe ponders over the "historical record"—presumably someplace outside the North—it is not Franklin that captures his attention, but an ordinary seaman—the "excellent old Mr. Hepburn" (Wiebe, 35)—and a young Yellowknife woman called Greenstockings.

In *Playing Dead*, Wiebe thinks about a north that is "here" and "now." The result is not just a complete "restructuring" of his artistic sense of the northern landscape—shifting him from a European's lineal conceptualization of space to an Inuit's areal one (Wiebe, 49–78)—but an effort to explore its aesthetic and artistic ramifications. It is significant, not just for Wiebe but for all of us who "desire true NORTH, not PAS-SAGE to anywhere" (Wiebe, 114), that Wiebe contemplates a world that begins with the words of two of the North's most eloquent Inuit—Ikpakhuaq and Uloqsaq—but ends with a contemporary writer saying, "So, I am trying to . . . prepare myself. To walk into the true north of my own head between the stones and the ocean. If I do, I will get a new song. If I do, I will sing it for you" (Wiebe, 119).

If Wiebe and other writers like him are successful—if they find new songs that integrate their own firsthand experiences with the Inuit's and Dene's understanding of the landscape—our literature will be the richer for it. Certainly, the northern frontier will, like some tired glacier warmed by a summer sun, retract even more. But, perhaps for the first time ever, the reading public will travel north and see a world that, as any number of Inuit and Dene will confirm, has existed here for millennia.

"Difficult Meat": Dialogism and Identity in Three Native American Narratives of Contact

James Ruppert

For years critics have explored historical accounts of the first contacts between Native Americans and European adventurers through written European-American accounts such as captivity narratives and travel journals. While extensively exploring the white images of contact, critics have been hesitant, with good reason, to examine the complexities of Native American oral accounts of early cross-cultural contact. Without a definitive text, critics felt their conclusions could always be undermined, and without the conventional certainty of the Western notion of "author," what could be safely concluded about style, rhetorical stance, voice, or authenticity of the text? Indeed, James Clifford warns that "oral societies—or more accurately oral domains within a dominant literacy—leave only sporadic and misleading traces. Most of what is central to their existence is never written."[1]

Recent studies in anthropology and literature have offered the exploration of "discursive paradigms of dialogue and polyphony" (Clifford, 41) as a way to generate a new understanding of the verbal domains of others. Based on theories of utterance, recent publication of the work of Mikhail Bakhtin and the serious commentary on that work by Don Bialostosky and Tzvetan Todorov have established the importance of dialogic discourse for literary criticism and linguistics by emphasizing the cultural context of discourse. While Bakhtin has been seized upon by literary critics who are finding a variety of voices in single-author texts, many of the voices culturally shaped, I want to look at more collectively generated oral narratives now recorded as written texts.

These texts express a multivoiced texture similar to that identified in Bakhtin's original investigations into utterance. An application of the insights of Bakhtin and his interpreters can aid in the appreciation of Native contact accounts by exploring the fabric of the cultural conversation that creates a context for oral history and that generates narrative discourses that are identity-creating as well as event-oriented. Applying Bakhtin's insights, Arnold Krupat has discussed the ways in which Native American autobiography reveals a model of the "collective self" in which the individual self defines an identity "by the achievement of a particular placement in relation to the many other voices without which it could not exist."[2] Similarly, contact narratives present a discourse in which differing voices define identity on at least three levels: social, ritual, and mythic. As these voices speak, presenting ideas and positions, they reveal a culture-oriented discourse characterized by the conflation of the various levels. It might even be possible to delineate these levels as the spheres of discourse that Bakhtin refers to as "languages."

Most critical assessments of oral contact narratives seek to identify and build an analysis on one of the modes of discourse identified by Aristotle: Dialectic, the proving of theses and the establishment of logical relations between theses; or Rhetoric, the art of convincing others through an understanding of their beliefs and a shaping of their judgment. Indeed, most literary analysis takes these modes as precritical assumptions necessary for further theoretical development, and then proceeds to erect an interpretation built on a perceived monological perspective. Even the most cursory look at contact narratives makes clear that neither of these modes is germane to an understanding of this discourse. What discursive activity can be identified that will aid our appreciation of the material? Building on Bakhtin's work, Bialostosky outlines dialogic discourse as distinct from Aristotle's two modes—not thesis-oriented or audience-oriented discourse, but culture-oriented and community-oriented: "In my account dialectic concerns impersonal relations among terms that are independent of those who hold them— relations of confirmation and contradiction, antithesis and synthesis, and the like. Rhetoric concerns relations of practical agreement and disagreement among persons—relations that can be effected, despite ideological differences, in the formation of consensuses among divergent interests and parties. Dialogics concerns relations among persons articulating their ideas in response to one another, discovering their mutual affinities and oppositions, their provocations to reply, their desires to hear more, or their wishes to change the subject."[3]

In his discussion of discourse, especially oral, Bakhtin insists that "the dialogic orientation is obviously a characteristic phenomenon of all discourse. It is the natural aim of all living discourse. Discourse comes upon the discourse of the other on all the roads that lead to its object, and it cannot but enter into intense and lively interaction with it."[4] Bakhtin's point is that no discourse can avoid reference to other discourses related to the object under discussion, nor can it avoid similar events or actions existing in an already ongoing cultural conversation. Bakhtin sees discourse composed of not just words but utterances— utterance being understood as a speech act that proposes social and cultural positions. Utterances establish relationships with previous utterances: "The utterance enters in relation with past utterances that had the same object, and with those of the future, which it foresees as answers" (Todorov, 53). This web of reference and meaning, this polyphony of voices and cultural positions, which Clifford refers to as "the intersubjectivity of all speech" (41), Todorov calls "intertextuality," but this term seems to privilege written discourse. Bialostosky, expanding on Bakhtin, calls this world of reference the "conversation" of dialogic discourse, and I will use his term.

As narratives handed down through generations, oral accounts of contact serve as excellent examples of dialogic discourse since they are an accumulation of text and interpretation, utterance that responds to previous utterance. Dennis Tedlock reminds critics to observe this interplay of text and interpretation in oral texts, and he encourages scholars to adopt "a dialogical point of view" when dealing with ethnohistorical documents. In his discussion of the Popol Vuh, he points out that the Christianized opening "tells us more about the sixteenth-century Quiche Maya than anything else in that document, precisely because it simultaneously shows us, with respect to the question of cosmogony, who those Quiches were and who our Spanish cousins were, how they met up and how they did not meet up."[5]

Oral historical narratives reveal identity as they incorporate the responses of others, their elaborations, appreciations, and comments. The various voices in a dialogic conversation elaborate and define the cultural context as individuals and cultural stances become synonymous, if only for a moment, if only for this round of conversation. Such conversations strive for "comprehensive responsiveness and responsibility to the consequential person-ideas of a time, culture, community, or discipline" (Bialostosky, 789). The oral contact narrative, specifically, exposes a moment of intense cultural conversation where "the primacy of context over text"[6] reverberates with questions of cultural identity.

It is my contention that dialogic conversation is at the heart of Native oral contact narratives, and rather than being mere records of events, these conversations/narratives are ultimately about cultural identities that in turn sustain individual identities. But they are coded and embedded in a manner not familiar to most Western trained readers because they challenge our definitions of history, identity, and narrative structure.

A first-contact narrative told by the Lipan Apache reveals some of the levels of the cultural conversation. The narrative opens with Percy Bigmouth relating that he heard the tale from his grandmother through his mother of a time when the Lipan were living by the gulf near the Texas-Louisiana border. Many good things would come from the sea like shells, fish, and turtles, but "one time they had a big wave. It was very bad. They thought the ocean was going to come right up . . . Living things from the water washed the banks, were washed up. Then when the sun came out and it was hot, all these things began to swell and smelled bad." One day they see a black dot coming over the water. Everyone comes out to watch and talk about what this thing could be. Eventually they realize that it is a boat. Surprisingly, the people who get out have blue eyes and are white. Bigmouth continues:

> They thought these people might live in the water all the time. They held a council that night. They were undecided whether they should let them live or kill them. One leader said, "Well, they have a shape like ours. The difference is that they have light skin and hair." Another said, "Let's not kill them. They may be a help to us some day. Let's let them go and see what they'll do." So the next day they watched them. "What shall we call them?" they asked. . . . Some still wanted to kill them. Others said no. So they decided to let them alone.[7]

While the names of those who speak are not retained, their utterances and the fabric of the cultural discourse is. Utterance follows utterance as positions are proposed. It is a discourse continued in contemporary tellings into which the old texts are woven.

The Lipan left them alone and most of the whites died during the year. Next spring the Lipan elaborated their conversation. Positions were taken as to the appropriate actions and attitudes toward the new people—positions emerging out of the proposed nature of the new people—and thus the status and relationship to be recognized were established. "Some said, 'Let's kill them now; they are only a few.' But others said, 'No, let us be like brothers to them.' " The conversation had resolved itself into a position where the new people were to be treated as "brothers." The Lipan would grant a social status with rights and responsibilities. They helped the whites with food and seeds, binding them into a chain of human sharing and mutual respect of which the whites had little idea. Bigmouth concludes, "The Lipan gave them venison. They were getting along very well. After that, they began to get thick" (Bigmouth, 28).

Understanding three features of this contact narrative will help us to redirect our Western historical expectations and begin to understand how the cultural conversation permeates the text. First, note that the discourse dwells on the nature of the whites' and the Indians' response. An Apache listener familiar with Apache oral tradition could reconstruct the suggested variety of positions on the nature of the whites and their origin, as well as the formulation of policy concerning them, and the incorporation of them into Lipan Apache worldview and self-concept. Clearly the wide variety of attitudes and subjects here is of primary cultural interest to the Lipan listener, since it is in that variety of stances that cultural values are expressed. As if to emphasize the cultural significance of the narrative, the speakers remain anonymous, never being named as would be expected in a Western narrative. The social level of identity is the first to be explored as the Lipan attempt to establish the nature of the new people and their place in the social network. But the discussion about the essence of the whites rises out of previous associations with the beneficial and violent things that come out of the sea. The sea will wash up fish, turtles, and shells, but it can also bring destructive storms. Ritual and mythic levels of meaning and understanding lie just below the surface of this discourse.

As they attempt to fit the whites into the Apache worldview, the Lipan Apache struggle to give the new people a name. Eventually the Lipan decide to abandon their posture of noninterference and act to pull the whites into the web of social interaction. The variety of voices in this conversation defines the nature of cultural response, thus the nature of culture; in other words, the conversation and the act of extending the human social world to the whites redefine and confirm who the Lipan are and their social order. The story has lived so long in oral tradition not because it establishes an identity for the whites—every Lipan knows that—but because it reveals Apache social values in dialog.

Second, the discourse does not attempt to establish the elaborate logical support of an Aristotelian thesis, because the native audiences accept the reality of conversation about the new experience as much as people who experienced contact did; rather, the discourse functions to encourage the conversation to continue over time, and indeed to continue to this day. The conversation's cultural purpose is more significant than any dialectical purpose that could be promoted, such as proving the thesis that the whites should be spared, or any rhetorical purpose, for instance to sway the audience to agree that they should be killed, though such positions might be explored in the cultural conversation. In many ways the contact story is told to reinforce the conversational process that determines who the Lipan Apache are.

Too often narrative significance for Western readers is encapsulated in the conclusion—that is, how did it turn out—but for the native audience oral narratives encode "culturally moral subjects."[8] The codes suggesting Lipan Apache expectations about cultural dialog, consensus, treatment of potential spiritual beings, hospitality, future kinship relationships, and social interactions dominate the conversation surrounding the event to the point of overshadowing the outcome. As dialogic discourse, the contact narrative takes its place in an elaborate weave of cultural discourse over time, relating similar events and discourses from the past whether from the personal, social, religious, or mythical realms.

Third, a personal level of the cultural conversation emerges when the "author," Percy Bigmouth, decides to tell the story so it will be written. A full development of the personal level of identity generated by the telling of the contact narrative would require an in-depth study of the biography of the storyteller, his performance of the text, and his performance of similar texts. Such an analysis is outside the scope of this paper, but let it suffice to observe that many contemporary Lipan listeners would enjoy the obvious irony of the narrative: that the Lipan Apache were dispossessed as part of an official Texas-Louisiana policy of extermination, despite the fact that they had helped the first white settlers, would require no comment from the storyteller. The white reader is also encouraged to engage the cultural voices in the conversation. Since the white reader also knows the outcome, he is drawn into the discussion and his voice creates yet another definition of cultural identity as he struggles to define not the whites who came to Lipan territory but who the Lipan were (and still are). Bialostosky underscores the identity-creating function of dialogic conversation when he writes: "Those who take their turns speaking and listening, representing others and being represented by them, learn not just who these others are, but who they themselves may be, not just what others may mean but what they themselves may mean among others" (Bialostosky, 792). The audience for the story, whether Native or white, allows itself to be represented and projected into a value-creating discourse by the cultural voices defining themselves and others in what is said. Bakhtin asserts: *"Discourse is oriented toward the person addressed, oriented toward what that person is"* (Todorov, 43). While the narrative was oral, the Lipan were addressing themselves and culturally defining themselves. When the white audience is allowed to eavesdrop on the cultural conversation, it imaginatively identifies itself with the Lipan Apache.

This sense of cultural conversation and self-definition is clarified by a narrative of contact between the Ahtna of Alaska and Russian explorers. Here the ritual level of the cultural conversation surfaces through the social level. The conflation of these levels of discourse guarantees the importance of the contact narrative in Ahtna oral tradition. The narrative tells of the first group of Russians exploring Ahtna country coming up the Copper River. As they do so, they find the local headmen along the way and whip them in order to establish dominance over them. After they whip the first chief, a boy walks out to check his traps and hears sobbing. "He listened carefully and it sounded like a person. He returned to his grandmother and he brought the news to her. 'It didn't sound like an animal. I heard a person sobbing.' "[9] The boy expresses confusion at hearing a grown man, a chief, cry. The man has been reduced to a state similar to that of animals. The cultural conversation hovers around the distinction between the two modes of being. Every Ahtna knows the outcome of this narrative, so the concern is with a definition of humanity. Storyteller Katie John says, "His grandmother went over to the people staying nearby there. 'My grandchild was checking traps downriver where people are staying and he says that you should be on guard. Someone let him know the Russians would be coming here. And this is how the situation seems to be,' and so she told the people" (John, 77).

The community is warned, but no action is taken. The Ahtnas seem to disbelieve that humans could act this way. The storyteller does not elaborate on the cultural conversation that must have surrounded the news of the new men in the Copper River territory, but the central poles of the cultural conversation have been established. Individual Ahtnas in tune with Ahtna oral history would imagine and recreate the conversation, perhaps even applying the narrative's significance to contemporary events. In facing the Russians, the Ahtnas' identity as true human beings would have been reinforced by their lack of action, by their noninterference and their expectation of social responsibility on the part of the newcomers. The Russians repeat their cultural violations of the bonds of human relationship and hospitality when they whip another chief, making him cry. The chief asks them if they know whom they are whipping. "You are doing this to Yalniil Ta, 'Father of He Is Carrying It.' Do you know you are doing this to someone who is vicious?" (John, 78). He calls out his personal name to challenge their right to act this way. Who are they? Are their names and positions higher than his? How do they fit into the social world of human interrelations and interactions? C'uket Ta', an Athabaskan who was serving as an unsympathetic guide for the Russians, does not translate this challenge. By this point the narrative has firmly established the social level of discourse as Ahtna utterance meets Ahtna utterance. After they whip the chief, the Russians take the men's weapons, enslave the women, and turn the men out naked and unarmed to freeze. Again they treat them like animals.

Taken in by other Ahtnas, the humiliated men engage in a social conversation about what they should do, but their conversation takes the ritual form of making medicine, joining their medicine power with other Ahtna to see if they will be able to get revenge. When the spirit world signs are favorable, they move in on the Russians. C'uket Ta' helps the Ahtna, counseling them as to the appropriate time to attack.

149

Anthropologists de Laguna and McClellan have noted that for the Ahtna warrior killing an enemy is a life-crisis situation where the strictest taboos apply, yet there are ritual ways to control the evil associated with killing, and these rituals are similar to hunting rituals.[10]

C'uket Ta' holds them back until the time is right, saying, "It would be difficult meat. You should wait!" (John, 84). C'uket Ta' warns that before the voices of the spirit world are heard, the attack would not be appropriate. Meat is hard to find when the spirit world does not help. It is easy meat when the Russians take themselves out of the human social world. They will be like the animal that gives himself to the hunter; indeed, they are already in the Ahtnas' lodges. The Russians have crossed the line dividing humans and animals; they have forced others to cross, and as such, they can now be hunted like meat. Fred John says, "At night then, after they had finished training for war, C'uket Ta' took the spears away from them (the Russians). Then the fight started at night" (John, 82). The Ahtna women jam the barrels of the Russians' guns. Katie John continues: "When they killed the Russians they did it at night. Then in the morning at daylight, as it was just getting light, 'Then they killed the meat, they killed the meat' (they said). In the morning they went back to them. With spears, bows, and weapons of war, they climbed up a hill. Then they sang a war song to them. I have forgotten some of it, just half (I remember). They sang of what C'uket Ta' had told them earlier. 'It would be difficult meat. You should wait!' C'uket Ta' had told them" (John, 83–84). The song that the Ahtnas sing to commemorate the event incorporates C'uket Ta' warning: "Now it would be difficult meat. Now the meat has been killed" (John, 84). The central image of the song "difficult meat" becomes a symbol unifying the various levels of identity in the song and the contact narrative. C'uket Ta's conflating utterance has provided a focus for the various levels of discourse.

The whole Russian party is killed except for a wounded half-breed, who is allowed to leave with C'uket Ta'. However, the survivor threatens to break the social bonds that might tie him to the Ahtnas by reporting their actions to other Russians. C'uket Ta' sends word to the Ahtnas. After an evening of discussion, the Ahtnas come and kill the half-breed. The half-breed is allowed to live at first because of his potential social position in the larger cultural conversation that defines the Ahtnas and attempts to clarify to what degree this individual is entitled to hospitality, to what extent he might be related, and who might be entitled to recompense and revenge if he is killed. All of these topics expand on the groundwork basic to this particular conversation and point out how the Russians have lost the right to be considered on this level of human relationship and identity. They reveal themselves to be nonhuman.

When the half-breed reveals his plan to inform on the Ahtnas, he aligns himself with the Russians and places himself in the "meat" category.

As with the Lipan Apache contact narrative, the conversation begins with an attempt to define the nature of potential social interrelationships, but the question of identity, of the true nature of the whites, keeps surfacing. When the social questions interact with ontological inquiry into the true nature of the beings encountered, we see Ahtna cultural values working. The exercise of these values solidifies cultural identity; moreover, the deep epistemological structure of the conversation begins to emerge as the spirit world is called into the conversation. Clifford reminds us that in many cases identity is not an either/or construct: "Yet what if identity is conceived not as a boundary to be maintained but as a nexus of relations and transactions actively engaging a subject. The story or stories of interaction must then be more complex, less linear and teleological" (Clifford, 344). In the Ahtna narrative, this nexus is engaged in intense questioning, in searching for illuminating cultural images and discourses. As the levels of the cultural conversation conflate, the intertextual or dialogic dimension becomes highly dynamic and less linear. Consequently, the ritual level of discourse starts to emerge from the subsurface. The discourse becomes a path to inquire of the spirit world, to let the spirit world speak, and it reaffirms the appropriateness of the utterance of the spirit world in the ongoing cultural conversation.

At first, the discourse swings around social ideas of hospitality, relationship, and the essentials of the nature of the new beings. The animal/human dichotomy establishes the prime axis of the cultural conversation and, of course, defines the identity of the Russians and thus the Ahtna. However, as the Russian actions continue to provoke the Ahtna, the conversation widens to include a ritual/spiritual dimension. The voice of the spirit world becomes predominant.

> Those who had come down at "Roasted Salmon Creek" were training (for war) among them. They made medicine, and the old men made medicine. They combined their medicine (powers). The people trained with medicine. The medicine men said, "You try to break the biggest spruce tree out there. If blood and hair come out of it, then you will get your revenge," so the shamans told them. So they did that. Out there they charged against the largest spruce tree and broke it and blood, hair with blood, came out (of the tree). "There you have made revenge. You will do like this. You will kill them," they told them. The shamans told them. Then they were trained. (John, 79–80)

Once the spirit world has taken a position, consensus can be reached, and action follows. The Ahtnas' sense of identity is reinforced by their renewed medicine power, their social rights and relationships are sanctioned by spiritual response, and the voices from other realms have been heard as required by Ahtna worldview.

Along with the social and ritualistic levels, the cultural conversation can center on a deeper mythic level as well. Contact narrative discourse can take many forms. The dialogic interaction can center on one level, then fuse with a second and third, or remain at one level leaving the other levels as subtext for the surface conversation. While all levels of conversation are possible, some narrative may leave one or more levels unrealized. The following story of contact between the Tlingit and Europeans presents a conversation that fuses all three levels.

The narrative told by George Betts begins with the Tlingits living in Lituya Bay. He tells, "There was a white object that could be seen way out on the sea bouncing on the waves and rocked by the waves. At one point it was coming closer. 'What's that? 'What's that, what's that?' 'It's something different!' 'It's something different!' 'Is it Raven?' 'Maybe that's what it is.' 'I think that's what it is—Raven who created the world. He said he would come back again.' Some dangerous thing was happening."[11] (Long ago in story time, Raven was all white before he turned black.) It is the white sail of a ship coming into the bay, and the people abandon the village for the protection of the forest. They fear that they will turn to stone if they watch Raven come to them, but they also are interested and excited. Uncertainty abounds as the people try to decide how to interpret the meaning of the event, and the mythic level of experience seems to make the most sense. They hear an unusual and fearful sound (an anchor being dropped). Soon they decide to roll skunk cabbage as a telescope (it will keep them from turning to stone) and they watch things climbing around on Raven. Only by ritual action can humans clarify the meanings that come from the voices of the spirit world.

Betts recounts, "When no one turned to stone while watching, someone said, 'Let's go out there. We'll go out there.' 'What's that?' Then there were two young men; from the woods, a canoe was pulled down to the beach" (Betts, 305–307). The men board and are shown many wonderful things like mirrors, and then are given food to eat that they take to be maggots and sand (actually it is sugar and rice) and liquor to drink. Betts concludes, "When they got ashore they told everyone: 'There are many people in there. Strange things are in there too. A box of our images, this looking glass, a box of our images; we could just see ourselves. Next they cooked maggots for us to eat.' They told everything. After that, they all went out on their canoes" (Betts, 309).

The Tlingits' first concern is for the safety of the village. The initial conversation that centered on what to do was resolved with the removal of the people from the village. The mythic level of the conversation quickly surfaces as the appropriate action of the community would ultimately be tied to a discovery of the nature of the being visiting the Tlingit. Its identity, as all identities in the Tlingit world, must have a mythic component as well as a social one, and as the conversation circles around social identity, it evokes mythic perception and thus mythic identity.

Concurrently, the identity of the arriving phenomenon redefines the Tlingit sense of identity, but the text records the weave of utterance and identity. If Raven has returned to the Tlingit, then they must act like those who are initiated into the knowledge of Raven's world (i.e., the Tlingit). They must act in a way ritualistically consistent with Tlingit attempts to gain knowledge from the spirit world, to hear its voice. Their actions reaffirm that they know how to act, that they can ritually assimilate spiritual/mythic knowledge, that they have a way to let the mythic world into the social. Their social identity as warriors and traders is backgrounded, while their ritual role as men of power who seek spirit knowledge emerges. They seek to act with the mythic identity of an actor from the Myth Age where all things are possible, where Raven will come to interact on a personal level. While the first action (leaving the village) is prudent only if you are dealing with enemy warriors, the second action (viewing with skunk cabbage leaves) is prudent only if you are dealing with mythological/spiritual beings. Ultimately as the social identity of the new beings resolves itself, the Tlingit reconstitute their social identities, and come out to welcome and trade with the strangers.

Again, as a contact story that still lives in an oral tradition, it is clearly not told for reasons that could be classified as rhetorical or dialectical in the Aristotelian sense. It is not told to argue that the Tlingit audience should decide that the non-Native visitors really were Raven or to prove the logic of the Tlingit position. The narrative serves to introduce the social and mythic levels (among others) of an ongoing cultural conversation. Tlingit values and thus Tlingit self-definition are created in the process of this cultural conversation. The first level attempts to determine the human or animal nature of the new phenomenon in order to establish the appropriate social customs and manners. The second level emerges from the attempt to establish the mythic qualities of the event so as to clarify the relation of the phenomenon (the coming of the different men) to a spiritual reality and thus to place it in a mythic context, to clarify its mythic identity. The interplay between two levels generates the narrative, and the narrative clarifies cultural values and cultural identity rather than arguing for or pronouncing a rigid position.

Readers trained in Western culture often expect contact narratives to reflect conventional plot structures and morals illustrated by the conclusions of narratives. However, the creation and continuation of oral narratives grow out of a more cultural set of concerns. The Natives may end up killing the newcomers or giving them food with little alteration to the dialogic nature of the discourse. Oral contact narratives have little to do with rhetoric and everything to do with cultural identity and a cultural conversation that interweaves with previous discourse. It is precisely this sense of Native American cultural identity and such texts as these that Arnold Krupat believes are necessary for a truly American literature and a better understanding of our national identity (Krupat, 202–215).

As these narratives are written and published, some collectors and compilers may attempt ironic and dialectical positions, but even then, these positions will work only as the narratives begin to draw the reader into the cultural conversation and assign him positions in a dialog of utterances. In other words, any dialectical or rhetorical stances one may perceive in the written narratives must be seen as one voice constantly yielding to a dialogic play of voices inside a cultural conversation.

For Bakhtin, this play of voices is more than a series of assertions; it is a way of knowing the world, of defining self, knowledge, and truth. Those cultural and context-oriented conditions that encouraged dialogic narratives (and thus dialogic thinking) he termed *heteroglossia*. While Bakhtin was referring specifically to novels, his comments were built on an understanding of oral discourse. If he had made a close study of oral tradition, he would have been impressed by the degree to which oral cultures maintain heteroglossia as a social and epistemological basis for meaning. Oral traditions thrive on the interplay of voices—the creation of identity and the building of meaning through an expanding context of utterance, growing richer as the stories are told and told again in a world of oral dialogism. Michael Holquist offers a succinct definition of dialogism at the end of his collection of Bakhtin's work: "Dialogism is the characteristic epistemological mode of a world dominated by heteroglossia. Everything means, is understood, as a part of a greater whole—there is a constant interaction between meanings, all of which have the potential of conditioning others. Which will affect the other, how it will do so and in what degree is what is actually settled at the moment of utterance. . . . A word, discourse, language or culture undergoes 'dialogization' when it becomes relativized, de-privileged, aware of competing definitions for the same things" (Bakhtin, 426). Oral tradition creates an environment that is similar to heteroglossia. Contact narratives record a cultural moment where definitions compete and discourse is highly dialogized. Identity is created and confirmed, and contact narratives continue the dynamic of the dialog in every retelling as well. In the narrative of first contact, the reader/listener becomes aware of a moment of intense dialogization of culture. Every action, every voice is understood only in a "greater whole" of social, ritual, and mythic meanings that interact and condition each other. Utterance at these moments is privileged by oral tradition—privileged not for the individual, the argument, or the plot, but in the way it redefines that greater whole, recreating identity and encouraging the competition of discourse. The hunt is for "difficult meat," indeed.

Notes

Notes–Heyne essay

1. Frederick Jackson Turner, *The Frontier in American History* (New York: Holt, 1948), 11.
2. In a profound sense all European-Americans are "Easterners." But I think it is nevertheless useful to note how few authors of the American frontier were actually there.
3. Annette Kolodny, *The Land Before Her: Fantasy and Experience of the American Frontiers, 1630–1860* (Chapel Hill: University of North Carolina Press, 1984), 173.
4. Henry Louis Gates, Jr., "Writing 'Race' and the Difference It Makes," *Critical Inquiry* 12, no. 1 (Autumn 1985):5.
5. John Seabrook, "Invisible Gold," *The New Yorker*, 24 April 1989, 73.
6. Annette Kolodny, *The Lay of the Land: Metaphor as Experience and History in American Life and Letters* (Chapel Hill: University of North Carolina Press, 1975), 149; hereafter cited in text.
7. Jacques Lacan, *Ecrits: A Selection*, trans. Alan Sheridan (New York: Norton, 1977), 27.
8. Edwin Fussell, *Frontier: American Literature and the American West* (Princeton: Princeton University Press, 1965), 17.
9. Ray Allen Billington, *America's Frontier Heritage* (New York: Holt, Rinehart & Winston, 1966), 25; hereafter cited in text.
10. John Cawelti, *The Six-Gun Mystique* (Bowling Green, Ohio: Bowling Green University Popular Press, 1984), 82; hereafter cited in text.
11. *The Writings of Henry David Thoreau*, vol.5 (New York: AMS Press, 1968), 237.
12. Melody Webb, *The Last Frontier* (Albuquerque: University of New Mexico Press, 1985), 307.
13. Harold Simonson, *The Closed Frontier* (New York: Holt, Rinehart & Winston, 1970), 48, 51.
14. Frederick Pohl, *Jem* (New York: Bantam, 1980), 304.
15. "Self-Reliance," *The Complete Works of Ralph Waldo Emerson*, vol. 2 (New York: AMS Press, 1968), 67.
16. "Nature," *The Complete Works of Ralph Waldo Emerson*, vol. 1, (New York: AMS Press, 1968), 40.
17. Herman Melville, *Moby-Dick* (New York: Norton, 1967), 284.
18. Richard Slotkin, *Regeneration Through Violence: The Mythology of the American Frontier, 1600–1860* (Middletown, Conn.: Wesleyan University Press, 1973); Slotkin extends his mythological analysis in *The Fatal Environment: The Myth of*

the Frontier in the Age of Industrialization, 1800–1890 (New York: Atheneum, 1985).

19. Although, as Ann Ronald observes, his novels were "patterned like romances" and all of his writing belongs to the American romantic tradition (*The New West of Edward Abbey* [Albuquerque: University of New Mexico Press, 1982], 3).

Notes–Barnett essay

1. Throughout this essay I will use John R. Searle's categories of illocutionary acts as presented in *Expression and Meaning: Studies in the Theory of Speech Acts* (Cambridge: Cambridge University Press, 1979); hereafter cited in text. Searle divides illocutionary acts into five types: assertives, directives, commissives, expressives, and declarations. As he describes these classes in his summary statement, "We tell people how things are, we try to get them to do things, we commit ourselves to doing things, we express our feelings and attitudes and we bring about changes through our utterances" (viii).

2. D. H. Lawrence, *Studies in Classic American Literature* (1923; reprint, New York: Viking Press, 1964), 60.

3. In the preface to *The Leatherstocking Tales* Cooper describes Deerslayer as follows: "Removed from nearly all the temptations of civilized life, placed in the best associations of that which is deemed savage and favorably disposed by nature to improve such advantages, it appeared to the writer that his hero was a fit subject to represent the better qualities of both conditions without pushing either to extremes."—James Fenimore Cooper, *The Deerslayer, or The First War-Path* (New York: Appleton, 1901,); hereafter cited in text as *Deerslayer*.

4. "Cooper's Tragedy of Manners," *Studies in the Novel* 11 (1979): 406.

5. Roland Barthes, *A Lover's Discourse: Fragments*, trans. Richard Howard (New York: Hill & Wang, 1978), 6.

6. In the Cooper/Deerslayer worldview, for instance, Indians lack the natural ability to master the white technology of the gun. In a shooting competition with Chingachgook, Deerslayer repeatedly triumphs. As he tells Judith, "Chingachgook, now, though far from being parfect sartainty with a rifle—for few redskins ever get to be *that*—though far from being parfect sartainty, he is respectable, and is coming on" (*Deerslayer*, 457).

7. Deerslayer's various Indian names, one of which is "Straight Tongue," overtly suggest personified abstractions, and his own description of himself and Hurry all but denominates them as "Good Deeds" and "Good Looks." Other characters may also be labeled: Hutter as "Rapacity," Rivenoak as "Guile," Chingachgook as "Fidelity," Hetty as "Simplicity." The only character to develop is Judith, who moves from "Vanity" to "Humility."

8. David Brion Davis (in "The Deerslayer, A Democratic Knight of the Wilderness: Cooper, 1841," in *Twelve Original Essays on Great American Novels*, ed. Charles Shapiro [Detroit: Wayne State University Press, 1958] describes Hetty as "impotent and inarticulate," suggesting "the nobility of mute nature itself" (7). Actually, Hetty is surprisingly articulate. Rather than "mute nature," she embodies unswerving devotion to an institutional value—religion—and although she is incapable of understanding that it cannot be applied everywhere, her discourse is far from impotent.

9. R. W. B. Lewis, *The American Adam: Innocence, Tragedy and Tradition in the Nineteenth Century* (Chicago: University of Chicago Press, 1955), 104. Natty is not master of all of the names of civilization, however. He imagines the chess pieces to be idols and has never heard of a buccaneer.
10. "Fenimore Cooper's Literary Offenses," in *The Portable Mark Twain*, ed. Bernard DeVoto (New York: Viking Press, 1946), 553. Harold C. Martin correlates the leisureliness and prolixity of Cooper's style with a separation from direct observation, "energy distributed rather than focused," in "The Development of Style in Nineteenth-Century American Fiction," in *Style in Prose Fiction*, ed. Harold C. Martin (New York: Columbia, 1959), 122.
11. Judith, who has been unduly influenced by settlement life, observes the conventions of social discourse up to the point of her proposal of marriage to Deerslayer.
12. Unlike Hurry's remarks, Hutter's message is not objectionable—only its form, which implies distrust. As Deerslayer agrees, the father of two daughters has a right to know why a stranger comes into his territory during a time of crisis.
13. Alan F. Sandy, Jr., in "The Voices of Cooper's *The Deerslayer*," *ESQ* 60 (1970): 5–9, distinguishes three levels of diction in dialogue: "the frontier-dialect of Natty and Hurry Harry, the Indian dialect, and the more or less standard English of the Hutters" (6).
14. *Biographia Literaria*, vol. 3 of *The Complete Works of Samuel Taylor Coleridge*, ed. [William Greenough Thayer] Shedd (New York: Harper & Brothers, 1864), 105.
15. " 'Voice' in Narrative Texts: The Example of *As I Lay Dying*," *PMLA* 94 (1979): 302–303.

Notes–Lawlor essay

1. This notion of character is to some extent distilled from Harold Bloom's discussion in "The Analysis of Character," which serves as the introductory essay to his *Major Literary Characters* series of anthologies (Chelsea House, 1989). Bloom argues that our present understanding of the literary representation of a human being still derives from Shakespeare. By inflecting his human figures with the will and the ability to change in "overhearing themselves, whether they speak to themselves or others" (ix–x), Shakespeare "reformed the universal human expectations for the verbal imitation of personality." The self-analysis implicit in the act of listening to their own utterances initiates a self-representation that mixes character "as a stable soul and a wavering self" (xii). I am interested, like Bloom, in the aesthetics of a simultaneously primordial and sublimated desire in fictions of subjectivity, but I intend to address not so much the desires themselves in Daniel Boone stories as the modes of their persistence or repetition, and I will consider them as such rather than as components of a soul. I am also borrowing from Bloom the idea that at least a part of what attracts us to Hamlet or Iago is their sense of outrage and their negative charisma, because in Daniel Boone, it is most often the overt rejection of normative social order, mixed with a sublimation of his distaste so that he may properly serve that order, that snags our attention.
2. Richard Slotkin, *Regeneration Through Violence* (Middletown, Conn.: Wesleyan University Press, 1973), 21.

3. John Filson, *The Discovery, Settlement and Present State of Kentucke*, ed. William Masterson (New York: Corinth Books, 1962), 6; hereafter cited in text.

4. Filson's map seems to downplay the presence of a self-conscious observing or reading subject as well, since it lacks perspective; its lines and curling rivers compose a flat, naive visual representation of Kentucky to accompany Boone's verbal one.

5. While Henry Nash Smith and Richard Slotkin also analyze representations of Boone in terms of economic and ideological values that the figure can absorb, their interests lie predominantly in Boone's mythic status. Whether representative of the myth of regeneration through violence or of virgin land, in these accounts Boone's position as a coherent subject is assumed, even if the specific historical dimensions of his character are called into question for any one account by virtue of the many variously politicized narratives of him. Slotkin's discussions of Boone's violence are directed toward analysis of myth and political ideology; mine are concerned with the implications of his violence for the paradigms of subjectivity that Boone presents.

6. John Bakeless writes that Boone "took an innocent joy in being written up" (395) and claims that he affirmed the accuracy of Filson's book on more than one occasion when in fact there were many mistakes in dates, population estimates, and descriptions of events. Nonetheless *Kentucke* made him famous in the United States and abroad. From Bakeless's discussion, then, it is easy to surmise that Boone adopted Filson's account as something of a script and his behavior in it as a paradigm, or role, for himself after publication. In any case, with or without Bakeless's evidence, the performative quality of Boone's behavior seems to precede Filson in the Kentucky promotion literature that drew the latter's attention. It seems as if Daniel Boone's life was always to some extent a public one and that his acts were simultaneously recordings.

7. James Hall, *Letters from the West, Containing Sketches of Scenery, Manners, and Customs; and Anecdotes Connected with the First Settlements of the Western Sections of the United States*, ed. John T. Flanagan (Gainesville, Fla.: Scholars' Facsimiles and Reprints, 1967), 236; hereafter cited in text.

8. Stephen Fender, *Plotting the Golden West: American Literature and the Rhetoric of the California Trail* (Cambridge, Cambridge University Press, 1981), 27.

9. In a discussion of Thucydidean and Hippocratic narrative procedures entitled "The History of the Anecdote: Fiction and Fiction" (in *The New Historicism*, ed. H. Aram Veeser [New York: Routledge, 1989], 49–76), Joel Fineman situates the importance of the anecdote in two of its features, its literariness and its way of being "directly pointed towards or rooted in the real" (57). As a pointed moment in a history, it has "referential access to the real" (56) which the larger design of a historiography cannot by itself maintain; these features of the anecdote allow us to conceive of it as a historeme. While Fineman underscores the referentiality of the anecdote, I am emphasizing its self-indulgence and its apparent difference from or resistance to the elaboration of an ideology or interested narrative of which it would simply be a part. Its resistance to a larger reality allows it, however, local authenticity and ignorance of narrative implication. In this sense Fineman's understanding of the historeme and mine are in accord.

10. Timothy Flint, *Biographical Memoire of Daniel Boone: The First Settler of Kentucky, Interspersed with Incidents in the Early Annals of the Country*, ed. James K. Folsom (New Haven: Yale University Press, 1967), 15; hereafter cited in text.

11. Henry Nash Smith, *Virgin Land: The American West as Symbol and Myth* (New York: Random House, 1950), 59.

12. John Cawelti describes a similar negotiation between the representation of

social order and the pursuit of individual desire in the cowboy of popular literature and film, in *The Six-Gun Mystique* (Bowling Green, Ohio: Bowling Green University Popular Press, 1984), 73.

13. Lucy Lockwood Hazard, *The Frontier in American Literature* (New York: Frederick Ungar, 1961), 109; Smith, 64; Slotkin, 409; Stephen Raillton, *Fenimore Cooper: A Study of His Life and Imagination* (Princeton: Princeton University Press, 1978), 90–91.

14. Jane Tompkins, *Sensational Designs: The Cultural Work of American Fiction, 1790–1860* (New York: Oxford University Press, 1985), 119.

15. Henry Nash Smith and others have addressed what they perceive as a problem for Cooper in giving such a central position in this novel to such a classless character; Smith explains this problem as caused partly by Cooper's ambivalence towards his father, figured as Judge Temple, and partly by his unwillingness to categorically celebrate nature at the expense of culture (68–69).

16. James Fenimore Cooper, *The Deerslayer: Or, The First Warpath*, vol. 2 of *The Leatherstocking Tales*, ed. Blake Nevius (New York: Library of America, 1985), 525; hereafter cited in text.

Notes–Barszcz essay

1. Frederick Jackson Turner, "The Significance of the Frontier," in *The Frontier in American Literature* (New York, 1920; reprint, New York: Holt, Rinehart & Winston, 1962), 3; hereafter cited in text.

2. *The Snow Image and Uncollected Tales*, vol. 2 of *The Centenary Edition of the Works of Nathaniel Hawthorne*, ed. William Charvat et al. (Columbus: Ohio State University Press, 1974), 49; hereafter cited in text as *Snow Image*.

3. R. W. B. Lewis, *The American Adam: Innocence, Tragedy, and Tradition in the Nineteenth Century* (Chicago: University of Chicago Press, 1955), 114.

4. Edwin Fussell, *Frontier: American Literature and the American West* (Princeton: Princeton University Press, 1965), 103.

5. *The Scarlet Letter*, vol. 1 of *The Centenary Edition of the Works of Nathaniel Hawthorne*, ed. William Charvat et al. (Columbus: Ohio State University Press, 1962), 67; hereafter cited in text as *Scarlet Letter*.

6. In establishing Hester's similarity to the Puritan authorities, some contemporary critics emphasize her methods of interpretation and reading. In *The Rhetoric of American Romance: Dialectic and Identity in Emerson, Dickinson, Poe, and Hawthorne* (Baltimore: Johns Hopkins, 1985), Evan Carton, for example, equates Hester's "reinterpretation of the letter" with the "play of significances that the magistrates' sentence . . . inaugurates" (196). My emphasis here is on the power of voice, the physiological rather than lexical or semantic aspects of language.

In the current wave of reaction to critics like Fussell and Lewis, which questions the value of "individualism" and "freedom," especially as defined by American critics in the 1950s and 1960s, this forest scene from *The Scarlet Letter* has not attracted much attention, though the issues raised by the scene have. For example, in *Visionary Compacts: American Renaissance Writings in Cultural Context* (Madison: University of Wisconsin Press, 1987), Donald Pease accepts (as I do not) Hester's position as an avatar of individualism. In this he agrees with critics who helped form what he refers to as "the cold-war consensus." He then argues in favor of Dimmesdale's repudiation of Hester's plan of escape from New England. For Pease, this repudiation demonstrates Dimmesdale's commitment to communal values that cold-war critics tended to disavow.

Albert J. Von Frank, in *The Sacred Game: Provincialism and Frontier Consciousness in American Literature, 1630–1860* (Cambridge: Cambridge University Press, 1985), argues judiciously that the "utter independence of Hester's inner life is of course the product of her reaction against the allegory that condemns her, and *as* its opposite is not more healthy or more tenable" (94). But, like Pease, Von Frank fails to acknowledge that Hawthorne repeatedly compromises the independence of Hester's thought.

7. The association of Indians and witches is made especially clear in the closing chapters of the book, where representatives of both groups dress with uncommon luxuriance. As described in chapter 21, "a party of Indians—in their savage finery of curiously embroidered deer-skin robes, wampum-belts, red and yellow ochre, and feathers, and armed with the bow and arrow and stone-headed spear" attends the election-day festivities (232). The suspected witch, Mistress Hibbins, appears at the same event "arrayed in great magnificence, with a triple ruff, a broidered stomacher, a gown of rich velvet, and a gold-headed cane." This character herself draws the connection closer as she confides to Hester some details of her nighttime excursions into the forest: "Many a church-member saw I, walking behind the music that has danced in the same measure with me, when Somebody was fiddler, and, it might be, an Indian powwow or a Lapland wizard changing hands with us!" (241). See also the diabolical ceremony in "Young Goodman Brown": "Scattered . . . among their pale-faced enemies, were the Indian priests, or powows, who had often scared their native forest with more hideous incantations than any known to English witchcraft."

8. Pearl is almost always taken as a symbol rather than as an image of a human child. (This is somewhat surprising, since Hawthorne is said to have based at least some aspects of her character on observations of his own daughter Una.) In *Hawthorne's Tragic Vision* (New York: Norton, 1957), for example, Roy Male maintains that Pearl "signifies truth and grace" (93). More recent critics hesitate to find a single, stable meaning for her but nonetheless talk of her in terms of what she means. In "The Obscurity of Signs" (*Massachusetts Review* 23 [1982]: 17), Millicent Bell regards her as typical of the symbols in the book, since they all offer multiple meanings. Evan Carton sees Pearl as a provocative but unstable symbol of the "generative act," the sexual union of Hester and Dimmesdale: "Despite Chillingworth's suggestion that an analysis of her character and mold might reveal the father, she is, like the letter, too elusive or too overwhelming a symbol to yield her source" (192). Harold Bloom, in the introduction to *Modern Critical Interpretations: Nathaniel Hawthorne's* The Scarlet Letter (New York: Chelsea House, 1986), associates Pearl with an anarchic, Gnostic strain sometimes found in Emerson. He adduces the *Gospel of Thomas*, in which "the pearl particularly represents . . . the best part of us, that which is capable of knowing, was never made, but is one with the original Abyss, the Foremother and Forefather who is the true or alien God" (4).

9. Hawthorne's recognition of the potential barrenness of individuality brings him much closer to D. H. Lawrence's view of social life than Lawrence himself ever acknowledged. Indeed, Hester Prynne exemplifies the intellectual and spiritual quandary of Americans, as Lawrence describes it in the opening essay of *Studies in Classic American Literature* (1923; reprint, New York: Viking Press, 1964): "Perhaps at the Renaissance, when kingship and fatherhood fell, Eu-

rope drifted into a very dangerous half-truth: of liberty and equality. Perhaps the men who went to America felt this. . . . Liberty in America has meant so far the breaking away from *all* dominion. The true liberty will only begin when Americans discover IT. IT being the deepest *whole* self of man, the self in its wholeness, not idealistic halfness" (6–7). Donald Pease has initiated a comparison between Hawthorne and Lawrence in *Visionary Compacts*, though he looks beyond what I take to be the central similarity between the two authors. Pease wants to show that the "self in its wholeness" can only flourish when people living in groups feel themselves to be a polity with shared values and myths. Lawrence and Hawthorne may well support such a vision, but to make the case in this way is to distort the emphasis of their work. For these authors the self achieves its wholeness not primarily in relation to a community but in relation to a husband or wife. The style of characters' political lives reflects the style of their marital lives.

10. Ralph Waldo Emerson, *Essays and Lectures*, ed. Joel Porte (New York: Library of America, 1983), 487; hereafter cited in text as *Essays*.

11. See especially Richard Poirier's essay "Resistance in Itself" in *The Renewal of Literature: Emersonian Reflections* (New York: Random House), 135–81.

12. Sherman Paul, *Emerson's Angle of Vision: Man and Nature in American Experience* (Cambridge, Mass.: Harvard University Press, 1965), 79–80.

13. Carolyn Porter, "Reification and American Literature," in *Ideology and Classic American Literature*, ed. Sacvan Bercovitch and Myra Jehlen (New York: Cambridge University Press, 1987), 202.

14. Ralph Waldo Emerson, *Emerson in His Journals*, ed. Joel Porte (Cambridge, Mass.: Harvard University Press, 1982), 432.

15. *Selections from Ralph Waldo Emerson: An Organic Anthology*, ed. Stephen E. Whicher (Boston: Houghton Mifflin, 1957), 413–14. The terms *monism* and *dualism* have sometimes been applied too generally to this aspect of Emerson's work. In a social sense, for example, Myra Jehlen is quite right to refer to Emerson's "urge to monistic resolutions of conflict and his sense that the dualities which may arise at any stage of understanding are only apparent and thus capable of being transcended by rising another level toward the ultimate abstract One" (Bercovitch and Jehlen, 130). As evidence in his journals, Emerson usually became bored or irritated with people who were merely argumentative or contradictory. He preferred to rise or imagine rising with them to "another level toward the ultimate abstract One." (The conversations with Thoreau bear this out.) But Emerson does not as strongly imagine blending with inanimate objects or the objects of thought in general. All individual human thinking might be dissolved into Man Thinking, but the objects of thought remain separate.

16. *The Writings of William James: A Comprehensive Edition*, ed. John J. McDermott (Chicago: University of Chicago Press, 1967), 34.

Notes—Dyck essay

1. Northrop Frye, *The Anatomy of Criticism: Four Essays* (Princeton: Princeton University Press, 1967), 136.

2. Leo Marx, *The Machine in the Garden: Technology and the Pastoral Ideal in America* (New York: Oxford University Press, 1964), 3; hereafter cited in text.

3. Richard Slotkin, "Myth and the Production of History," in *Ideology and Classic*

American Literature, eds. Sacvan Bercovitch and Myra Jehlen (Cambridge: Cambridge University Press, 1986), 70; hereafter cited in text.

4. Richard E. Sykes, "American Studies and the Concept of Culture: A Theory and Method," *American Quarterly* 15 (Summer 1963): 263.

5. For the purpose of illustration I have reduced the complex motivation of the Puritans to a single, economic cause. A more complete explanation would, among other things, need to consider the Puritan understanding of typology.

6. J. Hector St. John de Crèvecoeur, *Letters from an American Farmer* (New York: E. P. Dutton, 1957), 41. Describing the agrarian myth's depiction of the American farmer, Richard Hofstadter notes, "His well-being was not merely physical, it was moral; it was not merely personal, it was the central source of civic virtue; it was not merely secular but religious" (*The Age of Reform: From Bryan to F.D.R.* [New York: Random House, Vintage, 1955], 24–25; hereafter cited in text).

7. Frederick Jackson Turner, *The Frontier in American History* (Tucson: University of Arizona Press, 1986), 4, 37, 320.

8. Richard Slotkin, *The Fatal Environment: The Myth of the Frontier in the Age of Industrialization, 1800–1890* (Middletown, Conn.: Wesleyan University Press, 1985), 77; hereafter cited in text.

9. "Nothing so undermines the Western claim to a tradition of independence as this matter of federal support to Western development. The two key frontier activities—the control of Indians and the distribution of land—were primarily federal responsibilities" (Patricia Nelson Limerick, *The Legacy of Conquest: The Unbroken Past of the American West* [New York: W. W. Norton, 1987], 82; hereafter cited in text).

10. "The ideological function of the Myth of the Frontier had been to substitute the credible prospect of an infinite reservoir of land and economic resources as an alternative to the intense conflict of social classes, economic interest groups, or regional groupings of slave and free states. But in the real-world pursuit of expansion, American political leaders discovered that each new advance of the 'territory of Freedom' served to provide new occasions for the acting out of inescapable conflicts" (Slotkin 1985, 211).

11. Leo Marx explains that although Jefferson retained his pastoral ideal, he recognized the impossibility of implementing it because of America's changing internal and international situation. In a 13 October 1785 letter he explained that "this is theory only, and a theory which the servants of America are not at liberty to follow." On 9 January 1816 he wrote, "We must now place the manufacturer by the side of the agriculturist" (Jefferson, 33–41).

12. Blanche Gelfant, "The Forgotten Reaping-Hook: Sex in *My Antonia*," *American Literature* 43 (March 1971): 81.

13. Willa Cather, *Early Novels and Short Stories* (New York: Library of America, 1987), 921.

14. Cather's pastoral vision has an inadequate understanding of progress. For example, her natural aristocracy includes a railroad builder and a corporate lawyer for "one of the great Western railways." Their work helps to destroy the necessary isolation of the garden, which is preserved for Antonia but destroyed in *A Lost Lady*. Capt. Forrester and Jim Burden's love of the land masks the effect their occupations have on it. Because Cather excludes larger social dimensions from her work, she can only present threatening developments to her idealized world in individualistic terms, and thus she can only retreat into nostalgia rather than present a social analysis when confronted with modern developments.

15. Willa Cather, *A Lost Lady* (New York: Random House, Vintage, 1951), 123; hereafter cited in text.
16. Another important act of violence occurs offstage. After her husband dies, Miriam Forrester has Ivy invest what money is left. In his scheme, Ivy cheats Indians out of their land. He reveals a double disregard for nature in his quest for economic power by cheating those representatives of nature out of the land that sustains them.
17. Annette Kolodny, *The Land Before Her: Fantasy and Experience of the American Frontiers, 1630–1860* (Chapel Hill: University of North Carolina Press, 1984), 17; although this generalization does describe Alexandra and Antonia's attitude, it is not supported by a considerable number of novels and personal accounts of the prairie pioneers. Note, for example, Mari Sandoz's *Old Jules* (Lincoln: University of Nebraska Press, Bison Book, 1935) or Ole Rölvaag's *Giants in the Earth: A Saga of the Prairie* (New York: Harper & Row, Perennial Library, 1955).
18. Annette Kolodny, *The Lay of the Land: Metaphor as Experience and History in American Life and Letters* (Chapel Hill: University of North Carolina Press, 1975), 21–22; hereafter cited in text.
19. Henry Nash Smith, "Symbol and Idea in *Virgin Land*," in *Ideology and Classic American Literature*, eds. Sacvan Bercovitch and Myra Jehlen (Cambridge: Cambridge University Press, 1986), 28.
20. Canadian novelist Frederick P. Grove's *Settlers on the Marsh* (Toronto: McClelland & Stewart, 1966) exemplifies Kolodny's thesis by showing the parallels between one character's actions toward his land and toward his wife. Each day after working to make his land productive by forcing his will upon it, he returns to the house and forces his will sexually on his wife, who is in poor health. With already too many children to care for, she intentionally forces a miscarriage by overworking herself, which further deteriorates her health and eventually causes her death.
21. Ivy Peters is historically as much a representative of the pioneer as of the modern entrepreneur. Patricia Limerick in *The Legacy of Conquest* explains that instead of a garden most pioneers saw real estate, land as a profitable commodity often used for speculation. She imaginatively begins the second chapter, "Property Values," by stating that "if Hollywood wanted to capture the emotional center of Western history, its movies would be about real estate. John Wayne would have been neither a gunfighter nor a sheriff, but a surveyor, speculator, or claims lawyer" (55).
22. Oscar Handlin, *The Uprooted*, 2d ed. (Boston: Little, Brown, Atlantic Monthly Press Book, 1973), 4.
23. "On the Divide," *Willa Cather's Collected Short Fiction: 1892–1912* (Lincoln: University of Nebraska Press, 1965), 495–96.
24. Vernon Parrington, "Introduction," *Giants in the Earth*, by Ole Rolvaag (New York: Harper & Row, 1929), ix.
25. Harold P. Simonson, *Prairies Within: The Tragic Trilogy of Ole Rolvaag* (Seattle: University of Washington Press, 1987), 12; hereafter cited in text.
26. Julie Roy Jeffrey states, "Women identified these monotonous landscape [*sic*] as both visually tedious and psychologically overwhelming. Places that appeared to go on 'forever and forever,' without any clear definitions, a skyline that was only 'a hazy wobble,' without natural or human markings diminished human beings" (" 'There Is Some Splendid Scenery': Women's Responses to the Great Plains Landscape," *Great Plains Quarterly* 8 [Spring 1988]: 73).
27. June O. Underwood, "Men, Women, and Madness: Pioneer Plains Literature," in *Under the Sun: Myth and Realism in Western American Literature*, ed.

Barbara Howard Meldrum (Troy, N.Y.: Whitston Publishing, 1985), 51–52; hereafter cited in text.

28. Richard Slotkin, *Regeneration Through Violence: The Mythology of the American Frontier, 1600–1860* (Middletown, Conn. Wesleyan University Press, 1985), 4.

29. Robert Warshow quoted in John G. Cawelti, *Adventure, Mystery, and Romance: Formula Stories as Art and Popular Culture* (Chicago: University of Chicago Press, 1976), 250; hereafter cited in text.

30. James E. Miller, Jr., "The Nebraska Encounter: Willa Cather and Wright Morris," *Prairie Schooner* 41 (Summer 1967): 167; hereafter cited in text.

31. Wright Morris, *Ceremony in Lone Tree* (Lincoln: University of Nebraska Press, Bison Book, 1973), 117; hereafter cited in text.

32. As Lee Roy's use makes explicit, the automobile in many ways has become the modern equivalent of the six-gun.

33. Ginny Brown Machann, "*Ceremony at Lone Tree* [sic] and *Badlands*: The Starkweather Case and the Nebraska Plains," *Prairie Schooner* 53 (Spring 1979): 167; hereafter cited in text.

34. Lois has this world with McKee. Not all the female characters in *Ceremony* share Lois's fear. Etoile is more sexually obsessed and aggressive than any of the male characters. Daughter, in mocking Boyd's failure to become involved with Lois, implies that she doesn't share his fears and would act differently.

35. Madelon Heatherington, "Romance Without Women: The Sterile Fiction of the American West," in *Under the Sun: Myth and Realism in Western American Literature*, ed. Barbara Howard Meldrum (Troy, N.Y.: Whitston Publishing, 1985), 86; hereafter cited in text.

36. I am referring to the classic Westerns of, for instance, Zane Grey. John G. Cawelti carefully demonstrates how Westerns have continually changed in response to shifts in culture.

37. Jane Tompkins, "West of Everything," *South Atlantic Quarterly* 86 (Fall 1987): 373, 376. Tompkins presents a provocative case for understanding the Western as a reaction against the feminine values set forth in the domestic "sentimental" novel that dominated nineteenth-century culture.

38. Madelon Heatherington believes that Westerns, from *The Virginian* to *Little Big Man*, have failed to explore their full potential because "the basic dynamics of romance are aborted" (76). These novels follow the archetypal pattern of the hero quest, but the hero never faces the initiatory tests that will allow him to master himself and his world before he attempts the greater task of rescuing others. "Women play a crucial part in this preliminary testing and therefore in the preparation for deliverance, for because of his encounters with various female archetypes the hero learns to accept various aspects of himself" (81). Because this is missing in the pattern of Western novels, the Western hero never comes to a mature understanding of either women or himself, and "he wastes his regenerative energies in mere adventure for its own sake" (82). This corroborates Cawelti's assertion that the Western hero's motivation for using violence is to define himself rather than to save a community.

Notes–Pickle essay

1. Although many accepted Frederick Jackson Turner's frontier thesis in the century after he published his essay "The Significance of the Frontier in American History" (1893), others questioned the positive interpretation Turner put

on the implications of the frontier. Recent discussions have focused on the tragic cultural and literary mode arising from the realization of a finite, closed frontier, as in Harold Simonson's study *The Closed Frontier: Studies in American Literary Tragedy* (New York: Holt, Rinehart & Winston, 1970). Another Frederick Turner mused recently on the strong elegiac mode in American (including South American) literature: "Visions of the Pacific," *The Best American Essays, 1986*, ed. and intro. Elizabeth Hardwick (New York: Ticknor & Fields, 1986), 240–53. The latter Turner traces this elegiac mode to "the failure to realize paradise" in the new world, "the memory of bright hopes dashed by first encounters with magnificent lands and seascapes, paradise poisoned by dreams saved from a fantastic pettiness only by their size and tragic consequences, of death and utter disappointment, of blighted seaboards and blasted rain forests, of entire native cultures, fragile as feather, that disappeared" (249–50).

2. At least three other nonfiction works by German-speaking immigrants or their children should be mentioned here. Swiss immigrant Elise Dubach Isely's *Sunbonnet Days, As Told to Her Son Bliss Isely* (Caldwell, Idaho: Caxton, 1935) is an engaging memoir, full of fascinating detail about frontier conditions in early Missouri and Kansas. Mela Meisner Lindsay makes her mother Evaliz the first-person narrator of *Shukar Balan: The White Lamb* (Lincoln, Nebr.: American Historical Society of Germans from Russia, 1976). The first half of the book takes place in the German-speaking colony in Russia from which her family emigrated in 1905. Although the family comes to western Kansas after the early frontier days are past, most of their experiences resemble those of other rural immigrants. Pauline Neher Diede recalls the first few years of her German-from-Russia family's homesteading venture in western North Dakota in *Homesteading on the Knife River Prairies*, ed. Elizabeth Hampsten (Bismarck, N. Dak.: Germans from Russia Heritage Society, 1983). Her memoir testifies to the harshness of life for poor rural immigrants on the Great Plains. Interesting though these works are, they do not provide the close parallels for comparison to the works by Cather and Rölvaag as do those by Ise and Sandoz.

3. Page references to the four works are noted in the main body of this study and refer to the following popular editions: Willa Cather, *My Antonia* (Boston: Houghton Mifflin, [1949]); John Ise, *Sod and Stubble* (Lincoln: University of Nebraska Press, 1967); Ole E. Rölvaag, *Giants in the Earth* (New York: Harper & Row, [1929]); Mari Sandoz, *Old Jules* (Lincoln: University of Nebraska Press, 1962); hereafter cited in text as *MA, SS, GE,* and *OJ,* respectively.

4. In his chapter on *Giants in the Earth*, Paul Reigstad noted how often Rölvaag wrote his wife, who was visiting her parents in the summer of 1923, to confirm details of frontier life with his father-in-law (*Rölvaag, His Life and Art* [Lincoln: University of Nebraska Press, 1972]). Mildred K. Bennett's study *The World of Willa Cather* (new ed. with notes and index [Lincoln: University of Nebraska Press, 1961]) examines the biographical origins of Cather's writing. See James Woodress's comments on this as well: "American Experience and European Tradition," *The Art of Willa Cather*, ed. Bernice Slote and Virginia Faulkner (Lincoln: University of Nebraska Press, 1974), 53.

5. Paul A. Olson, "The Epic and Great Plains Literature: Rölvaag, Cather, and Neihardt," *Prairie Schooner* 55 (1981): 263–85; hereafter cited in text.

6. Helen Winter Stauffer, *Mari Sandoz: Story Catcher of the Plains* (Lincoln: University of Nebraska Press, 1982), 102.

7. Barbara Meldrum, among others, writes of two dominant cultural myths in the American concept of the West, that of the garden and the agrarian tending

it, and that of the frontiersman of the untamed land: "Agrarian versus Frontiersman in Midwestern Fiction," in *Vision and Refuge: Essays on the Literature of the Great Plains,* ed. Virginia Faulkner and Frederick C. Luebke (Lincoln: University of Nebraska Press, 1982), 44–63. It seems to me that Jules Sandoz incorporates both of these myths.

8. Melody Graulich's study of *Old Jules* as "a catalogue of male-caused tragedies in women's lives" is very convincing: "Every Husband's Right: Sex Roles in Mari Sandoz's *Old Jules," Western American Literature* 18 (1983): 9.

9. Reigstad (64–65), Olson (270–72), and Neil T. Eckstein ("*Giants in the Earth* as Saga," in *Where the West Begins,* ed. Arthur R. Huseboe and William Geyer [Sioux Falls, S. Dak.: Center for Western Studies, 1978], 35–39) discuss Per as hero in the Nordic and Faustian traditions. Meldrum identifies Per as a representative of the mythic Western hero who is "both frontiersman and agrarian," who becomes "a victim of the reckless western spirit he has helped to promote and seems to embody" (46, 49).

10. See Catherine D. Farmer's study for an interesting analysis of Beret's mythic aspect: "Beret as the Norse Mythological Goddess Freya/Gerthr," in *Women and Western American Literature,* ed. Helen Winter Stauffer and Susan Rosowski (Troy, N.Y.: Whitston, 1982), 179–93.

11. Olson speaks of Per "as epic hero, symbol of autonomy and western materialistic progress, [who] destroys himself at first in a series of acts of neglect of love directed toward wife and community and finally in a gesture of heroic self-justification" (270). Simonson says that Rölvaag believed that "the American promise is one and the same with its terrible cost": the spiritual disintegration that comes with the rootlessness of frontier independence. He notes Rölvaag's insistence that the immigrant, " 'especially the Nordic,' cannot uproot himself and move to a new land without paying the ultimate price, the sacrifice of his cultural soul" (94).

12. Evelyn Helmick examines the parallels between the final book of Cather's novel and what is known about the Eleusinian mysteries: "The Mysteries of Antonia," *Midwest Quarterly* 17 (1976): 173–85. (Also in *Willa Cather's "My Antonia",* ed. and intro. Harold Bloom, Modern Critical Interpretations [New York: Chelsea House, 1986], 109–117.) Bernice Slote writes of Cather's evocation of a sense of a "lengthened past" in her treatment of lives like Antonia's, and establishes the connection between such a sense of history and myth ("Willa Cather and the Sense of History," in *Women, Women Writers, and the West,* ed. L. L. Lee and Merrill Lewis [Troy, N.Y.: Whitston, 1979], 162, 170). Robert Scholes says that Antonia and the other hired girls "are figures of heroic and vital innocence, associated with nature and the soil" ("Hope and Memory in *My Antonia,"* in *Willa Cather's "My Antonia,"* 33). Phyllis Rose discusses Cather's emphasis on "heroic simplification" in her approach to character and on the mythic, timeless episode ("The Case of Willa Cather," *Modernism Reconsidered,* ed. Robert Kiely, assisted by John Hildebidle, Harvard English Studies, no. 11 [Cambridge, Mass.: Harvard University Press, 1983], 133).

13. Bernice Slote's discussion of "Willa Cather and Plains Culture" in *Vision and Refuge* examines the role of immigrant groups in the formation of culture on the Great Plains (see especially pp. 100–104). John J. Murphy identifies Cather's focus on the immigrant experience of the West as part of the "epic, almost archetypal dimensions" of the novel ("The Virginian and Antonia Shimerda: Different Sides of the Western Coin," in *Women and Western American Literature,* 163).

14. James E. Miller, Jr., says that the seeming structural weakness of books 2

and 3, in which Antonia almost fades completely out of the picture, actually "exemplifies superbly Turner's concept of the recurring cultural evolution on the frontier," in which a kind of cultural shedding to a primitive level of starting over again occurs. He concludes that "the successive cultural plateaus of the nation operate as ordering elements in the novel" ("*My Antonia*: A Frontier Drama of Time," in *Willa Cather's "My Antonia,"* 26).

15. Many critics have noted the subjectivity of Jim's image of Antonia and of frontier life in general. William J. Stuckey discusses the tension between Jim's "desire to convert Antonia into a beautiful image of agrarian life and Antonia's resistance to that conversion" ("*My Antonia*: A Rose for Miss Cather," *Studies in the Novel* 4 [Fall 1972]: 474). Similarly, Susan Rosowski finds that Antonia contradicts Jim's assumptions about her by working out her individual destiny "in defiance of her narrator's expectations" (*The Voyage Perilous: Willa Cather's Romanticism* [Lincoln: University of Nebraska Press, 1986], 88). Blanche H. Gelfant calls Jim a "disingenuous and self-deluded narrator" who fears sex and sexuality and whose narcissistic reminiscing becomes a negative distortion, rather than a creative act ("The Forgotten Reaping-Hook: Sex in *My Antonia*," *American Literature* 43, no. 1 [March 1971]: 79). Jean Schwind points out the subtext to this effect in the early illustrations of the novel that Cather approved ("The Benda Illustrations to *My Antonia*: Cather's 'Silent' Supplement to Jim Burden's Narrative," *PMLA* 100 [1985]: 51–67).

16. Albert J. von Frank, *The Sacred Game: Provincialism and Frontier Consciousness in American Literature, 1630–1860*, Cambridge Studies in American Literature and Culture (Cambridge: Cambridge University Press, 1985), 155.

17. Collections of letters by German-speaking immigrants can also be enlightening in this context. The immediacy of both subjective and objective frontier experience in such documents is invaluable as a point of comparison with secondhand narratives, for studies about the immigrant on the rural frontier. But it is precisely their immediate quality that causes them to lack a distanced perspective on events. The reader is referred to the letters of Henriette Geisberg Bruns in nineteenth-century Missouri, *Hold Dear, As Always: Jette, a German Immigrant Life in Letters*, ed. A. E. Schroeder (Columbia: University of Missouri Press, 1988); to Howard Ruede's letters as a Kansas homesteader in 1877–78, *Sod House Days*, ed. John Ise (New York: Columbia University Press, 1937); to Darlene M. Ritter's edition of *The Letters of Louise Ritter from 1893 to 1925: A Swiss-German Immigrant Woman to Antelope County, Nebraska* (Fremont, Nebr.: Siegenthaler-Ritter Publishers, 1980); and to the collection of letters from farmers in *Briefe aus Amerika: Deutsche Auswanderer schreiben aus der Neuen Welt 1830–1930*, ed. Wolfgang Helbich, Walter D. Kamphoefner, Ulrike Sommer (Munich: Beck, 1988), 55–273.

18. To some extent, this is perhaps less true of Jules and Mary Sandoz. Jules believed that hard-working Germans and Swiss Germans like his wife were superior settlers (*OJ*, 221). On occasion, Mary longed for Switzerland and for the cultural advantages of her European youth (*OJ*, 185, 212). But these were factual givens in their lives, not the central touchstones of their frontier experience.

19. Blanche H. Gelfant is not completely unfair to Cather when she says that *My Antonia* is "a representatively American novel" for its beauty of art and affirmation of history, but also for "how we betray our past when we forget its most disquieting realities" (97).

20. James E. Miller also asserts this of the fictional pioneers in *My Antonia* ("*My Antonia* and the American Dream," in *Willa Cather's "My Antonia,"* 103).

21. The message communicated by the lives of unsuccessful settlers might be

quite different. The reader is referred to *Far From Home: Families of the Westward Journey* by Lillian Schlissel, Elizabeth Hampsten, and Byrd Gibbens (New York: Schocken Books, 1989).

22. Wallace Stegner, "Willa Cather, *My Antonia*" (*Willa Cather's "My Antonia*," 49).

Notes–Scheckel essay

1. James E. Seaver, ed., *A Narrative of the Life of Mrs. Mary Jemison*, 22d ed. (New York: American Scenic & Historic Preservation Society, 1925), vi–vii; hereafter cited in text as *Jemison*. This edition contains the original 1824 text along with all changes and additions made by later editors.

To be consistent with the nineteenth-century terminology of the texts I discuss, I have chosen to refer to Native Americans as "Indians" throughout the essay. When I make reference to "the Indian," I mean to invoke a symbolic category, a product of the nineteenth-century tendency to define all Native Americans in terms of universal qualities (such as savagery, nobility, etc.) and to erase important distinctions among different tribes; I do not mean to embrace (or deny the dangers of) such a universalizing vision of Native Americans.

2. Frank Mott, *Golden Multitudes: The Story of Best Sellers in the United States* (New York: Macmillan, 1947), 306, lists the Jemison narrative as best-seller of 1824.

3. Roy Harvey Pearce, "The Significances of the Captivity Narrative," *American Literature* 19 (1947): 12.

4. Richard Slotkin, *Regeneration Through Violence: The Mythology of the American Frontier, 1600–1860* (Middletown, Conn.: Wesleyan University Press, 1973), 110, 179; hereafter cited in text.

5. Alden T. Vaughan and Edward W. Clarke, *Puritans Among the Indians: Accounts of Captivity and Redemption, 1676–1724* (Cambridge, Mass.: Belknap Press, 1981), 11–12; hereafter cited in text.

6. Far from feeling a sense of common ground and mutual understanding with Seaver and the white culture he represents, Mary Jemison is so uncomfortable about sharing her story that she will not speak unless her friend and neighbor, Thomas Clute, is present in the room.

7. Arnold Krupat, in *For Those Who Come After: A Study of Native American Autobiography* (Berkeley: University of California Press, 1985), 33, discusses Indian autobiography in similar terms as a composite text produced by a "principle of original bicultural composition . . . the textual equivalent of the frontier," defined as "the reciprocal relationship between two cultures in contact." Jemison's narrative, however, adds another level of complexity to this model since Jemison herself does not fully belong to either culture. Thus her perspective, itself, can be seen as a frontier where two cultures meet.

8. Victor Turner, "Liminal to Liminoid in Play, Flow and Ritual: An Essay in Comparative Symbology," *Rice University Studies* 60 (1974): 60–61.

9. Roy Harvey Pearce, *The Savages of America: A Study of the Indian and the Idea of Civilization* (Baltimore: Johns Hopkins University Press, 1953), 48–58.

10. Philip Fisher, *Hard Facts: Setting and Form in the American Novel* (New York: Oxford University Press, 1985), 20.

11. Richard Slotkin, *The Fatal Environment: The Myth of the Frontier in the Age of*

Industrialization, 1800–1890 (Middletown, Conn.: Wesleyan University Press, 1985), 404.

12. Henry Nash Smith, in *Virgin Land: The American West as Symbol and Myth* (New York: Vintage Books, 1950), 81–120, discusses the popularity of Western heroes, such as mountain men (1830s–1870s) and female Amazon characters (1860s–1870s), who violate conventional mores and inhabit the West as a realm of lawlessness and freedom from social restraint. Smith believes that the movement toward such unconventional heroes marks "a progressive deterioration in the Western story as a genre," a loss of "ethical and social meaning." The presence of such unconventional elements in Mary Jemison, whom Seaver nevertheless defines as a hero in quite conventional terms, shows that mainstream and subversive elements may be more closely intertwined than Smith's analysis would suggest and that the unconventional is not necessarily devoid of "ethical and social meaning." David Reynolds, in *Beneath the American Renaissance: The Subversive Imagination in the Age of Emerson and Melville* (New York: Alfred A. Knopf, 1988), examines a broad range of literature, both popular and elite, exploring ways in which "subversive" writings relate to more conventional forms.

13. It is difficult to believe that Jemison, who had been separated from her family (of Irish descent) since childhood, would still speak with a noticeable Irish accent. The fact that Seaver singles out this detail in his brief description of Jemison suggests that he considers it important for understanding her character. During the nineteenth century, even before the great waves of Irish immigrants during the famine years of the late 1840s and early 1850s, the Irish, associated with poverty and Catholicism, were viewed suspiciously as socially marginal, unwelcome additions to the American population. They were considered to be racially inferior—ignorant, idle, childlike, lacking self-control, fond of drink. One schoolbook in 1830 even quotes an anecdote from Robert Bruce in which the Irish are referred to as "barbarians." Seaver may have stressed Jemison's Irish descent because it would place her in a somewhat marginal position in white society without surrendering her identity as a white woman; such a position might have made her easy and willing adaptation to Indian ways seem more understandable and less threatening to white readers than if she had occupied a social position more firmly at the center of the dominant white culture. James Fenimore Cooper makes a similar move in *The Last of the Mohicans*, where Cora's attraction to Uncas can be explained by the taint of black blood that compromises her racial identity. This allows Cooper to play with the notion of miscegenation (although he never carries it into the world of present reality as does the Jemison text) without threatening the commonly accepted image of white womanhood or the values associated with it. For a discussion of attitudes toward the Irish in the nineteenth century, see Robert H. Wiebe, *The Opening of American Society: From the Adoption of the Constitution to the Eve of Disunion* (New York: Alfred A. Knopf, 1984), 335–37, and Ruth Miller Elson, *Guardians of Tradition: American Schoolbooks of the Nineteenth Century* (Lincoln: University of Nebraska Press, 1964), 124–28.

14. Natty Bumppo is the hero of the five books comprising James Fenimore Cooper's *The Leatherstocking Tales*, written between 1823 and 1841.

15. Such appendices were conventional in Indian ethnographic texts published at this time.

16. Cass's and McKenney's articles appeared in the *North American Review* (January 1826) and the *National Intelligencer* 26 (April 1825), respectively.

17. Richard Drinnon, *White Savage: The Case of John Dunn Hunter* (New York: Schocken Books, 1972); hereafter cited in text.

18. Annette Kolodny, in *The Land Before Her: Fantasy and Experience of the American Frontiers, 1630–1860* (Chapel Hill: University of North Carolina Press, 1984), 80, argues that the Jemison narrative is "revolutionary" because it is the first to depict a woman's willing accommodation to the wilderness, and therefore it is the first to bring "the baggage of communal and familial domesticity" into "the wilderness preserve of the male hunter-adventurers."

19. Jemison notes that, according to tribal legends, this land was not cleared by these blacks nor by Indians, but by a mysterious race, whose bones are sometimes uncovered there. Thus Jemison's frontier home is built upon the grave of a vanished race. Such theories of a vanished race, supplanted by the Indians, were often put forth by whites in an attempt to justify the Indians' supplantation by whites, making it part of a larger, natural cycle of the rise and fall of civilizations. Such theories also gave Americans the sense of history they were looking for as part of their larger search for a national identity, while assigning the Indian a liminal position in that history. An anonymous essay on "American Antiquities," published in 1828, illustrates this effect. Contending that America, far from lacking historical depth in its national identity, exhibits "a perfect union of the past and present; the rigor of a nation just born walking over the hallowed ashes of a race whose history is too early for a record, and surrounded by the living forms of a people hovering between the two." This essay is quoted in Brian Dippie, *The Vanishing American: White Attitudes and U.S. Indian Policy* (Middletown, Conn.: Wesleyan University Press, 1982), 17. In this formulation, the Indians belong neither to America's past nor to its present. Thus, with no place to fit into America's vision of itself, the Indians become less than real—mere "forms" "hovering" between worlds. In a similar way, the tendency to view the Indian as "vanishing American" made living Indians liminal, like troublesome ghosts who refuse to slip quietly into the past, haunting a present that has no place for them.

20. See William J. Scheick, *The Half-Blood: A Cultural Symbol in Nineteenth Century American Fiction* (Lexington: University Press of Kentucky, 1979) for a discussion of Americans' racial identification of "half-bloods" as Indians.

21. See Dippie, 3–78, for a full discussion of the causes and significance of this theory during the Jacksonian era.

22. Francis Parkman, *The Conspiracy of Pontiac*, quoted in Michael Rogin, *Fathers and Children: Andrew Jackson and the Subjugation of the American Indian* (New York: Knopf, 1975), 115; hereafter cited in text.

23. Nancy Cott, *The Bonds of Womanhood: Woman's Sphere in New England, 1780–1835* (New Haven: Yale University Press, 1977), 97.

24. Michael Rogin, "Liberal Society and the Indian Question," *Politics and Society* 1 (1970): 23.

25. Wilcomb Washburn, ed., *The American Indian and the United States: A Documentary History* (New York: Random House, 1973), 2556.

Notes–Singley essay

1. For detailed discussions of Sedgwick's uses of historical sources, see Michael Davitt Bell, "History and Romance Convention in Catharine Maria Sedgwick's *Hope Leslie*," *American Quarterly* 22 (1970): 216–18; hereafter cited in text; Edward Halsey Foster, *Catharine Maria Sedgwick* (New York: Twayne, 1974),

73–80; hereafter cited in text; and Mary Kelley, ed. and intro., *Hope Leslie; Or, Early Times in the Massachusetts* (1827; reprint, New Brunswick, N.J.: Rutgers University Press, 1987), xxi–xxxiii; hereafter cited in text as *HL*. Sedgwick also explains her fictional use of these materials in the preface to her novel (5–6).

2. Bell Gale Chevigny, ed., *The Woman and the Myth: Margaret Fuller's Life and Writings* (Old Westbury, N.Y.: Feminist Press, 1976), 190; hereafter cited in text.

3. Alexander Cowie, *The Rise of the American Novel* (New York: American Book, 1948), 204. Readers sometimes had difficulty distinguishing Sedgwick's and Cooper's fiction. Published anonymously in 1824, Sedgwick's *Redwood* was attributed to Cooper and actually appeared in France and Italy with Cooper's name on the title page. See Harold E. Mantz, *French Criticism of American Literature Before 1850* (New York: Columbia University Press, 1917), 43.

4. Nina Baym, "Melodramas of Beset Manhood: How Theories of American Fiction Exclude Women Authors," *American Quarterly* 33 (1981): 123–39.

5. Van Wyck Brooks, *The Flowering of New England* (New York: E. P. Dutton, 1936), 188.

6. Robert E. Spiller et al., *Literary History of the United States*, 3d ed., rev., vol. 1 (New York: Macmillan, 1963), 256.

7. See, for example, Joel Porte, *The Romance in America: Studies in Cooper, Poe, Hawthorne, Melville, and James* (Middletown, Conn.: Wesleyan University Press, 1969); hereafter cited in text: "Natty is the epic hero par excellence" (43), with *The Last of the Mohicans* and *The Pioneers* serving as Cooper's *Iliad* and *Odyssey* (39–52); and Georg Lukacs, *The Historical Novel* (New York: Humanities Press, 1965), who finds "an almost epic-like magnificence" in Cooper's portrayals (64). Addressing Cooper's aesthetics, H. Daniel Peck, *A World by Itself: The Pastoral Moment in Cooper's Fiction* (New Haven: Yale University Press, 1927), finds in his landscapes not so much a frontier consciousness but a timeless, classic pastoral ideal. Robert E. Spiller, *Fenimore Cooper: Critic of His Times* (New York: Minton, Balch, 1931); John McWilliams, *Political Justice in a Republic: James Fenimore Cooper's America* (Berkeley: University of California Press, 1972); George Dekker, *The American Historical Romance* (New York: Cambridge University Press, 1987); and others have noted Cooper's social and political criticism, but these interests appear mainly in Cooper's middle and late novels, not his early fiction, which is more appropriately compared with *Hope Leslie*. As Yvor Winters, *In Defense of Reason* (Denver: University of Denver Press, 1947), writes, "In the Leatherstocking Series . . . we have nothing whatever to do with social criticism, or at least nothing of importance" (185).

8. David Levin, *History as Romantic Art* (Stanford: Stanford University Press, 1959), ix.

9. See Leslie Fiedler, *Love and Death in the American Novel*, rev. ed. (New York: Stein & Day, 1975); hereafter cited in text; and R. W. B. Lewis, *The American Adam: Innocence, Tragedy, and Tradition in the Nineteenth Century* (Chicago: University of Chicago Press, 1955).

10. D. H. Lawrence, *Studies in Classic American Literature* (1923; reprint, New York: Viking, 1964), 78; hereafter cited in text.

11. Suzanne Gossett and Barbara Ann Bardes, "Women and Political Power in the Republic: Two Early American Novels," *Legacy* 2 (Fall 1985): 13–30; hereafter cited in text.

12. Sandra A. Zagarell, "Expanding 'America': Lydia Sigourney's *Sketch of Connecticut*, Catharine Sedgwick's *Hope Leslie*," *Tulsa Studies in Women's Literature* 6 (Fall 1987): 225.

13. Northrop Frye, *Anatomy of Criticism: Four Essays* (Princeton: Princeton University Press, 1957), 163.

14. Leslie Rabine, *Reading the Romantic Heroine: Text, History, Ideology* (Ann Arbor: University of Michigan Press, 1985), 7; hereafter cited in text.

15. Philip Fisher, *Hard Facts: Setting and Form in the American Novel*, New York: (Oxford University Press, 1985), argues that *The Last of the Mohicans* captures the spirit of the 1640s (39–40); but Cooper does not, like Sedgwick, take on the Puritan system of life in this novel. While one might argue that with its portrayal of the early stage of a hero's life, *The Deerslayer*, published in 1841, is a more appropriate companion text for *Hope Leslie*, this novel, even more than *The Last of the Mohicans*, reflects a timelessness and abstract yearning for lost origins and freedoms. Wayne Franklin, *The New World of James Fenimore Cooper* (Chicago: University of Chicago Press, 1982), even while defending Cooper's involvement with history, admits "even in *The Deerslayer*, as far back as he could push Natty, [Cooper] . . . introduced Tom Hutter and Harry March. . . . This bite of realism upsets what otherwise might become pure dream" (107–108).

16. Catharine Maria Sedgwick, *Life and Letters of Catharine Maria Sedgwick*, ed. Mary E. Dewey (New York: Harper & Brothers, 1872), 101.

17. Mary Kelley, "A Woman Alone: Catharine Maria Sedgwick's Spinsterhood in Nineteenth-Century America," *The New England Quarterly* 51 (June 1978): 209; hereafter cited in text.

18. Michel-Guillaume Jean de Crèvecoeur, *Letters From an American Farmer* (1782; reprint, New York: Dutton, 1957), 64.

19. Ann Barr Snitow, "Mass Market Romance: Pornography for Women is Different," *Radical History Review* 20 (Spring–Summer 1979): 150.

20. Quoted in Marvin Meyers, *The Jacksonian Persuasion: Politics and Belief* (Stanford: Stanford University Press, 1957), 52.

21. Unmarried, Sedgwick sublimated her erotic energies into an ethos of sibling love and comradeship: "The affection others have given to husbands and children I have given to brothers," she wrote (Kelley 1978, 213).

22. James Fenimore Cooper, *The Prairie* (1827; reprint, New York: Signet, 1964), 250.

23. Annette Kolodny, *The Lay of the Land* (Chapel Hill: University of North Carolina Press), 1975.

24. Leland Person, "The American Eve: Miscegenation and a Feminist Frontier Fiction," *American Quarterly* 37 (Winter 1985): 668–85.

25. David Mogen, "Frontier Myth and American Gothic," *Genre* 14 (Fall 1981): 330–31.

26. See, for example, *Wyandote; or, The Hutted Knoll* (1843), where Cooper's language is explicitly sexual and generative: "There is a pleasure in diving into a virgin forest and commencing the labours of civilization. . . . [This diving] approaches nearer to the feeling of creating, and is far more pregnant with anticipation and hopes. . . ." Quoted in Edwin Fussell, *Frontier: American Literature and the American West* (Princeton: Princeton University Press, 1965), 28; hereafter cited in text.

Notes–Dasenbrock essay

1. One particularly interesting example of the influence of other regionalisms on Southwestern regionalism is to be found in John Crowe Ransome [*sic*], "Regionalism in the South," *New Mexico Quarterly* 4 (1934): 108–113, a published version of a lecture Ransom gave in Santa Fe: the exponent of one regionalism telling the exponents of another how to go about it. See the introduction to Mabel Major and T. M. Pearce, *Southwest Heritage: A Literary History with Bibliographies*, 3d ed. (Albuquerque: University of New Mexico Press, 1972), 1–10, for a discussion of Southwestern regionalism that links it to regionalism as a broader phenomenon.
2. *Crumbling Idols*, quoted in *A Literary History of the American West* (Fort Worth: Texas Christian University Press, 1987), 340.
3. One critic to have seen this is Cecil Robinson: "The first American writers who began to work the vein of Hispanic lore in the Southwest were outlanders. They far from satisfied Allen Tate's requirement for the regional writer that he must have absorbed the culture of the region along with his mother's milk" (*Mexico and the Hispanic Southwest in American Literature* [Tucson: University of Arizona Press, 1977], 335). But he considers that the best Southwestern writing, like Cather's *Death Comes for the Archbishop*, shows that Tate was wrong: "Yet one of the outlanders, Willa Cather, produced a finished work of literary art in *Death Comes for the Archbishop* from the raw materials of history, tradition and lore in the Southwest, an accomplishment which suggests that one need not have been nurtured on tortillas and beans to respond aesthetically and with comprehension to the indigenous culture of the region" (Robinson, 335–36).
4. Lawrence Clark Powell, *Southwest Classics: The Creative Literature of the Arid Lands* (Los Angeles: Ward Ritchie, 1974), 13–24; hereafter cited in text.
5. This is a claim reiterated on the back of the reprint of Lummis's *The Land of Poco Tiempo*: "In fact, Charles Lummis was first to label that region as The Southwest." But Robinson quotes Whitman in 1887 as using the term: "I have an idea that there is much and of importance about the Latin race contributions to American nationality in the South and the Southwest that will never be put with sympathetic understanding and tact on record" (Robinson, 334). So the term's origins must lie farther back, though a use of it to refer to what we now think of as the Southwest must postdate the American conquest of 1846.
6. Charles Lummis, *The Land of Poco Tiempo* (1893; reprint, Albuquerque: University of New Mexico Press, 1969), 2; hereafter cited in text as *Poco Tiempo*.
7. Harvey Fergusson, *Wolf Song* (1927; reprint, Lincoln: University of Nebraska Press, 1981), 134.
8. Harvey Fergusson, *Grant of Kingdom* (1950; reprint, Albuquerque: University of New Mexico Press, 1975), 12.
9. Harvey Fergusson, *The Conquest of Don Pedro* (New York: William Morrow, 1954), 10; hereafter cited in text as *Don Pedro*.
10. David Lavender offers a parallel critique of Cather's portrait of Father Martinez of Taos (in "The Tyranny of Facts," in *Old Southwest/New Southwest: Essays on a Region and Its Literature*, ed. Judy Nolte Lensink [Tucson, Ariz.: Tucson Public Library, 1987], 65–68), making the shrewd point that Cather changes Lamy's name to Latour as if to deny the complete historical accuracy of her portrait but keeps Martinez's name the same, implying that her quite hostile portrait of Martinez is accurate.
11. Edward Abbey, *The Monkey Wrench Gang* (1975; reprint, New York: Avon, 1976), 25; hereafter cited in text as *Monkey Wrench*.

12. Willa Cather, *Death Comes for the Archbishop* (1927; reprint, New York: Vintage, 1971), 123.

13. Edward Abbey, *One Life at a Time, Please* (New York: Henry Holt, 1988), 89.

14. Edward Abbey, *Fire on the Mountain* (1962; reprint, Albuquerque: University of New Mexico Press, 1978), 167.

15. Elsewhere, in "Forms of Biculturalism in Southwestern Literature: The Work of Rudolfo Anaya and Leslie Marmon Silko," *Genre* 21, no. 3 (Fall 1988): 307–320, I have discussed some of the ways indigenous writers challenge the received forms of Anglo writing in their work.

Notes–Senkpiel essay

1. Quoted in Rudy Wiebe, *Playing Dead: A Contemplation Concerning the Arctic* (Edmonton: Newest, 1989), 5.

2. Louis-Edmond Hamelin, *The Canadian North and Its Conceptual Referents* (Ottawa: Supply and Services Canada, 1988), 12.

3. Margaret Atwood, "Canadians: What Do They Want?" in *75 Readings: An Anthology*, 2d ed. (New York: McGraw-Hill, 1989), 290–91.

4. Aron Senkpiel, "Of Kiwi Fruit and Moosemeat: Contradictory Perceptions of Canada's North," *History and Social Science Teacher* 23 (1988): 77–81.

5. Louis-Edmond Hamelin, *Canadian Nordicity: It's Your North Too* (Montreal: Harvest House, 1978), 17; hereafter cited in text as *Canadian Nordicity*.

6. S. D. Grant, "Myths of the North in the Canadian Ethos," *The Northern Review*, 3–4 (Summer–Winter 1989), 14; hereafter cited in text.

7. Northrop Frye, "Conclusion to *A Literary History of Canada*," in *The Bush Garden* (Toronto: Anansi, 1971), 220; hereafter cited in text as "Conclusion."

8. Thomas Berger, *Northern Frontier, Northern Homeland: Report of the Mackenzie Valley Pipeline Inquiry*, rev. ed. (Vancouver: Douglas & MacIntyre, 1988), 12.

9. Margaret Atwood, *Survival: A Thematic Guide to Canadian Literature* (Toronto: Anansi, 1972), 17.

10. Victor Hopwood, "Explorers by Land (to 1867)," in vol. 1 of *A Literary History of Canada*, ed. Carl F. Klinck, 2d ed., 3 vols. (Toronto: University of Toronto Press, 1976), 23; hereafter cited in text as "Explorers by Land."

11. Samuel Hearne, *Journey from Prince of Wales's Fort in Hudson's Bay to the Northern Ocean*, ed. Richard Glover (Toronto: Macmillan, 1958).

12. John Rae, *Narrative of an Expedition to the Shores of the Arctic Sea in 1846 and 1847*, referred to by Victor Hopwood, "Explorers by Land (to 1867)," 47.

13. Rudy Wiebe, *The Mad Trapper* (Toronto: McClelland & Stewart, 1980).

14. Thomas York, *Trapper* (Toronto: Doubleday, 1981).

15. Brian Fawcett, "The Secret Journal of Alexander Mackenzie," in *The Secret Journal of Alexander Mackenzie* (Vancouver: Talonbooks, 1985), 24.

16. J. Michael Yates, "The Hunter Who Loses His Scent," in *Man in the Glass Octopus* (Vancouver: Sono Nis Press, 1968), 52–61.

17. J. Michael Yates, *Hunt in an Unmapped Interior* (Francestown, N. H.: Golden Quill, 1967), 47.

18. Aritha van Herk, *No Fixed Address* (Toronto: McClelland & Stewart, 1986), 316.

19. Margaret Atwood, *Surfacing* (Toronto: General, 1972), 11.

20. M. T. Kelly, *A Dream Like Mine* (Toronto: Stoddart, 1987).

21. Allison Mitcham, *The Northern Imagination: A Study of Northern Canadian Literature* (Moonbeam, Ontario: Penumbra Press, 1983), 20; hereafter cited in text.
22. Al Purdy, *North of Summer* (Toronto: McClelland & Stewart, 1967).
23. This point is discussed by Eric Heyne in his article in this volume, "The Lasting Frontier: Reinventing America."
24. Carl F. Klinck, *Robert Service: A Biography* (Toronto: McGraw-Hill, 1976), 72.
25. This point is made by Richard Davis in his essay, "The North in Canadian Literature," which is to be published in *New Bearings on Northern Scholarship*, ed. Aron Senkpiel and Kenneth Coates, which is to be released by University of British Columbia Press in Vancouver in 1991; hereafter cited in text as "The North in Canadian Literature."
26. Aron Senkpiel, "Of Kiwi Fruit and Moosemeat," 78.
27. Richard Davis, "The North in Canadian Literature," 1–4.
28. Thomas Berger, *Northern Frontier, Northern Homeland*, 31–33.
29. This point is made by Reed Way Dasenbrock in his article, "Southwest of What?", in this volume.
30. *Dehco: Mom, We've Been Discovered!* (Yellowknife: Dene Cultural Institute, 1989).
31. S. D. Grant, "Myths of the North in the Canadian Ethos," 16.
32. Alootook Ipellie, "Damn Those Invaders," in *Northern Voices*, ed. Penny Petrone (Toronto: University of Toronto, 1988), 248–52.
33. Aron Senkpiel and N. Alexander Easton, "New Bearings on Northern Scholarship," *The Northern Review* 1 (Summer 1988): 15–17.
34. Nora Marks Dauenhauer and Richard Dauenhauer, *Haa Shuka, Our Ancestors*, vol. 1 of *Classics of Tlingit Oral Narrative* (Seattle: University of Washington, 1987).
35. Penny Petrone, ed., *Northern Voices: Inuit Writing in English* (Toronto: University of Toronto Press, 1988).
36. Hugh Brody, *Maps and Dreams: Indians and the British Columbia Frontier* (Vancouver: Douglas & McIntyre, 1981).
37. Robin Ridington, *Trail to Heaven: Knowledge and Narrative in a Northern Native Community* (Vancouver: Douglas & McIntyre, 1988), ix, xi.
38. Rudy Wiebe, *Playing Dead: A Contemplation Concerning the Arctic* (Edmonton: Newest, 1989), 40; hereafter cited in text.

Notes—Ruppert essay

1. James Clifford, *The Predicament of Culture: Twentieth-Century Ethnography, Literature, and Art* (Cambridge: Harvard University Press, 1988), 340; hereafter cited in text.
2. Arnold Krupat, *The Voice in the Margin: Native American Literature and the Canon* (Berkeley: University of California Press, 1989), 133; hereafter cited in text.
3. Don H. Bialostosky, "Dialogics as an Art of Discourse in Literary Criticism," *Publications of the Modern Language Association* 101 (1986): 789; hereafter cited in text.
4. Tzvetan Todorov, *Mikhail Bakhtin: The Dialogical Principle*, trans. Wlad Godzich (Minneapolis: University of Minnesota Press, 1984), 62; hereafter cited in text.

5. Dennis Tedlock, *The Spoken Word and the Work of Interpretation* (Philadelphia: University of Pennsylvania Press, 1983), 334.

6. Mikhail Bakhtin, *The Dialogic Imagination: Four Essays by M. M. Bakhtin*, ed. Michael Holquist (Austin and London: University of Texas Press, 1981), 428.

7. Percy Bigmouth, "Before They Got Thick," in *Native American Testimony: An Anthology of Indian White Relations*, ed. Peter Nabokov (New York: Crowell, 1978), 27–28; hereafter cited in text.

8. J. Barre Toelken, "Poetic Retranslation and the 'Pretty Languages' of Yellowman," in *Traditional Literatures of the American Indian: Texts and Interpretations*, ed. Karl Kroeber (Lincoln and London: University of Nebraska Press, 1981), 86.

9. Katie and Fred John, "When the Russians Were Killed at 'Roasted Salmon Place,' " in *Tatl'ahwt'aenn Nenn', The Headwaters People's Country: Narratives of the Upper Ahtna Athabaskans*, ed. James Kari (Fairbanks: Alaska Native Language Center, University of Alaska, 1986), 77; hereafter cited in text.

10. Frederica de Laguna and Catharine McClellan, "Ahtna," in *Handbook of North American Indians, Vol. 6, Subarctic*, ed. J Helm (Washington: Smithsonian Institution, 1981), 652.

11. George R. Betts, "The Coming of the First White Men," *Haa Shuka, Our Ancestors: Tlingit Oral Narratives*, ed. Nora Marks and Richard Dauenhauer (Seattle and London: University of Washington Press, 1987), 303–305; hereafter cited in text.

The Contributors

Louise K. Barnett is a member of the English Department and Associate Dean of Undergraduate Education at Rutgers University, New Brunswick, N.J. She is the author of *The Ignoble Savage: American Literary Racism, 1790–1890*, and she is presently working on a book entitled *Authority and Speech: Language, Society, and Self in the American Novel*.

James Barszcz teaches literature and composition at the William Paterson College of New Jersey. He frequently reviews books on classical rhetoric and architecture. Currently he is investigating relations between William James's theories of consciousness and modernist American poetics.

Reed Way Dasenbrock has taught at New Mexico State University since 1981. He is the author of *The Literary Vorticism of Ezra Pound and Wyndham Lewis* (Johns Hopkins, 1985) and *Imitating the Italians* (Johns Hopkins, 1991). He has also written on the Southwestern writers Rudolfo Anaya and Leslie Marmon Silko, and he has served as the nonfiction editor of the literary magazine *Puerto del Sol* since 1982.

Reginald Dyck, a recent graduate of the University of Washington, did his dissertation on Willa Cather, Wright Morris, and William Gass. His other publications include essays in *Modern Fiction Studies* and *Review of Contemporary Fiction*.

Eric Heyne teaches American literature and critical theory at the University of Alaska Fairbanks. He is currently working on a book on the theory and practice of literary nonfiction.

Mary Lawlor is Assistant Professor of English at Muhlenberg College. She has published articles on Frank Norris and Jacques Lacan, and she has completed a manuscript entitled *Fin de Siècle Naturalism and the Close of the American West*.

Linda Schelbitzki Pickle is Professor of German at Westminster College in Missouri. She has published in the areas of turn-of-the-century German literature, contemporary German women's literature, and German-American history. She is working on a book-length study of rural German-speaking women and their families on the nineteenth-century Midwestern frontier.

179

James Ruppert enjoys a joint position in English and Alaska Native Studies at the University of Alaska Fairbanks. He is a past president of the Association for the Study of American Indian Literatures, and he has published on written and oral Native American materials. He is the author of *D'Arcy McNickle* (Western Writers Series) and *Guide to American Poetry Explication: Colonial and Nineteenth-Century* (G. K. Hall).

Susan Scheckel's dissertation (University of California, 1991) is entitled "Shifting Boundaries: The Politics and Poetics of the American Frontier, 1820–1860." She is presently writing on Native American autobiography and works by James Fenimore Cooper and Francis Parkman.

Aron Senkpiel, Dean of Arts and Sciences at Yukon College, is a founding editor of *Northern Review*, the first scholarly journal published in Canada north of the sixtieth parallel. He has contributed to a wide range of publications, including *Northward Journal* and *Canadian Literature*, and is currently working with Kenneth Coates of the University of Victoria on two books dealing with northern Canada, to be published by University of British Columbia Press.

Carol J. Singley teaches literature, feminist theory, and American studies at American University. She has written articles on romance, the Gothic, and female initiation, and a book on the spiritual dimensions of Edith Wharton's fiction entitled *Edith Wharton: The Meaning of Longing*. She is coeditor, with S.E. Sweeney, of a volume of essays, *Anxious Power: Reading, Writing, and Ambivalence in Narrative by Women*.

Index